UNBROKEN

Mary Attenborough is a mathematician, software engineer, former lecturer and author of two third-level engineering mathematics textbooks.

Glasgow-born **Michael Gallagher** is an award-winning author of short stories, former civil servant and day-at-a-time recovering alcoholic. He enjoys walking, singing and playing freestyle football. The couple now live in north-west Donegal and, since 2000, have jointly run a web development business.

UNBROKEN

SECRETS, LIES & ENDURING LOVE

Mary Attenborough & Michael Gallagher

MERRION PRESS

First published in 2025 by
Merrion Press
10 George's Street
Newbridge
Co. Kildare
Ireland
www.merrionpress.ie

978 1 78537 560 6 (Paper)
978 1 78537 561 3 (eBook)

A CIP catalogue record for this book is available from the British Library.

Typeset in Minion Pro 11.5/17

Cover design by Fiachra McCarthy

Merrion Press is a member of Publishing Ireland.

Contents

Authors' Note

While this memoir is a true account of our experiences, some events and characters have been fused to maintain narrative pace. We have also changed some names out of respect for individual privacy but sought at all times to preserve the overall integrity of the story.

One

Please Don't Shoot!

Monday, 28 October 1996, around 4 a.m. – Michael

Our outside door came crashing in. Deafening thumps, steel banging on steel and shrill, piercing whistles filled the hallway.

Faraway voices called out in the dark: 'Armed police.'

Others, coming nearer, shouted orders: 'Get down on the floor.'

I half opened my eyes. Flitting in torchlight, shiny laced-up military boots slow-waltzed alongside white overshoes on our bedroom floor. Figures in full body armour, guns aimed at us, crowded around our bed.

Mary's shout, 'Fuck off, I'm naked', jolted me out of a dopey, disbelieving stupor. I'd never heard her swear in earnest at anyone, not even at me, in our eleven years together.

'On the ground,' ordered the voices. 'Get on the deck.'

I clambered crabwise off the bed, Mary's stomach against my back, the knee of her flailing leg clamping at my hip as we tumbled face down onto the floor. She lay next to me on the carpet, her arm looped tightly around my waist, a corner of the duvet bunched in her fist.

The overhead light came on. A man's voice sounded close to my ear. 'Move away from the bed and keep your hands where we can see them.'

Mary tightened her hold, but I pulled her arm free then crawled on my stomach along the tyre-track imprints of the intruder's muddy boots and stopped at his feet. His hands shook and the muzzle of his pistol moved erratically, close to my head. A bile uprush filled my throat as I pushed away a mental image of Diarmuid O'Neill, the young lad shot dead last month: *Jesus*, I prayed, *please don't shoot.*

The armed man backed off, and two plain-clothes detectives with forensic gloves and overshoes came to stand over me. One man tore open a package and unfolded a suit made of thick, white, puckered material. 'We'll get you dressed,' he said and, instructing me to slowly raise one leg at a time off the floor, drew trousers over my boxer shorts. He then fitted each arm into a sleeve, pulled the elasticised hood over my head and zipped up the front. The second officer handcuffed me and placed nylon bags around my hands and feet. With one captor on either side, they helped me stand.

Armed police closed in behind, and their combined pressure shunted me towards the hallway. I can't leave like this, I decided, and came to a dead stop, causing the squad to do likewise.

I looked down, my eyes searching for Mary, until they fixed on her face, drained of colour, shrunk into the billowing folds of the white duvet. An aching emptiness overcame me while my mind searched for some parting endearment.

All movement in the room had stopped and, it seemed, every eye was on us. 'Don't worry,' I said, the words sounding empty. 'We'll get this sorted out,' I added feebly, just as a leather-gloved hand on my head forced me around and out of the room.

As my nylon-bagged feet shuffled unsteadily, I lost my balance, almost fell over, and my head accidentally collided with the stairwell wall. The escorts, the same two who had dressed me, gripped my arms and used their rugby-player bulk to haul me upright. An instinctive feeling of gratitude was immediately replaced by resentment: these men had put me in this position.

Outside the closed door of our friend and neighbour Roy Wood's flat, a large, uniformed sergeant stood guard. Roy shouted from inside, 'You okay, Michael?'

I had a vision of him, glasses off, his good eye pressed to the spyhole.

Emboldened, I called back, 'Fine, Roy. Will you look in on Mary for me?'

'Yes, of course,' said Roy, the rest of his assurance smothered by the sharp crack of the copper's heel on his door.

'Get back to your bed, in there,' bawled the sergeant.

The two detectives led me downstairs, the armed guard still behind us. Three women wearing ordinary clothes stood in huddled conversation on the narrow first-floor landing. Their words were lost in the clatter of steps, but I heard one of my minders say, 'It's all yours, DI Williams.'

Pressing their backs against the wall, the women let us pass. I forgot my situation momentarily and acknowledged them with a neighbourly nod and half-smile. The eldest of the three raised her hand slightly and gave a half-smile back.

Outside our building, I walked in the light rain down the centre of the closed-off main road, between two long lines of squad cars, vans and ambulances parked at the kerb on either side.

I had a head full of stored secrets – surely inaccessible. Chaotic flashbacks of past behaviour crammed into my mind, not all innocent, but none that could have led to this morning's dawn raid. Police PR exercise, mistaken identity, I dared not think beyond those explanations. I listened instead to the rotating emergency lights on the vehicle roofs, clicking at each revolution and, high above, roaring jet engines on their Heathrow Airport flight path.

Minty mouthwash and musky aftershave odours wafted around the squad car's interior causing me to want to sneeze. Handcuffs and the plastic bags covering my hands like massive boxing gloves stopped me from taking the normal stifling measures. I tried to recall Mary's remedy for nasal irritation.

My mind jumped back to Mary. How was she? What did they do to her? I forgot about sneezing.

After we passed the Houses of Parliament and Big Ben, the car slowed to turn into a courtyard, stopping at a tall, stately looking building with a blue Metropolitan Police lantern hanging above the entrance. As we walked towards the open doors, I watched, almost with disbelief, my image reflected in a ground-floor Georgian window – handcuffed, covered head to foot in a white shroud, being led forward by my two minders.

Inside the building, we came to a landing above a flight of concrete steps. As my handcuffs and hand coverings were removed, I peered into the darkened stairwell. 'Where are you taking me?' I asked, instantly annoyed at myself for betraying my nervousness.

'Nearly there,' said one of the guards, pressing his hand lightly on my back, urging me downwards.

Fearful of an embarrassing slip, I moved my sweat-soaked, nylon-clad feet one step at a time. On reaching basement level, we emerged at the end of a long, low-ceilinged corridor, dusty with disuse. Directly in front of us, two officers sat at a reception counter, a single, naked bulb lighting the area around them.

On our arrival, they stood up. The older man, about the same height as me, looked portly in his buttoned-up sergeant's uniform; his taller colleague wore a suit and tie. Their grins were such that I vaguely expected them to reach out and shake my hand.

One of the escorts gave my name, address and date of birth and stated I'd been apprehended at home in Earl's Court, London SW5. The smartly dressed man, sporting cropped hair and a boxer's build indicative of a daily workout regime, had the demeanour of someone in charge. With a single nod, he simultaneously thanked and dismissed my two minders.

As the pair turned away from the desk, I had an involuntary urge to thank them, then cursed myself for the bizarre idea: their gun-wielding mates had endangered our lives and left Mary in a heap on the floor.

Mary! How could I have forgotten her again?

The uniformed man gave his colleague's name as Detective Inspector Sharp and his own as Custody Sergeant Packard, before reading out the rights afforded me under the Prevention of Terrorism Act. Without suggesting the reason for my detention, he asked if I had anything to say; I said no.

Beyond where the men stood, new storage crates with binders and box files were piled high. No way was this about me, I decided.

'Okay. Let's get you settled in, Mr Gallagher,' said DI Sharp.

Down the corridor we went, Sharp whistling under his breath and the officers' footsteps keeping time with the steely rhythm of the keys dangling from Packard's belt. We turned into a narrow passageway lined on one side with cells, their doors open, stopping at one halfway along, where Packard removed the plastic covers from my feet. I wallowed in momentary bliss as my sweltered soles pressed into the icy stone floor.

The sergeant ushered me inside. High grey walls streaked with drips from ancient leaks, brownish rings around the white ceramic toilet bowl and a pervasive dank smell offered a reassuring familiarity with the overnight cells of my Glasgow drinking days. The furnishings, too, were typical. No special treatment; it seemed I wasn't a major capture.

At the far end of the cell, a narrow, bed-shaped slab moulded a few inches above the rest of the floor had a stone upslope for a pillow. A folded horsehair blanket, a towel, a pair of canvas shoes at least two sizes too big for me and a shopping bag sat side-by-side on the flimsy plastic mattress. Sharp walked to the bed, grabbed the bag and turned it upside down, letting a bundle of clothes fall out. 'Something for you to change into.' He moved aside, leaving space for me.

I stepped forward and had a closer look. The crumpled arms of a faded yellow sweater lay tangled up with threadbare blue jeans.

'No thanks,' I said, 'I'll wait for my own clothes to be brought in.'

'Afraid you've no choice,' said Sharp. 'It's dabs and mugshot next: bunny suits not allowed.'

With one hand against the wall helping me stay upright and ignoring the two men's watching eyes, I stripped off the white coverall, pulled on the jeans and stretched the heavy jumper over my head, holding my breath to avoid the musty whiff from its acrylic fibres. The exertion of getting changed caused my hands to shake. I shoved them into my pockets and clenched my fists.

Smiling and nodding, Sharp rubbed his hands. 'Just the job,' he said, looking me up and down like a gents' tailor would a client he'd fitted out. Spruced up as the inspector was, in his expensive wool suit and shiny black Chelsea boots, he seemed as satisfied as I was embarrassed at our contrasting apparel. 'Now you're dressed, we can get you fed.'

Sharp's mention of food prompted recollections of Glasgow cell breakfasts past: lumpy, greasy, square sausages packed into bread rolls and giant mugs of scalding tea. I knew the gnawing in my gut wasn't from hunger. 'No thanks,' I said, 'I'm not hungry.'

'You might change your mind if you saw our breakfast menu,' said Sharp. 'We could organise a proper fry-up or an omelette, maybe.'

'Or a wee Arbroath smokie,' called the sergeant, from the doorway, mimicking my Scottish accent through his cockney dialect. Judging by his burgeoning waistline, it would take more than a wee smokie to satisfy his hunger.

These two old hands were winding me up, but I wasn't falling for it. 'I've already told you; I'm not hungry,' I said, trying to sound assertive. 'Now I'd like to be on my own, if you don't mind.'

'Okay, okay!' Sharp raised his hands in a mock gesture of resignation. 'Have it your way.' He moved past me towards the door.

'To think we opened up Canon Row especially for him,' the sergeant said, the cell key in his hand, 'and this is the thanks we get.'

He pushed the door until it closed with the familiar heavy clunk, a sound once experienced never forgotten, but one I hadn't heard since quitting drink twelve years previously.

Opened up especially for me? Did they think I was a big shot after all? I took my hands from my pockets. They still shook.

I started to walk around the cell, carefully avoiding, at each circuit, pools of water on the floor caused by a leak from under the washbasin. My mind was full of frenzied speculations. Could the arrest be related to Malachy, the fictional IRA character I'd introduced in recent weeks to my writing tutor and classmates? Another disturbing thought was of one particular day I'd become convinced I was being followed while doing some business around West London. When I got home and told Mary, she hadn't believed me, saying my fixation on the novel was blurring my sense of reality. Thinking back now, maybe I'd been right after all.

Was Mary okay? She had every reason to be outraged with the police, but would her wrath extend to me? What questions would they ask her? It wouldn't matter. She'd recently been too engrossed in getting her maths book published to take any interest in my comings and goings. Anyway, she'd probably regale her interrogators with exaggerated tales of my good deeds, which would make their eyes glaze over.

Would she be back in the flat? Would she go to work? Would she let my parents know? My sister, brothers and Cathie, mother of my three sons? Her own family?

I lay down on the mattress and, for a while, gazed numbly at my bleak surrounds. The walls began to close in, so I pulled the blanket tightly about me and over my head. When I'd blocked out all the light, I said the Serenity Prayer.

Monday, 28 October, around 4 a.m. – Mary

A bang, crash, some sort of noise, wakes me. Michael stirs as I head for the window. Forty feet below, the gardener's shed door is banging – slammed closed by the wind only to bounce open again. I move from the window and ease back into bed.

'What happened?' Michael mumbles.

'A noise, just the wind.'

He turns away, and I put my arm around him. He falls back asleep and so do I.

Another crash forces itself into my dream.

Michael stirs. 'What was that?'

'The shed door – go back to sleep.'

Suddenly, there is shouting from the outside landing, then it's inside the flat. 'Armed Police. Get down on the floor.'

Flashlight beams illuminate the room. I hear a shriek and realise it's from me.

Someone is tugging at the duvet. I shout, 'Fuck off I'm naked,' and try to stay covered by following the path of the bedding as it's being pulled away. Michael is being dragged from the bed and I hook my arm around his waist, landing on the floor behind him. I shout, 'I want to see your search warrant.'

Figures in body armour stand over us, the steel from their guns glinting in the flashlight beams. My befuddled brain is overwhelmed by its fight-or-flight response to the invasion, but self-protective common sense counsels me against further acts of defiance.

'Don't panic,' I hear Michael say.

'I'm not panicking,' I answer. 'I want to see their warrant.'

'I don't mean you,' Michael replies.

Someone switches on the ceiling light. My brain is rerunning scenes of police charges on picket lines joined during my student days. I lift my head, aware of the importance of a witness statement when this outrageous police assault is investigated.

'Keep your head down,' a gruff voice orders.

I lower my head then lift it again. My attempt to scrutinise the scene is futile, however, as nothing makes sense to my scrambled faculties. When a machine gun is pointed at me, I duck below the duvet.

A man's voice asks Michael to slowly follow his instructions. Michael takes my hand to move my arm from around his waist and our fingers briefly interlock. His gesture of reassurance is tempered by the tautness of his grip.

From under the duvet, I watch two men in plain clothes dress Michael in a white suit, stand him up, handcuff him and lead him towards the door. He stops, only his face visible, looks down and his eyes search until they lock onto mine. His mouth moves, but I don't hear what he says. He tries a smile, but it looks more like a resigned grimace.

I open my mouth. No speech comes. They lead Michael away. In the wake of his ethereal, white-suited figure, a dark swarm follows.

'You can go now,' a woman's voice calls from beyond the remaining members of the armed group. The invaders' feet file past me, some just missing my head.

'I'm Detective Inspector Williams, officer in charge,' she says, and I raise my head up to see a woman of about forty alongside two others, all smartly dressed. 'And these are DCs Wilson and Dixon,' she adds.

Detective Constable Wilson crouches down behind me, takes hold under my arms and lifts me to my feet.

'This is an outrage,' I say, gathering the duvet tighter around my shoulders. 'You only had to knock and we would have let you in.'

'I'm afraid we've no alternative in a rapid response situation,' answers DI Williams. 'We're investigating IRA activity relating to your boyfriend.'

'Michael has done nothing wrong.' My voice is raised now, hoping to sound in command of the situation, although the absurdity of my nakedness, covered only by a duvet, is not lost on me.

'We have to follow procedures,' continues Williams.

'Procedures? You've turned our place upside down, and you haven't even shown me a warrant.'

The inspector takes a sheet of paper from her briefcase and holds it in front of me. I see in bold print 'Warrant to Enter and Search Premises, Prevention of Terrorism Act [PTA], Detective Inspector Janet Williams,

Metropolitan Police' and 'Dr Mary Attenborough'; the rest is a jumble of letters. This must be the warrant I've asked for, but surely it should have been shown to me in advance of their entrance.

'You can get dressed now,' Williams says. 'State your intention before reaching for your clothes,' she warns. 'Don't make any sudden movements.'

I open the wardrobe door and catch sight of myself in the full-length mirror inside. My face stares back, its normal tanned ruddiness now the colour of bottled milk.

I indicate my work clothes and get dressed.

'Is there anything else you want before we go?' asks the inspector.

'Go where?'

'You'll have to leave with us.'

'I can't just go. I live here, and I've things to organise for work.'

'We have to carry out forensic examinations.'

'Do you have a legal right to deny me access to my own home?'

DI Williams ignores my question and moves into the hallway, returning with a raincoat over her arm. 'You'll need this,' she says. 'We don't want you getting wet out there.'

Wet! Her friends could have killed us – now she's protecting me from the rain.

Once I've put on the coat, DC Dixon puts my handbag strap over my shoulder. I wince as strands of my loose hair get caught. 'Sorry,' she says and frees the trapped hairs.

The detectives lead me outside. We step around our front door, now lying flat on the landing floor with a large hole in the middle where the police have rammed it.

'Was that really necessary?' I ask, as we start downstairs.

'Had to be done,' Wilson says, but Dixon gives an open-handed shrug I take to be apologetic.

On reaching the first floor, DI Williams hurries ahead, calling back, 'I'll arrange for transport.'

I determine not to use their transport but, as we reach the ground floor, thoughts crowd in on me: I'm without my flat and everything in it – my computer, books, clothes – and I've lost Michael.

'Where have you taken my partner?'

'Come to the station,' says Wilson. 'We'll find out there.'

'No, thank you,' I say, but I'm still in shock and not sure I'm capable of organising my next move.

I open the door slightly and look outside. Police tape festoons the iron railings around the entrance and, across the road behind metal crash barriers, TV camera operators and photographers stand in the drizzle. I quickly shut the door again. The media presence fits with the police-trawl publicity theory developing in my mind.

DC Dixon places her hand on my arm. 'Come along with us for now.'

It's only the second time I've heard this woman speak. She has pronounced the word now as 'nigh'. I can tell she is from somewhere in the North of Ireland.

I meekly nod my head. Through the door's frosted glass, I see the outline of a police minibus stopping on the pavement outside.

Two

Semtex? You've Got to Be Joking!

Monday, 28 October, 5.30 a.m. – Michael

Sergeant Packard led me into a room full of added light reflected from two tall windows. All along the grimy, yellowing walls, darker rectangles and squares, evenly spaced, hinted at long-gone bulletin boards. A man in brown overalls stood at a metal table lining up sheets of white paper alongside an ink pad and roller. Next to him a younger officer had his head bent over a tripod-mounted camera.

'Let me know when you're done,' Packard said, then turned and walked out.

Feeling strangely abandoned, I answered the beckoning nod of the photographer and sat down facing him.

He pointed his lens at me. 'Please remain still.'

I tugged at my jumper's sagging neck. 'Do I have to wear this?'

'It's only a mugshot: just try not to blink.'

Dazzling flashes followed, forcing me to blink several times, and I was still suffering from temporary blindness when the fingerprint man summoned me.

The officer, a burly guy, took hold of my left hand in his big paw. 'Now if you just relax, I'll do the rest.' He rolled my fingers one by one around his ink pad and onto the paper. After finishing one hand, he gave me a soggy, ink-stained rag.

'Can I have a clean one?'

'Sorry, it's all we have.'

'In these circumstances, everyone has to make do,' added the photographer, his remark, I assumed, including me into a collective forbearance pact.

'Bad result for the first fifteens on Saturday,' the fingerprinter said, as if to distract from our privations. He had cauliflower ears and probably played rugby when younger. 'But that referee did us no favours.'

'They never do with the Met,' agreed the photographer. 'Always like to stick it to the Old Bill.'

I vaguely recalled a rugby-playing friend of a friend from my civil service days.

'Had a good mate once who played for the Met,' I said, trying hard to remember the name of a guy I hardly knew. 'He was a great scrum half.'

A name-drop now, I calculated, might insinuate my innocence into the minds of these officers: serious suspects aren't likely to have had a great mate play for the Met.

'Oh yeah?' said the photographer, shooting a glance and a fleeting smile at his colleague.

'So what?' asked the fingerprint man, as he took hold of my other hand to finish his work.

I had nothing to say. Reminded of my place in this new order, I shrivelled into myself.

Monday, 28 October, 5.45 a.m. – Mary

When I rush from the building with the two detectives, camera flashes light up the rain-soaked pavement. A man steps nimbly from the minibus passenger seat and slides open the side door.

DC Dixon climbs in beside the driver, and I go to join her, but this man bars my way and, with a raised hand, ushers me through the side door.

I go quickly to the back row and sit down. The man clambers aboard just before the vehicle moves off, juddering and swerving, almost causing him to lose his balance. As he sits down opposite me, I catch the rain-damp smell of cotton from his flannel trousers and turn sideways to avoid contact with his long legs.

A buzzing noise draws my attention to a stubby aerial sticking out of his blazer's side pocket. He lifts out a phone.

'DS Greasley here,' he says, his tone slick and authoritative. After a short pause, he speaks again. 'Have you the room ready?'

He listens briefly. 'Fine, we'll be there in a couple of minutes.'

As my mystery journey continues, we pass several police cars parked outside the block of flats where Michael's friend Billy lives. They belong to the same addiction recovery group and chat regularly on the phone, although not much about Ireland, as Billy has never been there. It's bad enough, I think to myself, that they've targeted Michael, who at least identifies as Irish – Donegal has been his second home since childhood – but have the police cast their net so wide as to include people with an Irish granny?

After travelling a short distance, we stop, and I see we're outside the local Kensington Police Station. The two women in front alight; I follow DS Greasley onto the pavement. Pretending to hurry out of the rain, I catch up with DC Dixon.

'Is this where they're holding my partner?'

'It's unlikely,' she says. 'At our briefing they said you two should be kept apart.'

I'm encouraged by her frankness. We could talk later, in private, and she would maybe be more understanding: she is Irish after all. She would have suffered the stream of Irish jokes and subtle discriminations, just like any Irish person living in England.

A man stands alone in the station foyer. The others greet him, referring to him as 'Sarge'. He's in his mid-thirties and wears a sensible raincoat over his suit.

'I'm Detective Sergeant Byrne,' he says.

He leads us into a corridor and stops at the open doorway of a small room. The detectives usher me forward and, despite trying to hang back, I'm jammed into a space so confined that I'm compelled to move ahead of them. I make my way along the wall, carefully avoiding the spindly legs of chairs tucked under a table. By the time I reach the far end and sit down, Greasley and Byrne are already seated facing me, with Dixon and Wilson on either side. On the laminated tabletop, notepads and folders are laid out alongside a telephone.

I've been at events in small rooms before, such as student protest gatherings, where people had to sit on the floor, but this is more claustrophobic than any of them.

Greasley slides a foolscap pad in front of DC Dixon. 'My colleague here will write everything down and prepare a statement for you.'

'You can check it over when finished, Mary,' says Dixon, 'and then sign it.'

'We want you to help us here. It's in your interest to answer a few questions,' says Greasley. 'You've been living with Michael for some years now, so you must have had some suspicions about his activities.'

I'm on a mission to convince them Michael's arrest is a grave error, so decide not to question the potentially ominous implications of his words. 'I don't know what you mean. He's not involved in any illegal activities. Michael's a caring, considerate person.'

Michael is always helping his family, friends and other recovering alcoholics, but I know these good deeds have led him into less than entirely legitimate territory in the past. Could it be his ducking and diving that's brought down suspicion on him?

I mention the weekly money he sends to his ex-wife as atonement for his years of alcoholic neglect of his children. I mentally redact the little nuances, including his temporary work using a false identity; neither do I mention the time, recently, when he provided bogus documentation for a large homeless family in order to get them housed. After that episode, which I disapproved of, he promised not to blur legal boundaries in the future.

With the women, I think I'm doing well at painting a true picture of Michael. They nod sympathetically when I speak about his closeness to his three sons. As I end the speech about his noble endeavours, DC Dixon keeps writing.

Greasley drums his fingers on top of his manila folder. 'Is it a problem for Gallagher that you're the main breadwinner? Did it make him turn to the IRA to prove his worth?'

Such a question is not deserving of an answer, so I give him a sardonic smile.

'Where exactly does your money go? You're certainly not spending it on home comforts. Are you donating to the IRA?'

'Of course not.' I try not to laugh. 'I don't think our lifestyle is especially modest,' I continue. 'We've only got a new kitchen and dining suite for our housing association flat – it was nice before your armed friends stamped all over the woollen carpet with their hobnail boots. And we've just bought a cottage in Ireland.'

'Ah, yes, the cottage. Your car was packed, ready, was it not? Gallagher had got wind that his cover was blown, and you were planning a sudden departure to Ireland.'

I'm puzzled by this accusation. I had only put a new set of cutlery and a couple of rugs in the back of the car – hardly enough to indicate readiness to flee the country.

'We were going this weekend to finalise the purchase. Much as I'd like to leave the rough and tumble of city life permanently behind me, there's no way we could afford to move now – it's a holiday home.'

DC Wilson quickly moves on to an assertion that Michael is having affairs, naming Michael's ex-wife Cathie, his long-time friend from Acton Maxine, and his ex-work colleague Sonia. In my exhaustion and shock, I have a moment of manic amusement. Besides being a major IRA operative, Michael doubles as a rampant Lothario. My God, what a stud! Considering we've a pretty active sex life, he's certainly a goer.

I force my thoughts back to reality. Being something of a crime drama aficionado, I can see through their tactics: undermine our relationship and turn me against Michael.

'It's what men do,' Wilson says, insistently. 'They just can't help themselves.'

She may well be right in general terms, but it wouldn't take long to dismiss these particular claims as absurd. Cathie, during their marriage, had been many times bitten and was now twice shy of him; Maxine prefers her men twenty years younger; Sonia is enthusiastically gay.

Rather than refute the insinuations, I move on, explaining the frequent trips to Ireland, sometimes without me, which perhaps had made him a target of suspicion: our holidays visiting Michael's parents in Donegal; accompanying me on an academic visit to Dublin; helping sort out problems with a family land dispute; and, more recently, dealing with the purchase of the cottage.

I talk then about how things are changing in the North of Ireland and how there's no longer any need for violence, even in a defensive way – demographic changes will make a united Ireland inevitable.

DC Dixon finishes preparing my statement and passes it to me. I'm satisfied that it is a good description of the caring and law-abiding Michael. I sign it.

Having fulfilled my side of the bargain, I ask again about where Michael is being held and also about getting me somewhere to stay, now that my flat is off-limits. Sergeant Byrne blames the early hour for the communication delay. 'Perhaps we should all grab some breakfast,' he says, a suggestion greeted with assenting noises around the table. 'By the time we've finished eating, our admin people will have started work.'

Work! I'd forgotten.

'I need to get to work; I'm already late setting off.'

'Why don't you call in sick?' asks Greasley.

'But there's nothing wrong with me. I haven't had a sick day in five years.'

'Then just say it's your mother who's ill,' Greasley suggests.

'You're the police. Are you saying I should lie?'

Byrne is slowly shaking his head and smiling. He speaks before I can ask what he finds so amusing. 'I've never known of anyone going to work after being the subject of our Armed Unit's operation.'

The comment brings me a smidgeon of self-respect: they haven't completely shaken me, in spite of all that's happened to me and Michael.

Michael! How could I even think of going to work? I still don't know where he is, and staying close to this lot is my only hope of finding out.

'Okay,' I say, 'I'll contact my work and say I won't be in.'

I fish out a twenty-pence coin from my bag and ask to be excused. In the corridor I use a coin-operated telephone to ring my workplace.

When I go back into the interview room, Greasley is on the phone.

'For five, please. Yes, I realise it's short notice,' he says, his tone obsequious. 'Many thanks. We'll be along to the hotel shortly.'

He puts down the phone and then turns to me. 'We've arranged to get you something to eat.'

'But I'm not hungry.'

'You should try something, Mary,' says DC Dixon.

'You have to keep up your strength,' adds DC Wilson.

Greasley picks up his manila folder and makes his way out of the room. The rest of us follow.

In the comfortable boardroom of a local Kensington hotel, I'm hoping the detectives might be more helpful after their lavish meal. I look up from the forlorn remains of the toast I was cajoled into trying and ask again about accommodation and Michael's whereabouts.

'We should have some more information soon about where we're holding him,' says DS Byrne.

'But, meanwhile, I can show you the reason why,' says Greasley with emphasis. He reaches into the manila folder carried from the station and holds up an A4-sized envelope. 'In here I've a photograph of your boyfriend – when you see it, you might just have second thoughts about what a caring and loving person he is.'

It's the second time the word 'boyfriend' has been used in relation to middle-aged Michael. He may look at least ten years younger than his age, but the use of the term is ludicrous, a deliberate tactic to devalue our relationship.

Greasley then moves behind me. He leans over, places the photograph on the table and walks back to his seat.

The picture is shiny, good quality, with a date stamp of 04.05.1994, showing Michael, typically smart, wearing Armani jeans and a hoodie, holding a key to a padlock on what looks like a lock-up garage door.

'What do you have to say now?' asks Greasley. There's a certain triumphant finality in his tone which makes me want to laugh.

Thinking back to that time, over thirty months ago, I dimly remember overhearing a phone conversation between Michael and his friend Tom – the chap he helped get the council house – about storage needed for a removal.

'Yes, that's Michael outside a perfectly ordinary storage facility. So?'

'You don't get it,' says Greasley. 'It isn't what's outside the garage but what's inside that matters.'

'Like what?'

'RDX and PETN.'

'What's that?'

'Constituents of Semtex, an explosive substance often deployed by the IRA. You have to agree it's pretty damning evidence.'

'I'm sorry, I don't believe you.' I get angry now and push the photo back along the table. 'I've never heard of anything so ridiculous. Surely, after the mistakes of the past – the Birmingham Six, the Guildford Four, the Maguire Seven – the police should have changed their behaviour. The Birmingham Six were found guilty based on forensic tests that misinterpreted traces of nitrocellulose from playing cards on their hands as nitroglycerine. They were beaten up, tortured and spent sixteen years in jail. Now you're accusing Michael of serious offences for simply being outside a garage where inside, you claim, there were traces of explosives. It's like rerunning a bad film. You won't tell me where he is, and I've no idea how you might be treating him, and you say you are doing forensic analysis of our flat when you have just had about thirty armed police traipsing through the place. It's obvious any forensics will be subject to massive contamination by yourselves. It's an outrage of the highest order.'

During my lengthy monologue, I watch with satisfaction Greasley's attempts to fit the photo back into the envelope, resulting in it getting stuck half in and half out. Eventually, ignoring the instruction stamped 'Do Not Bend' on the envelope's cover, he rolls the glossy sheet into a baton shape and shoves it inside.

I take advantage of the embarrassed silence around the table. 'I need somewhere to stay and can you please tell me where Michael is?'

'We still haven't been told anything,' says DS Byrne. 'When we find out, we'll let you know.'

Their delaying tactics prompt me to remember the North Kensington Law Centre, which offers free legal advice. I have its number in my address book. When I ask to make a call, DS Byrne offers his mobile.

Unconcerned that the detectives around the table can overhear any conversation, I ring and am put through to a legal advisor. I tell him that the police, following an armed raid, have arrested my partner under the Prevention of Terrorism Act and have taken over my flat for forensic examination. He sounds slightly startled but composes himself enough to agree that the police would probably be responsible for providing my accommodation and that Michael can only be held for up to seven days without charge. I thank him, and he offers to speak to me again should I need more help.

Despite hearing only one side of the conversation, DS Byrne is spurred into action. He gets to his feet, takes his phone and steps into the corridor. Less than a minute later he returns and says they've booked me a hotel room.

Three

The Cavalry Arrives

Monday, 28 October, 9 a.m. – Michael

In a small, damp-smelling room, its only furniture an oak table and four chairs, Packard removed my handcuffs. 'Doesn't mean you can go wandering off.'

There was no malice in the sergeant's quip, so I gave him a rueful smile.

I settled into a chair and despite foam bursting liberally through the imitation black leather, I luxuriated in its softness after hours sitting on the cell's flimsy mattress. The wooden tabletop marked with cigarette burns and ingrained watermarks from scalding teacups implied hours of past interrogations.

My head still ached from its collision with our landing wall, and I wanted to check for bruising but, when I had tried to see my reflection in the cell's tiny stainless-steel basin, all it revealed was a blurry outline.

Looking around me, I saw a dark-tinted mirror shaped like a large TV screen fixed by four shiny metal corner studs to the side wall: its newness contrasted with the surrounding peeling plasterwork.

I got up and stood in front of this glass, where I made out matted wisps of red hair stuck to my forehead and dried blood on my beard. While going through a series of facial contortions, sticking my tongue in and out and feeling for bumps, I heard voices, barely audible, on the other side of the wall. I hurried back to the seat, cursing my stupidity for not recognising a two-way mirror.

Before my self-scolding had time to intensify, the door opened. A man dressed in a suit came in. His long arms wrapped around plastic water bottles, while his two hands grappled with his briefcase. He used the heel of his shoe to close the door.

'Mr Gallagher?'

'Yes. I'm Michael Gallagher.'

'Good morning, Michael, I'm Justin Kopelowitz,' he announced, setting down the bottles precariously on the table. 'I've been assigned to represent you.' He reached over, grabbed my hand and shook it. 'Please call me Justin.'

The cavalry had arrived.

I hadn't asked for a solicitor, not wanting the police to think I felt the need. However, I moved my head around, away from the view of the two-way mirror and, keeping my voice low, told the lawyer about the denial of due process, our violated rights and leaving Mary lying on the floor.

Justin interrupted my barely coherent rant. 'Mary's okay, she's not been arrested,' he said, his quiet tone matching mine in acknowledgement of the possibility of eavesdroppers. 'The police say they're arranging hotel accommodation for her while they search your flat.'

'What a relief,' I said, unable to keep emotion from my voice.

Justin smiled. 'When I got here, I overheard one of the arresting officers mention the suspect's bolshie partner.'

'Yeah, sounds just like her,' I said, elation sparking briefly inside me.

Justin asked if I knew why I'd been arrested, and I said I had no idea. He didn't know either but confirmed that the police had opened up the disused Canon Row, formerly New Scotland Yard HQ, just for me. He then recommended, as we hadn't been given time for a proper consultation, that I should answer 'no comment' to all questions. I'd have known to do that anyway, but his advice allayed any suspicions he could be a police stooge.

Two men walked into the room. The first, who wore dark-tinted glasses, had his arms full with an audio recorder and a large brown envelope; his colleague carried several bottles of water and a clipboard. There were no greetings as they laid down their props.

The detective with the recorder took the seat opposite me. He switched on the machine and gave his name as Detective Sergeant Fisher; his partner gave his as Detective Constable Burrows. He then asked us to state our names for the tape. Apart from Fisher's eyeshades and Burrows' weight – about eighteen stone – the two detectives seemed quite ordinary, their workaday appearance taking me by surprise, as did the lowly rankings. Perhaps I wasn't a significant suspect after all.

The square-shaped outline of a Nurofen handy-pack in Burrows' shirt pocket reminded me that my head still hurt. Annoyed at not taking a drink before the detectives' arrival, I knew if I picked up a bottle now, my hand would shake.

Fisher began the questioning.

'So,' he said, 'we are here to ask Michael Gallagher questions about the mortar attacks on Heathrow Airport in March 1994. Do you understand?'

Fisher's words thumped me like a kick in the balls. I was also confused. Do I answer 'no comment' or just say 'yes'?

Justin rescued me. 'As you have failed to supply me with sufficient information, I've advised my client to remain silent or answer "no comment" to your questions.'

'This is a very serious matter, Mr Gallagher, and you obviously must go on the advice of your solicitor,' said DS Fisher, 'but have I got a terrorist sitting in front of me? That's the question.' Staring directly at me, he paused, before adding, 'Or am I wasting my time?'

That was two questions. A few seconds passed where I didn't answer.

Fisher spoke again. 'For the benefit of the tape: Mr Gallagher at first shook his head. He's now nodding his head. Is that correct Mr Gallagher?'

'Aye, you're wasting your time,' I said, finally.

Justin shot me a look.

Fuck! I should have said 'no comment'. I'd fallen at the first hurdle.

The questions came rapidly, with Fisher leading and Burrows following up and maintaining the high tempo. They paused only to drink water, but these breaks were frequent, especially with Burrows. I became convinced the glugging sounds he made as the water went down his throat were deliberate.

The thrust of their probing suggested I was a high-ranking suspect. 'We know you are a valued member of the Provisional IRA and have been for twenty-five years. Isn't that the case?'

I was encouraged by this early question. If based on their knowledge, it was somewhat wide of the mark. 'No comment.'

'We didn't think you would be an easy nut to crack.'

'No comment.'

'You've undergone intensive training as to how to react to this kind of situation, haven't you, Mr Gallagher?' added Burrows.

'No comment.'

'And how to deal with people like us,' continued Fisher.

'No comment.'

The detectives continued with the same behaviour pattern. Burrows, slumped back in his chair, regularly rearranged the loose sheets on his clipboard. The downward angle of the board – as it rested on the rise of his stomach and the edge of the table – made it accessible viewing for both men, and they frequently referred to it. Sometimes Fisher would lift the brown envelope as if to open it, allowing himself a brief, self-satisfied smile before putting it down again; the bold lettering on the hard-backed cover read: 'Photographs. Do Not Bend.'

'You challenged your demons and overcame them, didn't you?' said Fisher. His abrupt change of tack from my alleged terrorism to my recovery from alcoholism threw me off guard.

'No comment.'

'Won your battle with the booze,' chimed in Burrows. 'Pulled yourself up by the bootstraps.'

'No comment.'

These remarks seemed genuine, compassionate even, but I wondered: how could they know so much?

Fisher turned to me again. 'Mary had her engineering maths book published recently,' he said. 'So, you started to write a book of your own, didn't you?'

'No comment.'

'You didn't like playing second fiddle, did you?' said Burrows.

'No comment.'

I should have known their earlier honeyed words would end with a sting.

Fisher picked up the envelope once more. But this time, instead of leaving it back down, he removed a photograph from inside and laid it down sideways on the table. The picture, taken from a high-up camera angle, showed me holding a key to the padlock on a lock-up garage door.

Holy fuck! They'd been following me after all.

'Do you recognise those premises, Mr Gallagher?' Fisher's eyes behind the dark shades gave nothing away, but his raised voice could not conceal a restrained excitement.

He didn't wait for my 'no comment'. 'Our forensic team has swabbed those premises and found traces of explosives,' he said. 'We need an explanation.'

'No comment,' I said, barely able to speak. I lowered my arms and wiped my clammy hands on the foam underside of the chair.

'Can you say what the quantity of explosives was?' asked Justin with perfect timing, as if he sensed instinctively when to intervene.

'One hundred and twenty nanograms,' said Burrows. 'Can you explain your association with certain individuals involved in the mortar attacks on Heathrow Airport?'

'No comment.'

'You thought we were onto you,' said Fisher. 'Didn't you tell Mary how you worried when hearing police sirens outside?'

'No comment.' For some reason I couldn't fathom, this question seemed out of kilter with earlier ones.

The audio machine made a clicking sound signalling the recording's end. While preparing to replace the cassette, Fisher paused and looked across at me.

'So, what do you think about the reward for information on those Heathrow attacks?'

'That's got nothing to do with me,' I said.

'Is a million pounds enough or should we have pitched it higher?' asked Fisher.

'No comment,' I said, reverting to interview mode.

'It's a no-brainer,' said Burrows. 'The money, a new identity and safe passage out of the country, in exchange for just two or three names.'

'You've a straight choice, Mr Gallagher,' added Fisher. 'Somewhere nice and sunny with Mary or many years' imprisonment.'

'No comment.'

Fisher inserted the new cassette and restarted the interview.

'There are a couple of roads open to you, Michael,' he said. 'Which one will you walk down?'

'No comment.'

'So, you're prepared to sit there and say "no comment" and to hang with the consequences.'

'No comment.'

'Doesn't leave you much of a future, does it?'

'No comment.'

'Where will you be in twenty years, Michael?'

'No comment.'

'And Mary?' asked Fisher. 'Where will Mary be then?'

I didn't answer. It was the final question of the session and the most disturbing of all.

Fisher looked at his watch. 'Ending the interview at 1 p.m.' He removed the cassette tape. 'We'll reconvene in two hours from now. Meanwhile, you might let your client know he's not doing his case any good by refusing to answer our questions,' he said, directing this remark to Justin as if I wasn't there.

The detectives stood up, gathered their things and walked out of the room. As soon as the door closed, I grabbed a water bottle, unscrewed the top and began to drink, each swallow down my parched throat more satisfying than all the ice-cold beers I'd ever had.

When I put the bottle down, Justin was waiting, pen in hand, poised over his notebook.

'Where would you like me to start? You'll want to know how I came to have the garage key I suppose.'

'I'm just here to ensure your legal rights are protected.'

Good, I thought. I was too tired to have to think quickly.

'With regards to the key, of course, we can discuss any evidence the police may have against you. I'm not sure there's been anything substantial so far,' added Justin.

'What about the 120 nanograms of explosives in the lock-up?'

'I wouldn't worry about those. Consider this.' Justin took up his pen again and pressed it down hard on the paper. He slid the notebook along the table.

There was a black dot on the page. 'So that's a nanogram?'

'No. That's a million nanograms.'

'Thank heaven for very small mercies,' I said, my weak attempt at humour barely concealing the immense relief I felt.

Justin put his notebook into his briefcase and glanced at his watch. 'If I'm to make contact with Mary, I should get a move on,' he said, getting to his feet.

'If you get the chance to talk, can you tell her …' I stopped, unable to carry on.

'Okay,' he said quietly. 'No problem.'

He gave the door a rap with his hand, a signal to the outside that our meeting had finished.

Sergeant Packard came into the room. I reached out to allow him to fit a pair of handcuffs around my wrists. As I said goodbye to Justin, I felt strangely emotional – like I was parting from a dear friend.

I lay on the mattress, my blanket wound tightly around me. Through missing panes of glass in the window high above me came constant sounds of revving engines from slow-moving traffic on the Thames Embankment, the racket enhanced by distant police sirens.

I sat bolt upright, recalling DS Fisher's words. 'Didn't you tell Mary how you worried every time when hearing police sirens outside?'

My mind rushed back to three months earlier. Before submitting the weekly chapter to my writing course, I had discussed a particular storyline with Mary that I'd neurotically sweated over for days. 'When I hear the sirens, I rush to the window and stare into the busy street.'

The fuckers had bugged our flat.

Monday, 28 October, 10 a.m. – Mary

DCs Dixon and Wilson take me to a tiny single en-suite hotel room in the grandly named Kensington International Inn, only five minutes from where I live. DC Wilson leaves to fetch some clothes and my mobile phone from the flat. While we wait, DC Dixon suggests it would be nice if the two of us could meet up later for a chat to help me make sense of all this. Her first name is Pamela, but I've to call her Pam, she says, handing me a card. 'You'll get me at this number anytime.' I politely take the card, mentally deciding that conversing more with a police officer is the last thing I need.

When DC Wilson arrives back, she calmly says, 'If you phone Scotland Yard from one o'clock onwards, you can find out where they're holding Mr Gallagher.'

At long last!

I thank the women and tell them I need a shower. After they leave, I take a shower and get dressed in sweater and jeans – no need for my work suit. While sitting on the bed and trying to figure out my next move, I turn on the TV. The BBC news is on, and the first words I hear are: 'Police are holding two men in connection with IRA attacks on Heathrow Airport in 1994. The arrests came during early morning raids in west London.' I see our building in Warwick Road followed by archive images of planes and Heathrow Airport. I'm shocked. Heathrow Airport? Oh my God, that's big. I experience a fleeting sense of awe.

I remember those attacks in March 1994. On the first day, mortars were fired from a car onto the airport runway. The following day, the police made a much-publicised search of the area, and the perpetrators were presumed to have gone back to Ireland. Two further attacks then took place, both timed to set off on separate days from the waste ground around the perimeter of the airport. There were no injuries and none of the mortars exploded, but the attacks caused massive disruption. They were clever, well planned and embarrassed the police and security services, who had failed to find the rockets that had been hidden underground. No wonder they were determined to arrest someone, irrespective of how bizarre their choice of person to pin the charges on. They must be still smarting from the ignominy of it all.

Then I remember I'm a pacifist and that the IRA should have loaded the mortars with leaflets or flowers.

I don't trust my mobile after it's been in possession of the police, so I go outside to a public call box and phone Michael's sister, Margaret, in Glasgow.

'Mary. Thank God! I tried to contact you earlier, but your phone went straight to the answering machine.'

Before I have a chance to explain, she speaks again. 'Eddie's lawyer told me about Michael's arrest and his friend Billy's also.'

'You must mean Michael's lawyer told you about them?'

'No. Eddie's: he was arrested at 6 o'clock this morning.'

'Eddie? That's terrible! How is he?'

'He is being questioned but has a lawyer friend in with him. I haven't heard any more news yet; what about Michael?'

'They won't tell me where he is, but they've promised to let me know this afternoon. That's if you can trust a word they say.'

I'm shocked. Eddie, Michael's younger brother, is a peaceable, artistically talented man, who, apart from spending his time doing oil paintings, has a furniture removal business. I'm relieved to hear he has a competent lawyer with him.

I recover some composure. 'Did the lawyer say anything about where Michael and Billy are being held?'

'He had no more details.'

'Did you see the news?' I ask. 'Apparently, the police are trying to claim a connection to the mortar bombing of Heathrow.'

'Yes, I heard it on the radio. Lucky they didn't arrest you as well.'

'Yes, but they've taken over our flat and kept me hanging around for five hours before putting me up in a cheap hotel. Have you told your mum and dad?'

'No, I wasn't sure what to do. I rang, eh … my youngest brother. We both agreed it best to hang fire, until we know more.'

I realise Margaret is deliberately not mentioning her brother, Johnny, by name. Presumably, she thinks her phone could be tapped.

'It's just a police trawl and publicity stunt,' I tell her. 'They had journalists lined up outside the flat. Anyway, they can only hold them for seven days at the most. Knowing Billy, he'll probably try and flog them a dodgy pension plan.'

I hear Margaret's laugh.

'I'm sorry, I shouldn't joke.'

We agree to talk again when one of us has more information. It had been comforting to hear her friendly voice. I end the call reluctantly.

Who else should I phone to let them know? My brother Keith will be at work and I'm not going to tell my parents until the whole thing has blown over. All my London-based friends will be at work, although I know I can rely on them to help out in any way they can. Roy, our neighbour, will be worried, so I dial his number.

He answers. 'Mary, are you okay? How's Michael?'

'I'm fine, Roy, but no news of Michael yet. I'll let you know when I know more.'

Roy promises to keep an eye on our flat and collect the post. He says the police have got the wrong man and he's working out ways to get him released.

With no more useful phone calls to make, I decide to buy some clothes for Michael. I set out to walk to Kensington High Street and take the route past Billy's flat, where I spot several police cars. I immediately make for the opposite side of the road, ignoring the cacophony of blaring car horns protesting at my dangerous meanderings through traffic.

A bit shaken up, I take to the quiet streets and old stable mews around Earl's Court. Twenty minutes later, I arrive at a shop Michael likes on Kensington Church Street. Concentrating on the matter in hand, I pick out black leather shoes, underwear and socks. I take care in selecting a pair of heavy cotton pyjamas, in case they turn the cell heating down at night – candy-striped, but they'll do – then take even more time selecting a shirt of dark-blue cotton and paler-blue chinos. Given the recent turn of events, my fussiness could seem shallow, but I want to help Michael retain some dignity in the face of adversity.

At exactly one o'clock, I phone Scotland Yard. After connecting to the extension, a voice tells me Michael is being held at Canon Row police station. The satisfaction at finding out his whereabouts dissipates somewhat when I realise that I've no idea where Canon Row is – my twenty years' foot-trodden knowledge of London streets is failing me. In a newsagent, I buy an A-Z of London, a notebook and a pen.

Catching the Circle Line tube from High Street Kensington station, I manage to find a seat and, with an enormous effort of will, begin to write a note to Michael: 'Dear Michael, I'm writing this note in case they won't let me see you. I hope that they are treating you well. I'm fine and I'm staying in the Kensington Inn in Earl's Court. Don't worry; they can't keep you long, so we will soon be together again. Love Mary xx.'

Nothing too romantic, as I'm sure my letter will be intercepted. I place it carefully inside the bag of clothes.

I divert my gaze to the window: a reflection of one of the living dead stares vacantly back at me. I try to compose myself but, after a few seconds, zombie Mary returns.

Leaving Westminster Station and heading along the road by the river, I reach an imposing building of red brick and white stone with small 'Police Property' signs outside, but there's no hint it's occupied and no doors are apparent. Just as I'm about to despair, a young, dark-haired man carrying a packed briefcase appears, exiting the end of the building from a basement flight of stairs.

I blurt out, 'I'm looking for Michael Gallagher.'

'Hello, I'm Justin Kopelowitz. I've just been talking to him,' he says. 'Are you Mary?'

Four

Homeless and Jobless

Monday, 28 October, 1.30 p.m. – Mary

'Thank heavens I found you,' I say to Justin, who has introduced himself as Michael's lawyer.

'Yes, a bit of luck,' he says, his earnest demeanour lightened by his kindly smile. 'This building's been in mothballs for years. The Anti-Terrorist Branch got special permission for its temporary use.'

'Have they brought in anyone else? His friend Billy McGhee?'

'They did arrest Mr McGhee, but I'm told he's since been let go.'

My satisfaction at Billy's release is fleeting. I look across the massive expanse of the old six-storey building. 'Michael's in there? By himself?'

I grope for the stability of the nearby railing. Why have they taken him to a disused building? A police space where no one can hear you scream?

'Is he okay?' I manage to ask.

'I'm sure no harm will come to him. He's coping well. And he sends you his love.'

I hold up my bag. 'Can I see him, get these clothes to him?'

Justin shakes his head. 'Unlikely.'

'But the police told me he was here; why do that if I can't make contact?'

'No harm in trying, I suppose,' Justin says, turning to retrace his steps.

At the basement door, Justin presses a bell. A uniformed policeman answers and beckons for us to enter. We follow him along a corridor to a room where several officers are gathered. I recognise DS Greasley as he approaches.

'I have Mary Attenborough here to see Michael Gallagher,' Justin says, now using assertive lawyer-speak.

I hold up my shopping bag. 'I'd like to hand in these clothes.'

Greasley gives me a hostile look as he takes the bag and rummages around. Finding my note, he reads it with growing animation and hands it, triumphantly, to another officer. He then says, 'Gallagher is being detained under the Prevention of Terrorism Act. He isn't allowed visitors.'

I start to protest, but Justin gives a curt tilt of his head. He turns away and I obediently follow. I call behind me, 'Please make sure Michael gets his clothes.'

Back outside, we pause on the pavement and I ask, 'Why would DS Greasley be so excited about my note?'

Justin looks perplexed. 'What did you write?'

'I gave my love and said they can't keep him for long.'

Justin laughs while trying to maintain his serious disposition. 'He may not have interpreted your words as being from knowledge of the PTA but as having a more sinister implication.'

'Oh my God, does he actually think I've a cunning plan to spring Michael?'

I walk along with Justin, nursing my despondency. Eventually I find my voice and recount my morning's experiences, including the BBC news claiming a connection between the arrest and the IRA's Heathrow attacks.

'Michael is adamant there's nothing to connect the garage with the IRA,' says Justin.

'In which case he should tell the truth; that would surely sort the whole thing out.'

'Maybe he will. Meanwhile, I've advised him to answer "no comment" to all their questions.'

At the next road junction, we prepare to part. Justin hands me his business card. 'You can reach me any time at those numbers.'

With a parting handshake, he promises to update me after Michael's afternoon interview.

Before continuing to the Embankment Underground station, I look back at Canon Row. I move my gaze slowly across the breadth of the building and wonder behind which of the barred oval windows Michael is languishing.

On my return to Earl's Court, I stop at a telephone kiosk and dial my friend Trish's home number in West Kensington. To my relief, she answers, and I pour out my news.

'You shouldn't be on your own,' she says. 'Come and stay here.'

I decline the invitation – I'm too self-absorbed to deal with the constant presence of another human being – but I gratefully accept her offer to have meals when I want and, even better, the use of her phone any time.

Monday, 28 October, 6.30 p.m. – Michael

When I heard the rapidly approaching footsteps in the corridor, I rolled onto the floor, as I'd done several times throughout the day. By the time an enquiring eye pressed at the spyhole and the cell door was unlocked, I'd already completed around ten press-ups. My feigned keep-fit routine, I decided, was preferable to being caught languishing morosely on the mattress.

The door opened. Sergeant Packard stood at the entrance holding a plastic shopping bag, which he left down just inside the cell. 'That's me finished for today. I thought you should have these before I go.'

'Thanks,' I said and paused, unsure if I should offer some pleasantries for the evening ahead. I could hardly say 'thanks for the hospitality'.

'Sergeant Snaith is officer-in-charge of night shift,' Packard said, filling the silence. 'He'll be with you shortly.'

'Eh … fine. I'll see you in the morning then.'

'Not tomorrow, you won't. It's back to base for me until Sunday.'

'I might not see you at all in that case.'

'You shouldn't want to set eyes on me again, ever,' said Packard, laughing to himself as he closed the door.

In the sergeant's light-hearted manner, I'd found welcome relief from the latent hostility and oppressive questioning of his CID counterparts.

One by one I lifted out Mary's purchases, holding each new item, cherishing her nearness.

I changed quickly out of the old clothes and into the new, starting with the pyjamas, which I put on under the shirt and trousers: this extra layer was necessary to combat the draught from the missing windowpanes.

After being served my evening meal, which I didn't touch, I lay on the mattress, miserably reflecting on the day's events. Without warning, the cell door opened, the sudden intrusion leaving me no time to get on the floor for my press-up pretext. Framed in the doorway stood a figure whose top half was shrouded in cigarette smoke. It gradually cleared to reveal a narrow, hunched, middle-aged officer. Sergeant Snaith, at around five foot ten inches, was the same height as Packard but was almost waif-like in comparison.

'Slop out time,' he announced, nodding his head at my meal tray on the floor. 'Come with me; we'll get rid of this lot.'

'And this lot too?' I picked up the carrier bag now filled with the police-issue clothes and trainers. 'Can I throw these in?'

'No.' Snaith took the bag from me. He led me along the corridor and then watched as I tipped the gooey mess of dinner into the metal dustbin. 'Many a prisoner would be glad of that clobber. And you should eat the food in here while you can. Might be the only healthy grub you'll have for a very long time.'

Monday, 28 October, 10.30 p.m. – Michael

In spite of the extra layer of clothing over my pyjamas and blanket wrapped tightly around me, I couldn't get warm. The earlier draught had become a chilling wind. I got off the mattress and banged on the cell door. Seconds later, the metal spyhole cover was slid across and Sergeant Snaith stood on the other side, his eyes peering through the opening.

'There's a gale blowing in here,' I said, pointing up to the window. 'Could I have another blanket?'

'You already have the standard amount of bedding,' said the sergeant.

'But it's freezing in here.'

'Well, maybe you should have stuck with our warm clothing; your fancy gear's not much good to you now,' he said, laughing as he slid closed the spyhole cover and walked away.

Tuesday, 29 October, 12.30 a.m. – Michael

The wind had died down, but sleep didn't come easy. Every few minutes when I fell into an exhausted doze, I'd be startled awake by the darts-playing night-shift staff at the far end of the corridor – groans or shrieks greeted most shots, with some followed by a stentorian announcer mimicking TV commentary, every sound amplified by the emptiness of the building.

After one such thunderous roar, I lifted my shoe and banged its heel on the cell door. 'Can you keep the noise down there?' I yelled.

The shouting stopped for a few minutes but then started again, louder than ever.

Fuck this. Without any rational thought, I slipped on my shoes and began dancing. I imagined the accompaniment of button accordions, fiddles and tin whistles from gatherings of neighbours in Gort a' Choirce during my school holidays spent in Ireland. It was there that I learned, through their songs, about emigration and rebellion, and the roles played by Patrick Pearse and Sir Roger Casement (regular visitors to the locality) but also our own local hero, Pádraig Ó Domhnaill, a member of the nineteenth-century Invincibles from the nearby townland of Mín an Chladaigh. At first, I stepped quietly, then a rush of adrenalin coursed through me as the clatter of my feet became faster and louder, the din echoing around the cell's high walls. Nearing the end of my dance, I had the added exhilaration of hearing, 'Keep down the bloody racket!'

I'd barely had time to savour getting my own back before the door opened. Snaith came hurrying inside, leaving a uniformed constable standing in the corridor, a guy twice as heavy as the sergeant, his darts clutched in his right hand.

'Right, Gallagher,' bawled Snaith, pointing at my feet, 'let's have those shoes.'

I took them off and handed them over. Without saying a word, Snaith turned, went outside and joined his constable. To my great relief, I watched the door close and heard the click of the key turning in the lock. For the first time ever, I was delighted to be safely banged up.

Tuesday, 29 October, 10 a.m. – Mary

I take the stairs to the sixth floor, locate the Human Resources office, knock the door and enter. Sue looks up and, with a lip-glossed smile and nod of the head, indicates the chair facing her. I sit down on the shiny leather seat. She fixes her stare directly on me, in the manner of a frank-talking but wholly sensitive, empathetic HR officer.

'I wanted to explain to you personally, Mary, that the future direction of your project is changing and your team is due for downsizing. I'll be contacting your agency giving a month's notice. Clearly, this is no reflection on your excellent standard of work and, with your qualifications, along with your extensive computer programming experience, you should easily get placed elsewhere. We are, of course, sorry for any inconvenience.'

Management may not have told Sue the real explanation for my early contract termination – the connection between Monday's arrest and me – but I could have been reassigned to another project had the team downsizing explanation been correct.

I can't think of an appropriately cutting response so decide on a dignified retreat. I head to the door and force a barely audible rasp: 'Thanks, Sue. I've enjoyed my time here. I'll use the remaining month to tie up any loose ends on the project.'

Looking for somewhere I can be alone, I find a ladies' toilet near the sixth-floor lifts. It's empty. I go into a cubicle, close the door, lower the toilet seat cover and sit. I grab a handful of toilet paper and blow my nose.

I've lost my partner, my flat and now my job. I'm tempted to go back in there to tell Sue she's just doing her bosses' dirty work and ask her to say straight out that I've been sacked.

When I come out of the cubicle and approach the sink, I see a face with thin, twisted lips looking back at me from the mirror. 'Where are your priorities?' I ask myself. 'Michael needs you to stay focused.'

I head straight back down to my desk.

Tuesday, 29 October, 6 p.m. – Mary

My watch shows barely two minutes past six as I rush along Piccadilly towards Albemarle Street. Slightly out of breath, I get to the second-floor reception of Arbeid, Goldstein and Oshry, where Justin is waiting. I mutter an apology for my delayed appearance.

'That's okay, I'm not back long myself. Michael's afternoon interview only finished half an hour ago,' Justin says as he indicates to enter his office.

'So, how is he?' I ask tentatively, taking a seat across from him at his desk.

'Still holding up well,' Justin says.

He hands me a plain white piece of paper, folded in two. 'I managed to get this note out.'

I open the paper. It says, 'My Mary, you are always in my thoughts. It won't be long now before we're together again. Stay strong. Love from your Michael xx'.

I battle to suppress the tears welling up in my eyes and readily accept Justin's timely offer to make tea. By the time he has returned, I've read Michael's letter several times.

'When do you think I can see him?'

'Under the act they don't have to allow visits,' Justin says, 'but hopefully, they'll release him soon. Their evidence is very flimsy.'

'But how could there be traces of explosives in a garage that Michael had the key to?'

'I wouldn't worry too much. Such a minute quantity could have arisen from cross-contamination in the police lab. Some studies have even shown traces found on the seats of London buses.'

'Can't Michael just tell them why he had that key?'

'He's made it clear to me that he didn't hire the garage personally,' Justin says, choosing his words very carefully. 'And that he's sure the IRA had no involvement.'

Assuming that's true, it could still have been used to store something dodgy. I dismiss drugs. Cigarette smuggling, maybe, or VAT-evaded imports? I wonder if I should tell Justin that not everything Michael does is completely above board; he might be protecting someone he was helping. But Michael may not be pleased if I speculate about a friend's business dealings to the extent of incriminating them; it could also prove professionally awkward for Justin. I decide to say nothing for now.

Justin mentions that he's given Michael a biro and notebook and will bring him mints and *The Guardian* each morning. The police have provided toiletries. I can tick those off my list.

I finish my tea and get up to leave. We arrange for Justin to phone me with updates. After I've left, I realise I should have given him a few pounds to cover the cost of the newspapers and mints.

Thursday, 31 October, 7.30 p.m. – Mary

I'm determined that my early contract termination won't leave my current project in disarray. I've never left loose ends in the past, and I'm not going to do so now. I curse the lack of seats as I catch the District Line, bustling with late commuters and early revellers. A seat is vacated at St James's Park and I gratefully plonk down, earning a disgruntled look from the woman in the next seat, disturbed from her engrossment in the *Evening Standard*. As the train moves off, I glance over and read a couple of lines, but gradually my eyes close and I descend into temporary unconsciousness.

I'm wakened by loud music. A burly male is standing a few metres away, dressed entirely in black. A shiny steel helmet completely covers his head, and he's carrying a cardboard machine gun adorned with childishly exaggerated red and yellow flames. His companion, dressed as an elf in a green felt costume with a large floppy hat, is carrying a ghetto-blaster and a small green bucket with a sign: 'Treat a child for Halloween.' While the cheerfully smiling elf vigorously shakes the bucket, his sidekick moves around the carriage, pointing his 'gun' at everyone in turn.

I clench my fist on the armrests between the seats, knocking the elbow of the *Evening Standard* reader and earning another annoyed glance. The figure in black is moving closer now, 'threatening' the passenger three seats from me. As we stop at Victoria, he shakes the 'gun' in my direction – I let out an involuntary yelp and jump up. I push through the standing passengers, jump off the train, run along the platform, down an escalator and don't stop until I feel sufficient time and distance has separated me from the scene.

Finding an empty bench on a platform, I sit shaking, my hand gripping the shoulder strap on my bag. It shouldn't be allowed, I think, scaring people like that. But somewhere my rational brain knows I had been terrorised not by that joker in his bizarre costume but by the real-life gunmen I'd faced on Monday. It's taken three days for me to flee.

Five

The Ford Sierra

Friday, 1 November, 3 p.m. – Michael

DS Fisher laid his folder on the table and sat in his usual seat opposite me, as Burrows took his, facing Justin.

'We've saved the best till last, Mr Gallagher,' Fisher said. 'When you see what we have in this file, you might change your mind about not talking to us.' He lifted the flap slightly, giving me no more than a glimpse inside, before letting it fall.

With his tinted glasses and straight face, DS Fisher was like the poker player savouring the last seconds before the royal flush reveal. After a dozen interviews, I'd grown used to his ways, but it didn't stop the uncontrollable fluttering of my insides.

Fisher took a green-coloured form from the folder. 'I have here the registration for a Ford Sierra car.' He held up the document. 'This was your vehicle, was it not, Mr Gallagher?'

'No comment.'

'Purchased just before the Heathrow attacks and sold two days afterwards by you, wasn't it?'

'No comment.'

'Does the registration document have my client's name on it?' asked Justin, interrupting the exchange.

'No, but one evening a local resident, a Mr Garneys, spotted from his window a couple of men acting suspiciously around the lock-up at Elmcroft Mews,' said Fisher. 'Our concerned citizen took a note of their car registration number.'

'And did Mr Garneys supply you with descriptions of these men?'

'No: he was unable to, as it was nearly dark.'

'So, how does this affect my client?'

'Let me explain how it affects your client,' answered Fisher, matching Justin's combative tone. He brought out two sheets of paper from the folder. 'What I have here are witness statements provided by the person we believe your client purchased the car from before the terrorist outrage at Heathrow and the other to whom your client sold it just days afterwards.'

He laid down the statements in front of Justin and me. 'The descriptions given here quite accurately represent Mr Gallagher's appearance.'

Justin began reading, his eyes scanning each line. I stared at the jumble of text, unable to concentrate, while the two detectives waited in silence.

'So, you say these describe my client quite accurately?' said Justin, finally raising his eyes.

'By and large,' answered Fisher.

'But not the height,' said Justin. 'The seller of the Sierra describes the suspect's height as nearly six feet, whereas the buyer says five feet seven or eight inches. And the seller also describes the hair colour as grey while the buyer says it was brown. And as you can see, my client has auburn-coloured hair.'

'In that case, he should have nothing to fear from an identification parade,' said DC Burrows, speaking for the first time.

'But maybe he does have something to fear,' said Fisher. 'Which is it, Mr Gallagher. Do you or don't you?'

'No comment.'

'You do realise, if you make the correct decision, you could be home by teatime.'

Fisher then spoke into the recorder to declare the interview over.

'Very well,' said Justin. 'I'll have a discussion with my client and let you know shortly.'

The two detectives manoeuvred their chairs back from the table and stood up. Burrows led the way out, but Fisher stopped in the doorway. 'Thanks for your time and patience, gentlemen,' he said, slowly closing the door. 'This afternoon's interview was our last.'

The last of the questions! There were times I thought they would never stop. An instant end-of-term feeling of nostalgia came over me, followed immediately by one of great relief at not having yielded to their pressure. I said a silent prayer of thanks.

While Justin checked the witnesses' accounts, I weighed up the possible consequences of a line-up. What if I'm picked out, even by mistake? It happens all the time.

'You think I should go for it?'

'It's up to you. I'm only here to advise.'

'But can you think of disadvantages?'

'If you don't, the prosecution could say you failed to co-operate, if it ever comes to a trial.'

'There's no chance of it getting that far, surely?'

'I seriously doubt it,' Justin said, 'but it's my duty to make you aware of any foreseeable downside.'

'Okay, I'll go for it, but I'd rather you don't mention this to Mary beforehand. I wouldn't want to build up her hopes.'

'I won't. By tomorrow, hopefully, you'll be free and things back to normal.'

Hopefully, I thought, but a voice in my head told me things would never be the same again.

Saturday, 2 November, 4 p.m. – Michael

Coming out of Canon Row police station, the dazzle of the low afternoon sun made me blink. Fisher and Burrows led me to the waiting minibus.

Casually dressed, they seemed younger and less formidable than when behind their interviewing desk.

I sat handcuffed to Burrows on a raised seat behind Fisher. The driver clutched the steering wheel with leather-gloved hands as if he was on the starting grid at Silverstone. He gave a hand signal to two police motorcyclists parked on either side and we set off.

I waited until the noise from whirring helicopter blades overhead faded slightly, then said, 'Isn't all this a bit much?'

'It's there in case your friends try to rescue you,' Burrows replied, his face expressionless. I couldn't tell if he was joking or not.

We travelled northwards on Park Lane and, after six days locked up, I had a brief, exhilarating feeling of setting out on an excursion. Tourists sauntered along the pavement bordering Hyde Park, many with elaborate-looking cameras slung around their necks; as we passed at speed, some directed their lenses towards us.

When we turned onto Edgware Road, our journey was brought almost to a standstill by slow-moving traffic and jaywalking shoppers. The driver fidgeted, then turned to Fisher. 'At this rate, Sarge, it's going to be midnight before we get there.'

'Go route one,' ordered Fisher.

'Right away, guv.' The driver rolled down his window and with a deft over-arm movement attached a magnetic box to the roof. A deafening siren blasted out. The two outriders spearheaded our charge and for the next mile or so, we sped past countless vehicles, their drivers obligingly pulling over, while every pedestrian head turned in our direction.

Our destination was Kilburn Police Station. Much to my relief, Justin was waiting at the entrance. Going inside, we were led by Burrows along a corridor and into a small room. 'The parade gallery is through there,' said the detective, indicating a door in the corner. 'Sergeant Thomas, the identification officer, will see to you shortly.' He then unlocked my handcuffs and left.

Shortly afterwards a grey-haired man in uniform ducked his head through the connecting door. 'Getting ready for the volunteers,' he said, holding up a pile of white envelopes. 'Won't be long.'

A notice was pinned inside a glass-fronted case fixed on the side wall with the heading 'Identity Parade Regulations'. I began to read it and was instantly distracted by the reflection of my wide-eyed, hairy face. Initial bemusement changed to shock at my ragged appearance, a reminder I'd been sleeping in my clothes all week. Inwardly, I cursed those at Canon Row for not allowing me a mirror.

Only half-listening while Justin gave me details about the order of the ID witnesses, my fingers busily realigned my shirt buttons. I'd scarcely finished when Sergeant Thomas called, 'We're ready for you now.'

I walked with Justin towards the connecting door. 'I'll probably stick out like a sore thumb through there.'

'You'll be okay; just try to blend in.' Justin placed his hand lightly on my back, urging me through the doorway, as if encouraging a reluctant protégé onto the stage.

Once inside, it took a few seconds for my eyes to acclimatise to the subdued lighting. The ID officer sat at a desk at the end of the long narrow room, his hands busy stuffing banknotes into envelopes. 'You can choose any one of those positions,' he said, nodding his head at a line of evenly spaced floor markings, numbered one to nine, with a chair at each. 'Stand or sit down as you wish.'

I took position five and stood with my back to the height measurement chart, clasping my hands behind me.

The line-up volunteers came shuffling into the room, one with a canvas bedroll, which he pushed under a table. The group formed a huddle no more than ten feet from me. None had a red beard or auburn-coloured hair: whatever hair they had was white or grey, with one man's shaven head mottled with dabs of the antiseptic Gentian Violet. As they spoke quietly, self-consciously, amongst themselves – predominately in Irish accents – they darted knowing smiles at one another and occasionally at me.

I shot sly glances back and felt an unexpected sense of kinship and a weird nostalgia for my days in The Spike homeless shelter at Camberwell. Such sentiments were quickly replaced by puzzled annoyance: twelve years striving to maintain a distance from my former life, yet the ID parade profilers judged I was similar in appearance to this group of rough sleepers.

The ID officer called, 'Get in line please.' The men moved in a swift regimented manoeuvre, their flurried activity in the confined area generating a familiar doss-house whiff: urine, surgical spirits, stale tobacco and musty clothing. They formed a line on either side of me, each with his hands joined at the front as if protecting his most vulnerable parts. I unclasped my hands from behind me, undid my top two shirt buttons, quickly mussed my hair and adopted the same posture.

The man on my left was several inches shorter than me. I tried to remember what the witness statements had indicated about height, but my mind went blank. The formaldehyde smell from the Gentian Violet on the man to my right hung around his head like an invisible halo.

Without warning, the room was flooded with a brilliant yellow glow. Momentarily stunned, I stared at the mirrored glass, the barrier separating me from the scrutinising eyes of the witness. I heard no sound except for the faint thrum from the fluorescent tubes on the ceiling. After about a minute, the brightness abruptly dimmed. The participants, including me, relaxed our rigid poses.

The ID officer came to my side and spoke quietly. 'You're entitled to change places for the next witness. Do you want to move? Or to sit down?'

My capacity for rational thought had, by this time, deserted me.

'I'll remain standing, thanks.'

The bright lights came on again. I fixed my eyes straight ahead.

The other men in the line-up were veterans, relaxed in the knowledge that the sergeant's waiting envelopes solved their single anxiety – where the money for the next drink was coming from. What hope could a suspect have, I silently asked myself? I was the one who must have looked and felt guilty.

Fuck it! I've no chance, I thought.

The parade finished, and the sergeant ushered me through to the witness-viewing gallery. The room was empty except for Justin, smiling broadly. 'No positive identification from either seller or buyer.'

'So they'll have to let me go now,' I said, quietly ecstatic, but not daring to believe I could simply walk free.

Justin seemed about to reply, but Fisher and Burrows walked into the room.

'I'd like to see you in private, Mr Kopelowitz,' said Fisher. 'DC Burrows can look after your client, meanwhile.'

'Okay, Mr Gallagher,' said Burrows stepping forward. 'Let's be having you.'

The big detective ushered me into the corridor and along to a tiny cell, a sweatbox no bigger than a dressing-room changing cubicle, which he locked me inside. It had a vinyl-cushioned bench, and I sat down and luxuriated in the hot air rising from a vent near the floor – it was the warmest I'd felt since my arrest. Although my expectation of immediate release had now waned, I hadn't completely given up hope. After all, Fisher had said if I attended the ID parade, I could be home by teatime. Maybe there was some paperwork to complete – release forms and so on. Stay calm, I urged myself.

Sounds of animated voices filtered through from outside. I got off my seat and peered one-eyed through the narrow gap at the side of the door. Sergeant Thomas was shepherding the parade volunteers along the corridor towards a Way Out sign at the end.

'That helicopter wasn't up there for sightseeing,' said the volunteer with the Gentian Violet marks. 'Yer man must be a real bad bastard.'

'We should be on danger money,' another voice insisted.

The officer laughed, as he ushered the men outside. 'Save your negotiating skills for the night shelter,' he shouted as the door closed.

Settling back onto the seat, I mulled over the convergence of circumstances that had caused my homeless past to collide head-on with this present crisis.

Late 1983 – Michael

The overnight coach from Glasgow to London Victoria crawled along the North Circular Road in Monday morning rush hour traffic. A young guy asleep next to me in the back seat had his Sony Walkman going, the same song in a loop, repeated over and over. My half-waking senses couldn't escape the tinny sound carrying the voice of Christy Moore singing:

> Where the hares and lofty pheasants are plain to be seen,
> Making homes for their young round the cliffs of Dooneen.

Stuck in traffic at Marble Arch, I opened up the letter from Cathie's lawyer, sent three months earlier, stating the reasons my wife had applied for a legal separation – they'd advised me at the Glasgow Council for Alcoholism to read it often to strengthen my resolve to abstain from drink. The lawyer had written: 'Through your habitual drinking, you have subjected your wife to psychological, financial and emotional abuse, and have abrogated your responsibility to care for your three children.'

That same month Cathie had moved 500 miles from Glasgow to a new home in Bournemouth with our three sons. It was on that day I stopped drinking – and I hadn't touched a drop for twelve weeks. Now I'd arrived in London to start a new life and, once in a job, I'd send her money regularly and maybe get to see my three boys – despite my drinking, we'd always had a loving relationship. And Cathie? I had a notion, in spite of everything, that she might take me back.

When I got off at the bus terminal and began my short walk to the nearest job centre that September, still stuck in my brain was the phrase 'making homes for their young'. I was weighed down by these words and those in the lawyer's letter and was overcome with shame and remorse. There was only one way I knew to rid myself of that feeling.

On the last day of the year, enjoying the winter sunshine, I sat on my own, rucksack at my side, on a bench at Westminster Cathedral Piazza, reading a newspaper I'd found. In common with the eight or nine other homeless men gathered around the next bench, I was waiting for the cathedral's soup kitchen to open. I glanced up from my paper and returned their tentative nods to mark our mutual recognition as fellow inhabitants of the Camberwell Spike.

Worshippers began to come out of midday Mass. An elderly couple approached and I politely shifted nearer to the end of the bench.

The man smiled. 'It's okay, we prefer to stand.' He took a Polaroid camera from its case. 'Get some pictures while the weather holds.'

'We're on holiday from the States,' the woman said. 'Is it okay for my husband to take your picture with this magnificent building as background?'

'Yes, fine.' I put down the newspaper and straightened my back. 'I'm not very photogenic though.'

The woman bent her head forward, looking intently at me. 'You sound like you're from Ireland?'

'Scotland. But my family's roots are in Ireland.'

'My husband and I are Irish, from Philadelphia.'

'Oh yes?' I said. 'My mother has an uncle and four aunts there. You might even have heard of them.'

'Very unlikely. Philly's a big place.'

'But it's a small world, you never know.'

Just as I was about to give names and 1920s emigration background, Ellis Island included, the husband focused the camera. 'Okay. Big smile please.'

I tried to oblige, pleased to be able to help. The picture duly appeared, sliding, still damp, from the exit slot on the camera. The woman took it and, her fingers carefully holding the hard plastic, came over and laid the photo down next to me on the bench.

'That one is for you,' she said. 'We need just one more for our album.'

As I posed again, there came a call from the neighbouring bench: 'How about us, missus? Are we not good enough?'

'It's okay, folks, no need to worry,' answered the woman, with a wide smile. 'It's your turn next.'

My second photo completed, the husband trained his camera on the group, who had already arranged themselves: several sat on the bench while the others stood behind, all with arms folded, posing like a football team.

As the man readied himself to take their picture, his wife interrupted. 'Hold fire, dear.'

She turned to me. 'Sorry about my manners. Would you like to join in with your buddies for the photograph?'

Fuck! Was she being serious?

'No thanks,' I blurted, shaking my head politely, as I fought to hide my shock at this woman's absurd suggestion. Without another word, I picked up my rucksack and photo, rose from the bench and rushed away.

Once out of sight of the cathedral, I stopped and looked closely at the photograph. The American woman must have given me the wrong picture. Certainly, in the background was the towering grandeur of Westminster Cathedral. The foreground though, showed a middle-aged, malnourished vagrant. The photographer had captured perfectly the man's glaring eyes, sunk in his head, and a wan smile that failed utterly to camouflage his misery.

I looked closer. The snapshot *was* of me, my face almost hidden by a month-long growth of beard, my silhouette bulging with layers of shirts and sweaters, a faded white ski hat askew on my head. Next to me sat my rucksack, with the long neck of my flagon of cider sticking out from its top, as if claiming the right to be included.

I tried to tear up the photo, but the thick plastic wouldn't yield. I found a bin and forced it down amongst discarded food takeaway wrappers and soft drink cans but, despite being gone, its alien image stuck in my brain.

I took the tube as far as Brent Cross and then, my arm out to thumb a lift, walked along an access road to the M1 motorway. A lorry stopped and the driver took me 400 miles back to Glasgow. I arrived at my sister Margaret's house in time for the Hogmanay bells to ring out for the start of 1984. In the six months since receiving that lawyer's letter, I hadn't contacted Cathie or my children once.

Saturday, 2 November 1996, 6 p.m. – Michael

I had dozed off but was roused by the clatter of feet outside the sweatbox. The door opened and Justin stood at the entrance. His grim expression, and the presence of Fisher and Burrows loitering in the corridor just a few yards away, told me all I needed to know.

'I'm sorry Michael. They're going to charge you.'

'With what? Why?'

'They say there's a recording where you told Mary you're in the IRA.'

My shock and growing despondency were tinged with a certain relief as I realised that was something I'd never have said, not to Mary, not to anyone.

'Don't they have to produce the actual recording before they can charge me?'

'The police say they're waiting for the relevant tape to be handed over to them by MI5. They're allowed to charge a suspect where there are reasonable grounds to believe that further evidence will become available.'

Burrows, holding out a pair of handcuffs, walked briskly towards me. 'Let's go, Michael,' he said.

Six

The Smartly Dressed Man from Glasgow

Sunday, 3 November, 9 a.m. – Mary

I've just got back to the hotel from my run in Holland Park, when the phone rings.

'Justin here. Sorry about the early hour, Mary, but I have some news.'

'Hello, Justin. Not bad I hope?'

'I've just been talking to DS Greasley,' the lawyer says. 'They'll let you see Michael if you agree to a formal police interview. They're suggesting this afternoon at three.'

'Sounds okay.'

'That's the good news, Mary, but if you don't agree to this interview, Greasley says they'll arrest you. Clearly there's nothing they could be thinking of charging you with,' adds Justin. 'Personally, I think it's a sign of their desperation.'

'Of course, it is.'

'There is one other thing. Michael is keen you give a "no comment" interview.'

'And what do you think?'

'It's up to you.'

'I'll go along with that, if it lessens Michael's anxieties. I've already given them an interview and statement; they know I've nothing to hide.'

Sunday, 3 November, 2.45 p.m. – Mary

At Kensington Police station, DS Greasley meets me in the foyer. 'Mr Kopelowitz isn't here yet. You can wait in the interview room.'

Robotically, I follow him along a corridor and we enter a room with a long table; he points me to the far end.

'Would you like a newspaper to read?'

'Okay.'

Returning with a Sunday tabloid, Greasley places it in front of me. 'Thanks,' I say as he walks out of the room.

I look at the newspaper but don't open it. My lack of sleep doesn't help thought retention. I stare blankly before me and wait for Justin's friendly face to enter the room.

Instead, it's Greasley who comes back in, this time carrying documents and a cassette-recording machine. He looks at me, then at the newspaper.

'It's not been touched,' he says. A smirk forms around his mouth. Maybe he doesn't understand the effects of extreme shock or perhaps he's celebrating reducing me to a barely functioning state, but his reaction is not sensible if he thinks I might have useful information about the alleged offence and could be induced to co-operate.

I'm prepared for more barbs but, mercifully, Justin walks in. Greasley takes his seat, and Justin sits next to me.

'Sorry for the delay,' he says, speaking quietly. 'I called in at Canon Row with Sunday papers and sweets for Michael.' He then turns to Greasley. 'We're ready to start, I think.'

The sergeant switches on the machine and we state our names. He then opens his folder and starts his questions: Do I have any knowledge of any other activities of the PIRA? Do I have an explanation for our regular trips to Ireland? Do I know of any legitimate reason why Michael Gallagher would have rented a lock-up garage in Hampstead? Do I know the police had him followed on many occasions?

I repeatedly answer 'no comment', but the last one has me thinking of the time Michael told me he was being followed. I had dismissed his claims, saying his fiction writing was distorting his sense of reality.

'It's in your own interest to co-operate now, Mary,' says Greasley, sitting forward in his seat. 'Cast your part in a better light when all this comes out.'

'No comment.'

'You do know there has been a listening device installed in your flat.'

Although Justin has mentioned covert surveillance, I'm somewhat shocked at this: surely, they cannot legally bug a person's home?

'On 23 September this year, Gallagher admitted to you he was in the IRA, did he not?'

I'm perplexed at the absurd suggestion.

'No comment.'

'And he wanted you to arrange for him to case the city.'

Now I'm convinced they haven't bugged our flat but just looked up the 'Special Branch Manual of Terrorist Stock Phrases' and plucked a few out to see if any hit the mark.

'No comment.'

'It's all going to come out about the codes, Mary – the codes.'

I work as a computer programmer: I code for a living. Has some bright spark in the security services fed this line of questioning to Greasley as a bizarre joke? Despite my confused and disorientated state, I have to stifle a laugh.

Greasley must have gathered from my manner he has said something I find amusing. He closes his folder and switches off the recorder. 'Interview concluded at 3.45 p.m.,' he announces.

I've done it! Now I'll get to see Michael.

'So, I can visit now?'

'Yes, shortly.' The smirk reappears as he leans back in his chair. 'I think you should know – we charged Michael Gallagher on three counts relating to the mortar attack at Heathrow Airport,' he says, not bothering to hide the tone of triumph in his voice.

I'm devastated but try to compose myself. 'You've no evidence. Michael is completely innocent. What possible point is there in charging him?'

'You'll soon find out,' says Greasley, getting to his feet.

'You've learnt absolutely nothing from your Birmingham Six or Guildford Four scandals,' I call out as he picks up his recorder and turns towards the door.

Justin glances at me and holds up his hand in a calming gesture.

'You're still pursuing innocent people.' I'm shouting now, as Greasley walks from the room. 'Saves you having to find who was really responsible.'

When we leave the police station, I readily accept Justin's offer of a lift.

'I'm sorry I didn't let you know about the charges earlier,' he says, as we move off. 'I didn't want to upset you before your interview. The charges will be formally presented when Michael appears at Belmarsh Magistrates' Court in the morning.'

'Can't we ask for the case be thrown out through lack of evidence?' I say with feigned composure.

'When the judge is made aware of the covert recordings, he's almost certainly going to allow the prosecution time to strengthen their case.'

'But we never said anything remotely like those quotes from Greasley. I think the bug could be a complete invention.'

'Their point is, although they don't have tapes or transcripts from MI5 yet, they've been provided with written samples of some incriminating passages allegedly from your conversations.'

'What about bail?'

Justin draws in a deep breath. 'Unfortunately, in matters of this nature bail is unlikely.'

'Surely, though, given the flimsy nature of the prosecution case, when the court hears from me, the person closest to him, the reasons for my total belief in his innocence, the judge would dismiss the case or at least grant bail.'

The car draws up outside Canon Row. 'We've engaged a very good civil rights barrister, Stephen Kamlish. Get there before the court starts tomorrow and we can discuss the best approach.'

A blonde-haired policewoman answers my ring on the basement's doorbell.

'I'm Mary Attenborough.' I try to sound assertive without being overbearing. 'I'm here to see my partner, Michael Gallagher.'

'Come in,' she says, smiling. 'We're expecting you.'

This woman exudes a kindness absent from most of her fellow officers.

She gives me a cursory pat-down search. We go along a corridor and pass a room where, through clouds of cigarette smoke, I catch sight of uniformed policemen seated around half a dozen joined-together canteen tables, the top strewn with playing cards; a portable TV in the middle is screening a football match.

We come to another room and go inside. A sergeant seated at a table near the door puts down his newspaper. 'Okay, miss,' he says, 'you can sit down over there.'

There's a faint sound from the opposite corner and I turn to look. Michael stands between two empty chairs. His beard has grown shaggy and his hair is falling over his forehead, but it's him. At last!

Sunday, 3 November, 5 p.m. – Michael

I felt my insides churn as Mary came towards me. We hugged, and I held her tighter and longer than I'd ever done before.

Packard called out, 'no physical contact please', his tone uncharacteristically formal. We ignored him at first but, when he called again, we broke apart and took our seats, facing each other.

'I was afraid they wouldn't let you in.' I stopped then, not trusting my voice. Mary had never seen me cry; I didn't want this to be the first time. I definitely didn't want Packard to see me blubbering – after a week coping with threats and jibes, how pathetic would it look to break down now?

I leaned forward in the chair and put my arms around Mary's shoulders. She drew me in and I burrowed my face into the crook of her neck, savouring the fresh-washed smell of her woolly scarf. We stayed like this until there was another 'no touching' warning.

We parted abruptly. Mary, her back to the sergeant, rolled her eyes and grimaced. She looked tired.

'You're looking well,' I said.

'No, I'm not.'

'Okay. You're looking terrible.'

'You look terribler,' she said.

'I'm only kidding, you look great.'

The colour of her beret and scarf matched the red rims etched around her eyes. She was beautiful.

Sunday, 3 November, 5.15 p.m. – Mary

'I should tell you what's happening out there,' I say hurriedly, anxious to make the most of our time. Michael is pleased to hear about the support from our families and friends, and their disbelief that he could be involved in such an affair.

'Hold on,' he says and moves his chair a few inches to his right. 'They can't see either of our faces now,' he continues, speaking quietly. 'Stops them lip-reading.'

I don't argue, although the police officers are less than thirty feet away and could probably hear us if they wanted to.

In Michael's altered position, an overhead light on the ceiling shines on him like a spotlight and I see him clearly for the first time. His new shirt is crumpled, grimy and spattered with what looks like ketchup – not blood, I hope. I try not to appear shocked, but the words just come out. 'What have they done to you?'

He smiles. 'They wouldn't let me get scrubbed up for my special visitor.'

'Are those the new clothes I brought in?'

'I've been sleeping in them over my pyjamas: there's no heating and some panes are missing in the window.'

'But you have bedclothes?'

'One blanket: the night sergeant knocked me back when I asked for an extra one.'

I turn my head and look sternly towards the sergeant; he has his head down, reading his paper.

'Not him,' Michael says quietly. 'He's the good cop.'

When I try to mentally summon the questions that need asking, I keep getting distracted by his appearance. 'Have you been sleeping?' I ask.

'I get three or four hours.'

I'm not tempted to suggest he asks for sleeping pills. I'm fearful of addiction, particularly given his past, and they don't provide proper sleep anyway.

'How about the food, can you eat?'

'They have it delivered from a fancy local restaurant, but I've no appetite.'

'Are you exercising?'

'I've been doing press-ups in the cell and dancing too.'

'Dancing?'

'Yea. Just some set-dancing steps. When I get into the rhythm, I lose myself and think I'm somewhere else.'

I'm pleased he's looking after himself but, so far, we've both avoided talking about tomorrow's court hearing, so I whisper in Michael's ear. 'Can you tell me anything about the lock-up? They showed me the pictures.'

'That was outside, Mary. How could I know what went on inside?' he says. 'The whole thing's ridiculous.'

'But if you told them the truth, they'd be forced to let you go.'

'Justin advised me to answer "no comment". I trust him.'

'Can't you at least tell them who gave you the key?'

'Drop it, Mary. Please.' An anguished expression crosses his face, the one I see only when he has acute back pain. 'Once I'm out, I'll explain everything.'

It's enough for me to stop. 'Okay,' I say.

Michael clutches at his shirt-front, bunching the cotton in his fist. 'I was hoping you could get me a clean shirt for tomorrow.'

I'm struck with the realisation that he has nothing respectable to wear and I can't have him looking like a criminal. I look at my watch. 'I'll have to try and get you clothes.'

'You can't go yet,' he says, hurriedly, his disappointment audible. 'I could wash the shirt in the cell.'

'That's not good enough. You need a suit.'

Michael grins suddenly. 'What do they call the man from Glasgow wearing a suit?'

'I don't know. What *do* they call the man from Glasgow wearing a suit?' I reluctantly repeat.

'The accused.'

I groan, remembering the old joke now.

'Okay, very funny, but where can I buy clothes at this time on a Sunday?'

As I finish speaking the policewoman calls towards us.

'The Army and Navy Stores in Victoria Street is open until six.' Her helpful intervention confirms what I suspected earlier – the officers could hear us.

We stand up. Michael smiles, but his eyes are sad. I lean close and tell him I love him.

'Love you too,' he replies, as we hug.

As the policewoman and I once again pass the tea-break room, I stop in my stride and call into the room. 'You lot are in there all day doing nothing but playing cards and watching TV and not one of you could arrange for Michael's clothes to be washed?'

There's no reaction, save for sheepish looks, and as we move towards the exit, the policewoman's shrug and smile tell me she doesn't have a problem with my outburst. She opens the door to let me out.

I look up at Big Ben's clock. It's twenty to six. I alternate between walking and running, dodging past tourists and Sunday shoppers, and reach the store with minutes to spare. I don't fancy the grey and black suits: too funereal. Then I spot a light-green jacket matched with pale grey trousers – just the thing. I grab a shirt, tie, underwear and a belt, and pay.

Pleased with my purchases, I walk quickly back to Canon Row. They haven't got him yet, I think. With my statement and Michael looking like a good, upstanding citizen, the judge can't possibly remand him.

I ring the bell, and the same policewoman lets me back in. We go no further than the vestibule. I hand over the bag. 'Will you let Michael have these for court tomorrow?'

'I'll make sure he has everything,' she says and then shows me out again.

Sunday, 3 November, 6.30 p.m. – Michael

Packard came into the cell and handed me a bag with clothes, along with a pen and a piece of paper. 'Before I go off duty, I need your moniker for this lot.'

I sign.

'You can't say she's not good to you,' he said, taking back the pen and his receipt. 'Just one thing,' he continued, turning around in the doorway. 'If you don't mind?'

'Go on.'

'I wouldn't bother with a lawyer. Let your missus speak in court; she'll have you back outside in no time at all.'

I smiled. In ordinary times I'd have offered to shake his hand.

Monday, 4 November, 5.45 a.m. – Michael

I had just finished dressing for court when I heard the familiar sound of Snaith's hacking cough from the corridor. His regular 5.45 a.m. call.

'Good morning, Gallagher,' he said and came inside. 'I trust you slept well.'

'Okay,' I said – every day the same untruthful salutations, the same untruthful replies.

The sergeant took up his usual position against the wall.

'Your last day,' he said, taking a drag from his cigarette. 'I hope you won't miss us too much.'

I took a step back, keeping my clothes clear of the smoke. 'I think I'll just about cope.'

'Believe me: this place is kosher compared to Belmarsh,' Snaith said. He took another drag on his cigarette, holding the smoke in his lungs, his eyes fixed on mine. It was a gesture I'd come to recognise, his prelude to recounting some Belmarsh horror story created by his warped imagination. I'd already heard of the rapists in the showers, the vengeful cook's mouse-dropping risottos and the cockroach curries.

'Remember when doing bird, Gallagher, and you're two-upped in the peter with another con, it's just your Donald Duck who you're landed with. Your oppo could be queer or a twenty-stone weightlifter, maybe even want to use you as a barbell, a dead-weight substitute, have bad breath or always farting, and you're locked in together, maybe for months at a time. It's not the same as an away trip with Arsenal or Spurs where you could be two-upped with your twin striker or centre-back in a five-star hotel bedroom.'

When Snaith's comment warranted a reply, I'd nod or shake my head. Sometimes I caught myself doing the opposite to what was appropriate but came to realise it didn't matter. So enamoured was the man with his grim forebodings that, as long as I reacted somehow, he was satisfied.

I decided Snaith's career had been wasted. His Home Office gaffers could have sent him and his jail stories to areas with rising levels of juvenile delinquency: he would have the errant kids terrified and reverse the crime rate in no time at all.

Snaith flicked cigarette ash into my wash-hand basin. 'Now I'm not saying you'll end up in Belmarsh,' he said, 'but it does no harm to prepare.'

Mercifully, before he could deliver another morale-sapping scenario, the door opened and DI Sharp walked in. I hadn't seen the inspector since my arrest. He came up to me, smiling and vigorously rubbing his hands together.

He looked me up and down. 'That's a sharp piece of clobber, Michael.'

I didn't answer, just nodded in agreement.

'Big day coming up. Are you all set?'

'Hopefully,' I said.

Sharp then asked about the food, which I agreed was good, though I hadn't much of an appetite.

'And the staff,' he asked, glancing across at Snaith, no longer smoking, 'the sergeant here and the lads – they've been fair, haven't they?'

'They've been okay,' I said, truthfully. There had been no more incidents after our darts and dancing conflict on my first night.

'We can take it then you've no complaints,' said Sharp, speaking like a tour operator having just completed a satisfaction survey of my foreign package holiday.

I was then handcuffed to a uniformed constable and, with Sharp and Snaith following us, we walked outside to the courtyard and climbed into the minibus parked at the pavement.

'Good luck, Michael,' said Sharp. Just as Snaith slid the door closed from outside, he called, 'Don't say you've not been warned.'

Seven

A Judge's Tough Love

***R. v Michael Anthony Gallagher* – Charge Statement**

The Director of Public Prosecutions (DPP) has instituted proceedings against Michael Gallagher for an offence under Part 11 of the Prevention of Terrorism (Temporary Provisions) Act 1989 in that on Sunday 3rd November 1996 Gallagher was charged with the following offences:

1. Between the 17th February 1994 and 4th May 1994 within the jurisdiction of the Central Criminal Court you did give, lend or otherwise make available to any other person whether for consideration or not a lockup and Ford Sierra motor car knowing that the lockup garage and Ford Sierra motor car would be used in connection with acts of terrorism to which Section 9 of the Prevention of Terrorism (Temporary Provisions) Act 1989 applies.

Contrary to Section 9 (2) of the Prevention of Terrorism (Temporary Provisions) Act 1989

2. On or before 16th March 1994 within the jurisdiction of the Central Criminal Court, you did unlawfully and maliciously conspire with a person or persons unknown to cause by an explosive substance an explosion of a nature likely to endanger life or cause serious injury to property.

Contrary to Section 3 (1) (a) of the Explosive Substances Act 1883

3. On or before 28th October 1996 at 111E Warwick Road, London SW5 you belonged or professed to belong to a proscribed organisation, namely the Provisional Irish Republican Army.

Contrary to section 2(1) (a) Prevention of Terrorism (Temporary Provisions) Act 1989

Monday, 4 November, 8.30 a.m. – Michael

Locked inside a two-way interview cubicle in the basement of Belmarsh Magistrates' Court, I sat reading the charge sheet. Insistent chants from mainly female voices outside disrupted my concentration – their three most used words: Belmarsh, SSU and Torture.

The cubicle door opposite opened and a man came in. His black gown hanging loose around his squat frame, he leant forward and pressed his hand against the plate-glass screen dividing us. Unsure what to do, I stood up, reached out and let my palm briefly cover his. I'd never been greeted in such a way, but the man's broad smile helped me relax.

He looked at me over the top of his glasses. 'I'm Stephen Kamlish, here to represent you, Michael.'

'Glad to meet you, Stephen.'

From within the folds of his gown, Stephen brought out a copy of my charge sheet. 'Are we all set?'

'More or less.' My hand swiped at wisps of hair on my forehead. 'A comb would be handy.'

Stephen patted the top of his bald head. 'No use asking me.'

'Sorry.'

'I like your suit,' he said, diplomatically diverting from my gaffe. Smiling, his fingers made a twirling motion.

Obediently, I turned a full circle. 'Mary, my partner, bought my clothes yesterday.'

'Yes, very smart.' His own pinstripe three-piece suit and starched white collar made his compliment meaningful.

Seating himself on the plastic chair, Stephen crossed his legs and rested his charge sheet copy on them. 'We've got District Judge Walters. He knows the law and is a stickler for procedure. He's reasonable, though, and doesn't care for gimmicks from either defence or prosecution. We should get a fair hearing.'

'You think he might let me go?'

'Well, let's see the charges, Michael,' Stephen said, his biro hovering over the sheet.

'Now, this lock-up, did you hire it?'

'No, I was there just once, to get the £50 deposit returned.'

'Not very sensible if you had suspected it was used for an IRA action,' he said, with a wry smile. 'And the lock-up would only matter if the prosecution was successful in proving its connection with the Heathrow mortars. On this point, we can discount the explosives evidence.' He made a tick on the page.

'But the police reckon that's their ace card.'

Stephen smiled. 'One hundred and twenty nanograms is such a minuscule amount, we can make a persuasive case for innocent contamination.'

'Fine,' I said, trying not to sound too excited.

'In relation to the Sierra car. You weren't picked out at the ID parade, so we don't think they'll proceed with this. Okay?'

I nodded back. 'Yea, sure.'

Stephen made another tick on the page.

'This third charge: from MI5's covert recording, where you told Mary you were in the IRA.' Stephen raised his eyes from the sheet and looked at me quizzically.

'There's no problem here. Their bug has recorded me reading to Mary some of my writing about an IRA volunteer in London – his mates have got back home safely, but he's left behind clearing up.'

'No need to go on, Michael. Justin has already explained this.'

'Mary will be here too. She can give an account, first-hand.'

Stephen shook his head. 'It's better if she's not involved.'

'Why not?' I asked, worried now that I'd overstepped the mark by implying this professional needed help. 'She could clarify the misunderstandings.'

'Mary could say something now that may be inconsistent with comments she's made in the past. Apparently, they have many months of recordings.'

'So, why haven't they already produced them?'

'They may still be sifting through their tapes and transcripts for evidence.'

'They're going to be disappointed,' I said, squirming inwardly at the thought of our conversations being pored over. 'Could I get bail if they won't drop the charges?'

'We would certainly try.'

'And what if I can't?'

'Don't worry, Michael. All going well, it won't come to that.'

Monday, 4 November, 9 a.m. – Mary

I arrive at the court exhausted and clammy but on time. I banish the paranoid feeling that the numerous hold-ups resulted from a security services directive to London Transport. On the positive side, my engendered state of hyper-alertness has helped me maintain the required running pace for the final mile from Plumstead Station. My journey has taken me twice as long as expected, but I'm here, notes written up, ready to give testimony and convince the judge of Michael's innocence.

When I get near the courthouse, I see Justin at the entrance. He stands, cigarette in hand, watching a line of women protesters outside the prison.

A man wearing a barrister's gown approaches us after we pass through security and Justin introduces Stephen Kamlish. Stephen's broad smile and welcome as we shake hands put me instantly at ease. He leads us to a small meeting room at the side of the concourse.

'How's Michael?' I ask Stephen. 'Is he wearing his new clothes?'

'Yes, Mary, he did a twirl for me in his new suit – very dapper.'

I'm reassured that Michael relates well to Stephen. I had hoped this would be so based on the barrister's experience: he was junior counsel to the Lawrence family for their private prosecution following the racist murder of their son Stephen and has also assisted leading human rights lawyer Michael Mansfield in other high-profile cases.

'Currently the prosecution case is extremely slim,' Stephen says. 'They haven't provided any hard evidence linking Michael to their allegations.'

'At what stage will I be allowed to speak?' I ask, impatient to know my placing in the order of proceedings. 'I think I'll be able to clarify to the judge that it's just a terrible misunderstanding.'

'Michael was very much in favour for you to plead his case,' Stephen says. 'I had to advise him there could be more recorded conversations not yet mentioned.'

'We've never said anything even remotely incriminating,' I say, ready to elaborate, when I hear a shouted announcement from the concourse outside.

'We're on,' Stephen says. He gets to his feet and heads for the door, Justin following.

As I make my way upstairs to the public gallery, I feel quite useless. Michael's fate is now out of my hands.

Monday, 4 November, 9.30 a.m. – Michael

A uniformed policeman led me upstairs and along a short corridor. We stopped at a plain wooden door that he opened and ushered me inside. After a faltering step forward, I found myself standing at the rail in the dock of the courtroom. At that moment, it seemed like every single person crowded below sneaked a look up at me. I sat down immediately, to make myself smaller.

My eyes scanned the room. Besides legal and media people, there were court staff and two policemen with sub-machine guns stationed on either side of the entrance but no sign of Mary.

Stephen stood in conversation with a barrister at the adjacent prosecutors' table. A sudden burst of optimism came over me at the sight of this pale, gangly lad looming over Stephen. I decided he could not be as guileful or experienced as our man.

I'd almost forgotten about Justin, but then I spotted him seated at the far right of the defence team's table, wearing a smart blue suit. I was impressed at the trouble he had taken with his attire: far removed from the slept-in look of his duty-solicitor working clothes. The fact he had seen fit to get dressed up, however, further frayed my nerves.

Members of the media occupied the back row of two benches situated on the room's left-hand side. Seated in the front row were two women I thought I recognised. They threw dour glances in my direction. A young woman carrying a flat canvas bag squeezed into the crowded back row. She struggled awkwardly along, her blue jeans and brashly coloured T-shirt incongruous amongst the suits and skirts of the other occupants. On reaching the end, no more than fifteen feet from me, she took an artist's sketchpad from her bag.

Holy Jesus, that's all I need! I instinctively reached for my tie and tightened the knot.

The clerk called out 'Be upstanding in court' and we all obeyed. A man wearing a plain grey suit came through a side door and strode to the middle of the long wooden desk, where he stopped. He made a downward motion and everyone sat, except for the armed policemen.

The judge called out, 'Will the accused please stand?'

I stood up straight, remembering Mary's warning not to slouch.

The clerk read out the charges and, when finished, asked, 'How do you plead?'

'Not guilty.'

I was greatly relieved to hear those words. So fearful had I been of saying 'guilty' by mistake, I had silently rehearsed my critical one-line speaking part.

Prosecutor Richard Horwell, in his opening statement, referred to the ruthless violence meted out by the IRA, gesticulating frequently. He regularly injected, 'If it pleases you, sir', and turned towards the judge; I wondered if such obsequiousness would impress Mr Walters or be seen as a sign of weakness. Stephen had said this judge had no time for gimmicks – I hoped this would include flattery. Finally, Horwell referred to taped conversations from our flat, in which he claimed I had discussed details of my IRA activity with Mary.

When it came Stephen's turn to speak, he stood at ease, looking fully prepared to systematically deconstruct the prosecution's case.

'My client has voluntarily undergone an identification parade and was not picked out by the two witnesses, the seller or buyer of the Ford Sierra. And relating to the lock-up garage, Mr Gallagher was merely returning the lock-up key for the deposit and was not party to the hiring of the garage. No evidence has been produced to place him there at any other time.' Stephen paused then and smiled. 'That said, the minuscule quantity of explosives allegedly discovered in the garage, 120 nanograms, is an amount that I could quite easily have picked up on the seat of my pants while sitting in my taxi on the way here.' His words prompted laughter around the room.

'On charge three, the so-called evidence here relates to MI5's covert audio surveillance of my client's flat. Mr Gallagher was in the process of writing a novel about an IRA fixer. He and his partner, Dr Mary Attenborough, had been discussing a storyline.'

Stephen picked out a sheet of paper from his folder and read from it. '"I hear their sirens and rush to the window, standing still, not daring to move, looking into the busy street." Now, I've no doubt those were his spoken words; indeed, he has confirmed so,' said Stephen. 'They have, however, been cleverly misinterpreted by the prosecution. A correct reading of the transcript in full, makes it clear Mr Gallagher, while quoting aloud his written words in the first person, is referring to the man, Malachy, his novel's protagonist.'

Slightly embarrassed as I was at Stephen's grandiose description of my humble project, his rational explanation should have dispelled any doubts of my innocence on the final charge. He finished by asking that the charges be dropped or, if not, that I should be granted bail.

'If it pleases you, sir,' said Horwell, getting immediately to his feet and holding up his copy of the transcript, 'it's the prosecution's belief that the Malachy character is, in fact, the alter ego of Michael Gallagher and that this so-called fictitious account is the actual lived experience of the accused.'

'Thank you, Mr Horwell,' said the judge. 'Unless the prosecution can produce more substantial evidence very soon, especially with regard to the covert MI5 surveillance, I would have to consider ruling that there is no case to answer. Meanwhile, I'm prepared to consider a bail application.'

That's it! I was going home.

Undeterred, Horwell was on his feet again. As he was about to speak, he turned and exchanged fleeting nods with two women I'd noticed earlier. I remembered then where I'd seen them: they were the plain-clothes officers I'd exchanged neighbourly smiles with when being led downstairs following my arrest.

'If it pleases you, sir,' said Horwell. 'I have here Detective Inspector Williams representing the Metropolitan Police. She has asked that any request for bail be rejected. Can I respectfully ask, before making your decision, you consider a further aspect of the taped conversation between the accused and his cohabitee?'

Judge Walters nodded. 'Go on.'

'I alluded earlier to the merciless nature of the Provisional IRA: this also extends to those within the ranks who betray its rigid code of discipline. The rule breached here is one forbidding members to discuss its activities with outsiders. If there is any doubt whatsoever this is the case with Mr Gallagher, then the Crown has a duty of care to protect him, as his very life may be at risk. I'm asking, therefore, that you remand him in custody, to keep him safely out of harm's way.'

I waited for Stephen to reply, but he remained seated, the smiling countenance he had maintained throughout now gone.

The judge reached his hand over the front of the bench. 'May I?'

Horwell handed up the transcript.

Walters lowered his head and began reading. The room went quiet, apart from the occasional scratch of crayon by the court artist, her head tilted, scrutinising my face.

Justin stood up and came tiptoeing around to the dock. I moved forward in my seat and leaned over the rail.

'The judge may have no alternative here. Should you get remanded,' Justin said, rushing his words, 'just keep your head down until we can get you moved.' Before I could ask him to explain, he was on the way back to his seat.

The judge called out, 'Will the accused please stand?'

I stood up straight.

'On this highly contentious argument about the interpretation of the covert recordings, I'm unable to rule.'

Walters paused then. I silently let out my breath.

'Nonetheless, this court considers the Crown would be in dereliction of its duty if it endangered you in any way. Application for bail is therefore denied.'

Horwell and his staff swapped broad smiles; DI Williams and the other plain-clothes officer clasped each other's hands in celebration.

The room began to empty. The artist put her sketchpad away, then paused and had another look at me. For a split second I thought she might offer me a copy of her work.

Justin and Stephen began packing away their documents. Justin gave me a nod but, before we had a chance for further exchanges, the police guard came and led me from the dock.

Monday, 4 November, 11.30 a.m. – Mary

I strain to look over the balcony, but there's a glass barrier and no hope of seeing Michael in the dock. I can see DC Pamela Dixon, though. She's leaving with DI Williams, both smiling broadly.

I hurry downstairs and find Justin and Stephen in the building's foyer. 'What was all that nonsense about Michael's safety? It's absurd. One minute they claim the IRA could help him escape, and next they're saying this same lot could be after his blood.'

'It seems the police are determined to have it both ways,' says Stephen.

'Exactly! So, why didn't you complain about it?'

'Horwell's new angle took us all by surprise,' says Stephen defensively. 'Walters had no alternative; he wasn't going to take chances with Michael's safety.'

Justin tells me I should apply at the prison information centre next door to be included in an approved list of Michael's visitors, so I take my leave of the two lawyers. Exiting the court building, I walk alongside the thick outer concrete wall of the prison where I pass a high, barred gate giving glimpses of neatly arranged, modern, red-brick blocks. I imagine Michael underneath, being led through the tunnel towards his cell, and hope he doesn't fall into despair.

The visitors' centre is empty except for a woman about my own age behind a snack counter. 'I'm Christine,' she says as I approach. 'You're new, aren't you? Can I help?'

'My partner was remanded to the Special Secure Unit [SSU]. I need to find out about visiting, sending money and things,' I say, almost matter-of-factly. The woman's concerned expression induces in me an onrush of deep sadness, but I'm determined not to break down.

Christine leads me to a cushioned bench at the window. 'If you'll just wait here,' she says, 'I'll get you an information booklet and a cup of coffee.'

I glance across to the prison gate, then turn to Christine. 'Thanks. Coffee would be nice.'

I sit down and immediately start to cry.

Monday, 4 November, noon – Michael

In the corridor two men in black-suited uniforms stood waiting. On the ground at their feet lay a large clear plastic bag stamped with 'HMP Belmarsh'. One of the guards unsealed the bag, which I now saw contained my clothes, pen and notebook. 'Let's have your tie and belt, Gallagher,' he said in a Scottish accent.

I handed them over.

'Arms at your back,' the other guard said and, moving briskly behind me, he fitted on handcuffs.

We walked along an underground tunnel, and I practically had to jog to keep up. The officer to my right, small and overweight, took short, splay-footed strides, while his colleague marched with a wiry energy, stamping a rapid beat on the stone floor. As the Scotsman swung my bag back and forward, his jacket sleeve rode up to reveal a tattoo on his forearm reading *Falklands Iraq Belfast*.

Without my belt, I was worried my trousers might fall down. The knowledge that this was illogical – the trousers wouldn't have got lower than my hips – didn't stop me keeping my handcuffed wrists pressed hard against the back of my waistband.

At steel gates barring our way, the Scots officer stooped and spoke into an intercom box. 'PO Muir here, along with PO Baggot. Category A, Exceptional High-Risk prisoner coming through.'

Exceptional High-Risk? How ludicrous! Was he actually referring to me?

The metallic screech of a banshee's wail signalled the gates parting, and I took my first steps into prison.

Eight

Belmarsh SSU

Monday, 4 November, 12.30 p.m. – Michael

Once inside the prison, Baggot held up a flimsy piece of paper: 'I'm duty bound to inform you of Rule 43. This regulation allows you to go on the vulnerable prisoners' wing,' he said. 'It's your choice, Gallagher.'

I knew my options well: get locked in with paedophiles and police informers or possibly face a Provo military 'tribunal' anxious for answers. I decided to take my chances with the latter and, should I be unlucky enough to get locked up with any Provos, hope to talk my way out of it.

At the end of the tunnel, we went outside and onto a gravel pathway bordering a two-storey, red-brick cell block. Along the line of barred windows appeared a wave of human silhouettes, bobbing in and out of sight, as though following a pre-assigned choreography. I lent a slight swagger to my forced-march gait.

To the right of our path, a steel-meshed, twenty-foot-high fence and razor-wired roof enclosed a tar-covered yard. Near the perimeter of this cage, two prisoners walked briskly. One, tall and bearded, wore a flowing white shirt that billowed in the breeze. His much smaller companion was wrapped in an oversized donkey jacket.

The two smiled and nodded through the fence, and I returned the gesture. Hurrying, they came out of the yard and reached the cell block building just ahead of us. A sign, fixed above the entrance read: 'Special

Secure Unit, Spurs 1, 2, 3, 4'. As the building's electronic gates opened, a guard stood aside to allow the men past and then waited for us to follow. We entered a big room dominated by a conveyor belt on the left, an upright scanner in the middle and a long table on the right.

Baggot removed my handcuffs. 'We'll get you searched here, Gallagher.' He walked off with Muir towards the security apparatus, leaving me to stand with the two prisoners. Feeling awkward, still dressed in my suit, I nodded at the men in a companionable but reserved sort of way before diverting my attention to a poster on the wall headed: 'Search Guidelines'. The first item stated: '(a) Searches of body orifices, e.g. intrusive exploration of the anus, should not be performed with the use of instruments.'

At the conveyor belt, Muir began transferring the contents of my property bag into a plastic tray. Meanwhile, at the metal uprights, Baggot began fitting a pair of latex gloves round his podgy fingers. As if recognising my discomfiture, the tall prisoner turned to me and held out his hand.

'I'm Rachid: this is *mon ami* Mustafa.'

I shook hands with both. 'Are you French?'

'No,' said the two, speaking together. 'Algerian.'

Mustafa's finger prodded his chest. 'Peckham also.'

We laughed.

'I'm Michael Gallagher, from Glasgow.'

Mustafa whistled and made a downward swooping motion with his hand.

'I'm sorry,' I looked at one, then the other, 'I don't understand.'

'On the radio,' answered Mustafa. 'Heathrow.'

'But I'm innocent.'

'Your friends are in our spur,' he added, ignoring my protestation.

'What friends?' I wanted to ask but turned around at the sound of the conveyor belt. My property tray had begun its journey on the moving rollers.

From his stance at the scanner's uprights, Baggot summoned Rachid forward. After a brisk pat-down he waved the big Algerian on. The warder took from the table a long metal rod with a small mirror attachment, which he held like a golf putter. He turned to Mustafa and me, his gimlet eyes shifting slowly between us, before beckoning the Arab prisoner forward. When Mustafa got there, Baggot waved him on, then called out, 'Right, Gallagher, let's be having you.'

Trying hard to remember the search guidelines, I walked slowly forward and had just reached Baggot when a clanging sounded from the entrance. A food trolley, its chrome hotplates shrouded in steam, came trundling inside, pushed by a warder who wheeled it on into the building's interior.

'Okay, Gallagher,' called Muir from the end of the roller conveyor. 'Let's go.'

Deliberately unhurried, I took measured steps until I reached him. The Scots warder handed over my property tray. 'In here,' he said. 'Everyone stops for the chow wagon.'

I nodded enthusiastically. No need to let him know the knots bunched so tightly in my stomach didn't leave any room for food.

We came to a central area and turned into one of four passageways. With only a dull glow from embedded ceiling lights and no windows, I had difficulty seeing along the corridor. Even so, I glimpsed Rachid being ushered through a cell door by his guard. Shit. I'm in the same spur as IRA men.

A small, brightly lit office, bubble-shaped, its outer shell constructed of clear Perspex, was centrally situated against the back wall. Behind a window hatch stood a female officer, her blonde head bowed, arranging glossy brochures and leaflets into a folder.

Baggot called out to her. 'A new arrival for you, Officer O'Brien.'

'Be with you in a minute folks,' the woman murmured, without raising her head. 'Just preparing induction information.'

While we waited, my eyes were drawn to the CCTV screen fixed to the rear wall of the office. The foreground showed a red-bearded, forlorn-looking man, standing flanked by two prison officers, his arms wrapped around a plastic tray piled high with clothes.

I stared at the image, graphic proof of my new status: Michael Gallagher, Prisoner, Special Secure Unit, Belmarsh.

'Okay, I'm ready,' I heard O'Brien say. Only then did I see her properly – fine-featured with blue-grey eyes, she seemed young and fragile compared to her two brawny colleagues. A Claddagh ring on her right hand made her seem less alien.

She nodded her head, indicating my property tray. 'You do realise you're not allowed those clothes.'

Vague feelings of kinship towards her quickly dissipated. 'How was I supposed to know what was allowed?' I heard my whingeing words echo in the spur. 'I had my own clothes in Canon Row.'

'It's not the Old Bill you're dealing with now,' said Muir. He lifted out the candy-stripe pyjama jacket from my tray and held it up with his two hands like an exhibit, before dropping it back in. 'And, believe me, Gallagher, we're doing you a favour not letting you wear this in here.'

O'Brien reached through the hatch and took the tray from me. 'Everything here we'll send to your old address.'

Old address? I still live there, I wanted to tell her.

'Can I have my notebook and biro?'

'No problem.' O'Brien handed me the pen and, after a brief look inside my notebook, began ripping the pages from their wire spine.

Too shocked to object, I waited till she finished. 'Why did you have to do that?'

She twirled the spindly coiled wire around her middle finger. 'The prison authorities consider this could be used for self-harm.'

'You're joking! How could I even consider garrotting myself in such genial surroundings?'

O'Brien raised her hand to her mouth, too late to cover a smile. She placed the notebook pages inside the folder with the induction material and pushed it through the hatch.

'Best of luck,' I heard her mutter as I turned away.

Baggot and Muir led me to the nearest cell to our left, the only one in a line of four with its door open.

'Welcome to your new abode,' said Baggot, his fingers pushing me inside. The door slammed shut, its thunderous bang reverberating through my body. I stood surveying the cell's interior. A narrow, steel-framed bed jammed tight into the right corner occupied most of the floor space, with a pre-school size toilet, washstand and wooden bedside cupboard the only other furniture.

It took only one step to reach the bed. A green crocheted top cover fitted snugly around white cotton sheets and at one end lay a white, puffy pillow. I sat down and savoured the softness: this was real pampering after the roll-up plastic mattress and musty-smelling horsehair blanket of Canon Row.

Among the information documents I found some lined paper stamped at the top with 'XK1660', along with a printed slip: 'Prisoners allowed a maximum of four free letters weekly'. I smoothed out a page on top of the cupboard and began to write:

> Dear Mary,
> It's not even one o'clock, but it's been a long day.

On and on I wrote, keeping my news upbeat. I'd reached the bottom of the page when I saw the very small print: 'Letter to be handed to officer on duty. N.B. Sealed envelopes will not be sent.'

Without another thought, I tore up the paper.

At the metallic rattle of the key in my door, I quickly got off the bed. I heard the sounds of other locks being released and, then, in a local London accent, 'Is that fella they've just brought in the one we heard about on the news?'

'I've not got a clue, was asleep,' said a second speaker, in a sing-song Dublin drawl.

Holding my breath, I put an eye to the door's spyhole. Squinting through the fish-eye lens, I saw two prisoners on the opposite side of the spur. Togged out in tracksuits, they stood talking outside an open cell door. Tall and slim, hair shorn, they looked to be in their late twenties. Let your shoulders relax, breathe normally, I urged myself.

Just seconds later, my door was thrust open and the two lads crowded into my cell along with an older man. I was hemmed in, unable to move. My eyes searched beyond the group as I watched my door slowly close.

The older man carried a lumpy-shaped gunnysack, one hand wrapped around the white muslin material, the other gripping it tightly at the top. An unruly black beard obscured most of his face but not the swollen discoloured skin around his left eye. As he slowly edged his way along the side of the bed, I couldn't decide if he was smiling or sneering.

'We heard about you on the radio, Mick,' he said, his muscular arms raising the sack up and down in front of my face. This movement, as much as his words, spoken in a business-like Belfast accent, caused me to flinch inwardly. 'So, we've brought you a little something.'

Before I could say anything – had I been capable of speech – he released the drawstring on the sack and, stretching out his arms over my bed, he turned it upside down. I watched, fascinated, as a cascade of oranges, apples, bananas, several Mars bars and a bottle of orange juice tumbled onto the bedspread.

The three IRA prisoners, smiling and laughing, then took turns to shake my hand and introduce themselves: the older man, Shane from Belfast, Dubliner Benny and Londoner Steve.

On hearing that my clothing had been confiscated, Steve and Benny went off and returned with tracksuit and trainers, an Aran sweater and T-shirts.

In answering their quick-fire questions, I told them about Glasgow, my family in Bournemouth and Donegal, and life in London with Mary. After letting me talk at length, Shane spoke. 'That's a wild mad thing they say you've done, Mick.'

I shook my head. 'Innocent of all charges.'

'So, what the fuck are you doing in here?' asked the Belfast man.

Everyone laughed, including me, but the earlier turmoil in my head instantly returned. How much should I tell them about myself?

'It's a long story,' I said.

Shane turned towards the door, and the others did likewise. 'Save it for the yard, Mick: exercise starts in fifteen minutes. We can give you the grand tour meanwhile.'

I knew in English jails, unlike in Ireland, there was no command structure, but Shane's actions and tone of voice carried a certain authority.

We left the cell and I followed them to the spur's back wall and through a wide doorless entry into a washroom. With a shower stall, a toilet cubicle and a stainless-steel urinal, the room looked quite ordinary: except there was no toilet door or shower curtain.

'Not much privacy here,' I said.

Shane shot a glance towards the office. 'They see everything from the bubble.'

We left the washroom and stopped in a nearby corner area, where, in front of a large TV, several iron armchairs were bolted to the floor. The sight of them sent spasms to my lower spine. Alongside the TV, a wooden bookcase had neat stacks of *Ideal Home* and *Global Holiday* magazines.

'So, where are the menus for your Chinese takeaways the *Daily Mail* keeps telling us about?'

The men laughed.

Encouraged, I went on. 'At least you have a television.'

'Not anymore.' Shane nodded at the blacked-out screen. 'That stays off until we get a certain issue sorted. And take note, Mick: the staff aren't allowed TV viewing without a prisoner present. It's the one area in here where we've control over the screws.'

'What about the two Algerians lads; don't they like to watch?'

'Rachid and Mustafa have no interest in TV,' said Shane. 'They just listen to their radios.'

At the sound of activity from the other end of the spur I turned and saw O'Brien looking towards us through her open hatch.

'Looks like we're being watched.'

'They're worried we're cooking up something ever since our ruck last week with the Mufti squad.' Shane's revelation gave me the first hint about the origins of his black eye, the bruises on Benny's arms and Steve's swollen neck. The Belfast man then explained what had happened: after the three had acted on a plan to resist a body cavity 'squat' search, they'd been attacked by the screws. When they had fought back, reinforcements were called in. 'Anti-Irish fuckers the lot of them,' concluded Shane.

'How about O'Brien?' I asked, remembering her Claddagh ring. 'Isn't she half Irish?'

Benny laughed. 'I thought that too, but whenever her boot connected with my balls, I just knew she was full-on English.'

I waited till the laughter died down. 'How often do the squat searches take place?' I asked, as casually as I could. 'I'm up for any protest you organise.'

'Best keep out, Mick. You don't want to go to your next court appearance covered in bruises,' said Shane.

We walked up and down the middle of the yard, a prison-issue donkey jacket with collar turned up protecting me from chilly gusts of wind.

When I told the men of my narrow escape from the squat search, they bombarded me with rules, all three seeming to speak at once: 'the screws can make you open your mouth but can't make you cough'; 'they can't order you to strip completely: only the top or bottom half at a time'.

They advised me to have a cheque sent in to my account for phone cards and stamps. I could also spend a fiver weekly on luxuries, such as sweets and shampoo.

'We can help out till your money gets here,' said Shane.

'But don't go getting released before you pay us back,' added Steve.

Shane stopped walking and we stood huddled in the middle of the yard. 'Kidding aside, Mick, I don't suppose you know how long you'll be around?'

'It could be just weeks,' I answered, not sure if he was probing but sensing these men wanted to know more. 'Or it might be years. MI5 bugged our flat and recorded Mary and me discussing a story I was working on for my writing class about a fictitious volunteer involved in the movement. The prosecution maintained I was talking about myself and could face reprisals from the IRA for loose talk.'

I paused to catch my breath, ready to say more, but Shane spoke.

'It's typical, Mick: the prosecution at their usual tricks, trying to set you up.'

We resumed our walk. Greatly relieved, I switched to my other preoccupation. 'I was hoping to borrow a phone card for a quick call to Mary: only for a couple of minutes …' my speech faltered. 'Just so she knows I'm okay.'

Shane shook his head. 'Sorry Mick, we can't help you there. Phone contacts have to get vetted first.'

'But you're allowed a letter,' suggested Steve.

'I know, but I wouldn't want it going through the censors.'

'Patrina, our brief, might be able to help,' suggested Benny. 'She's visiting us in the morning and could take your letter out.'

'Just like that?' I asked.

'Put Mary's number somewhere inside. Patrina can then phone her to arrange a pick-up,' said Benny.

'This would be just a one-off, Mick. Knowing the screws can read our open letters is just something we've had to deal with; we take care what we write about,' explained Shane.

'Not a word about where you've stashed your armoury,' whispered Steve.

More from politeness than amusement, I joined in with their laughter.

Monday, 4 November, 3 p.m. – Mary

I speak into the intercom. 'Hi Roy, it's me, Mary.' He buzzes me in, and I go upstairs to find his door already open. Roy is filling the kettle while Peter, his budgie, is chirping from a cage suspended in the corner of the room. My feet negotiate a route around Hi-Fi equipment, radios and boxes of records cluttered around the floor.

'What happened at court?'

'Not good, I'm afraid. Michael has been remanded to Belmarsh Prison until 12 November.'

'They're crazy. It's not Michael they should lock up: he's innocent.' Roy has his voice raised, aimed at my flat on the far side of his kitchen wall. 'It won't end well for them.'

Roy, diagnosed with a mental health condition, is of a kindly disposition, if a little eccentric, so I'm sure there's no violence implied in his consequential prognosis for the police occupiers of our flat.

'Don't worry, Roy. They'll have to release him unless they come up with some real evidence.'

He hands me a cup of tea. 'Sorry I wasn't with you today. I have to look after my nerves.'

'No problem, I know I can depend on you; well, you and Peter, of course.'

Roy lets go with his raucous cackle.

The budgie is squawking louder and flapping its wings. Roy opens the cage door. 'It's okay, all the windows are closed. Peter likes to fly around.'

I'm not sure your guests like the budgie droppings, I think, discreetly covering the top of the cup with my hand.

He points at some letters on his kitchen top. 'These arrived this morning for you.'

I grab the five envelopes and search through them – nothing to substantiate myself as Michael's common-law wife to allow inclusion on the official visitors' list: just bills and a bank statement in my name only.

Roy tells me how to leave the room to prevent Peter's escape: go through his hallway door, close it and only then open the outer door. The irony of this sequence isn't lost on me and, as I imagine the protocols in Belmarsh Prison, I'm struck by the implausibility of Michael, handcuffed, being inducted into the prison system.

Now out on the landing facing my own flat, I knock on the door and shout, 'It's Mary Attenborough, hello, can I talk to you for a moment?'

The door barely opens revealing a man's partially hidden face and behind him a couple of officers bent over, apparently picking up fluff and placing it into plastic bags.

'Who are you?' I ask.

'Detective Constable Hook. How can I help?'

'I've called to collect my passport and some bills. I need them to be allowed to visit my partner in prison.'

'Most of your belongings have been bagged back at headquarters,' DC Hook says. 'I'll need to check if forensics has been completed. Give me a ring on Wednesday, and I should have some idea.'

'Thanks. When will you be finished with the flat?'

'Another team will be dusting for prints; once on site, it should just take another day or so,' DC Hook replies.

'It's only one room, kitchen and bathroom. You surely could have searched and minutely forensically examined every inch of it by now? Meanwhile, I'm separated from my belongings and living in a cubby-hole hotel room.'

'I'll mention that you should have a better hotel,' he says, almost kindly.

'I'd rather get back home,' I say, somewhat surprised, and not expecting anything to come of it, 'but thanks anyway.'

Trish is working late and has left me the keys to her flat. After spending three hours on calls to family members, I now have enough sureties to pledge over a quarter of a million pounds, ready for the next bail application. It isn't just the amount that's important, it's the demonstration of the faith in Michael that it represents.

After brewing myself a much-deferred cup of tea, I dial my friend Becky's number.

'Hi, Becky, it's me, Mary – I have some bad news.'

'What? Has there been an accident?'

'Michael's in jail.'

'You're kidding. What the heck's he doing there?'

'He's been charged with conspiracy to cause explosions – connected to the mortar bombing of Heathrow.'

At Becky's shriek, I momentarily take the phone from my ear.

'Mary. Please tell me you're kidding.'

'I wish I was. Last Monday morning armed police broke down our door, dragged us out of bed and took Michael away.

'Oh my God,' says Becky.

'It's completely ridiculous – some weird mix-up. Michael had been caught on camera outside a lock-up garage where the police had found minute traces of explosives – probably the result of innocent contamination.'

'Where? Why did he have a lock-up?'

'It was in West Hampstead – it wasn't Michael's hire. For some reason he went there to retrieve the deposit. As if anyone would, if they thought that place had been used to prepare bombs.'

'And that's it?' asks Becky.

'Afraid not. They also claim he bought a car to be used in the attack.

He wasn't identified at an ID parade by witnesses, but they still charged him, and he's now in Belmarsh.'

'How awful. Can't you get him out on bail?'

'That's our next move, Becky, but it's an expensive business because the charges are so serious.'

'How expensive?'

'It could be anything up to half a million.'

'God Almighty.'

'Both our families have committed to helping and we're getting there. I'm phoning friends to see if they can make up the difference but only if that becomes necessary.'

I pause here, waiting for a reply. There is none.

'Mates like you, for example, who could maybe help, if only with a small amount.'

'Mary, I don't have a brass farthing; it's all tied up.'

'That's the point. You just have to show you have equity in your house or business to pledge. It doesn't actually get handed over. There's no risk. You know yourself; Michael wouldn't do a runner.'

'Of course, he wouldn't,' she says. 'Let me think about it. Poor Michael, we need him out of that hellhole. And poor you,' adds Becky.

'They turned me out of our flat too, and I lost my job.' I'm about to relay the saga but hear Becky's doorbell ring.

'Get back to me in a couple of days,' she says quickly. 'You hang on in there.'

'Hey-ho, got to keep going,' I say and end the call.

My last call is to Margaret in Glasgow. She tells me Derry Treanor, owner of a pub there – where Michael was a regular patron before getting sober – has left a phone number for me.

When I get in touch, Derry offers £10,000, not as part of the collective bail bond but as a gift. I suspect he thinks Michael is guilty; nevertheless, I'm really touched by the gesture but decline to accept.

Back at the Kensington International Inn, the receptionist is busy on the phone. With barely a glance, she hands over a note: 'Room booked for Dr Attenborough at the Hotel George, Templeton Place. Phone message 4pm 4/11/1996'.

As I pack my luggage, I wonder if the caller had said they were from Scotland Yard and, if so, would the receptionist speculate that I could be an undercover agent rather than a displaced suspect's partner?

I enter the reception area of my new digs through double glass doors; much of the space is occupied by trestle tables and step ladders with dust sheets covering the furniture. The young receptionist confirms the booking. 'Room 104, in the basement. I'm afraid the hotel is undergoing decoration at present, and we're only half open. However, bar food is available, and a full breakfast service is being offered in the restaurant.'

Room 104 turns out to be much larger than the one in the Inn, with plenty of wardrobe and drawer space. Next to the TV are a chair and dressing table with a pad of 'Hotel George' notepaper, envelopes and a pen. Sitting down, I write the date on the top sheet and under the hotel's address I write 'and potentially of 111e Warwick Road, London, SW5 9EZ'.

> Dear Michael
> I'm missing you terribly but I'm kept very busy on the phone. I hope you have applied for me to visit on at least one occasion for the weekend.

After a bit of general information and suggestions about exercising to keep up the spirits, I sign off:

> Write as soon as you can
> Lots of love Mary xxxx
>
> P.S. in a better hotel at the moment – hope yours is OK!

I head outside to catch the last post office collection of the day, then remember I've not eaten since a breakfast banana in Earl's Court Station. I decide on a Turkish kebab place, which also serves fish and chips, my favourite crisis meal.

Back at the hotel, I'm just in time for the nine o'clock news on the BBC: 'A man charged with offences relating to the mortar attack on Heathrow Airport in March 1994 was refused bail today at Belmarsh Magistrates' Court and remanded in custody until November 12th, 1996. Michael Anthony Gallagher with an address in Warwick Road, Earl's Court, London, denied the charges.'

There follows an archive newsreel about the Heathrow mortar bombings. Clearly the whole report is based on the police press release: through grit and hard work they 'got their man', making the world a safer place. I'm angry they've not included the defence's easy rebuttal of the evidence.

Nine

Everyone's Innocent in This Place

Tuesday, 5 November, 6 a.m. – Michael

Come daylight, I began my letter to Mary, so it would be ready in time to hand to the IRA men's lawyer. Determinedly upbeat, I described Spur 4 as cosy but omitted the fact that the tennis-court-sized cramped space was intended for twelve prisoners and sixteen staff, had no windows or ventilation, and my sealed cell window caused me to yearn for the missing panes allowing the icy wind to blow into the police cell in Canon Row. I told her we could exercise outside without mentioning how the thickly packed razor wire of the yard's roof blocked any view of the sky. I ended by saying I loved her very much.

At morning unlock, a screw pushed the door open and handed me a copy of *The Irish Times*. 'This is McCarron's regular order.'

'So, why haven't you given it to Shane?'

'He was moved during the night with the other two.'

I was gutted. Now how would Mary get my letter? I tried to speak but couldn't.

'You might as well have it,' the screw said. 'You're IRA too, aren't you?'

'No … no, I'm innocent,' I blurted out.

'No difference there,' he called over his shoulder as he walked away. 'Everyone's innocent in this place.'

I went outside into the spur. Shane's door lay wide open, his bed stripped, his belongings gone; the cells of Steve and Benny were likewise empty.

Back in my own cell, I leafed through the newspaper until stopping abruptly when I came to an article headed 'Airport mortar attack accused is refused bail'.

Overcoming the creepy feeling of seeing my name in print, I read: 'In opposing bail for Mr Gallagher – "for his own safety" – the prosecution stated he was a "committed member of the IRA" but had breached the rules of that organisation by speaking to an outsider about their activities.'

Holy fuck! With the IRA men gone and no one to spread a good word for me, my mind ran riot: maybe a nonce cook, unaware I was in the clear with the IRA, would, with a single plunge of his kitchen knife, hope to achieve instant release from his pariah status, or a desperado lifer, with no prospect of parole, would throw a bucketful of acid over me just for kicks.

My eyes scanning every word, I searched in vain for the account of my barrister's rebuttal of the prosecutor's claim. Stephen Kamlish had clearly told the court the recordings were of Mary and me discussing the IRA character I had created for my book. This inclusion would have put a completely different slant on the journalist's story, and threats to my life from the IRA – or its proxies – would not have been an issue. This reporter, and by extension their editor, also failed to highlight the perverse logic of the Crown, which had placed me right in amongst my potential attackers.

I wondered if it was more than the prosecution who were trying to set me up.

During midday lock-up I picked up a letter pushed under the cell door. The envelope, slit open by the censor, was addressed in Mary's handwriting. My hands shook as I took out its single page.

She wrote that she was over her shock but was missing me terribly, was still not sleeping but had eaten some food. Everyone sent their love. She carried on:

> Now you've no official duties, try to get fit again. Remember how I fought off high blood pressure by joining a gym. You can do the same with your back problem. I've sent £200 to your account and bought you gym clothes, so I must hurry to catch the post.
>
> Write as soon as you can
>
> Lots of love Mary xxxx
>
> P.S. in a better hotel at the moment – hope yours is OK!

I read the letter, over and over. It was a precious gift.

Thursday, 7 November, 7 p.m. – Mary

Justin rings to say that my discretionary visit has been booked for Monday. Michael has applied for the inclusion of our home phone on the approved list, since prisoners aren't allowed to call mobiles, but there is still no news about when I'll be allowed back into the flat.

I decide on a small act of defiance in the hope it will make me feel less helpless. I take an A4 sheet out of my notepad and, using a felt-tip pen, start writing. Just then Roy rings.

'There are two letters for you addressed in Michael's handwriting.'

'Put the kettle on,' I yell out, 'I'll be round in a jiffy.'

'Hold your horses, Mary,' I hear him say, but I interrupt.

'From Michael, at last; thanks so much. I was so worried. I've written twice but this is the first time I've heard back.'

'I'm on my way out to see Maggie at her mother's place. This is my access night.'

'Oh. How will I get the letters?'

'Don't worry, I'll leave them on the ledge in the hall,' Roy says.

I'm not reassured: I've never had a letter stolen from the shared hallway in fifteen years, but now my paranoia takes hold, and I get to Warwick Road in half the normal five minutes' walking time. The envelopes written in Michael's lovely script look out of place among the leaflets and circulars scattered around the ledge. Grabbing them, I climb the stairs to the second floor, knock and shout through the door of my flat, 'Is anyone there? It's Mary Attenborough. I live here.'

There is no reply, so I use some Blu Tack to attach the colourful announcement that I crafted back in the hotel:

> Private Property. Do Not Enter.
> Trespassers Will Be Sued.

I sit on the stair, open the letters and skim through them. His words seem cheerful and, now that I've put the police on notice to vacate my flat, I leave Warwick Road in better spirits.

Back at the hotel I make myself a cup of tea and, lying on the bed, begin to read Michael's letters properly:

> You asked me to make sure I don't come to any harm. This must be one of the safest places in the world. There's absolutely no chance of getting run over by a bus or getting hit on the head by a tube of scaffolding, so physically I've got a great chance. As for my mental state, nobody can take control of my mind, in here or out there.

He writes how welcoming the other prisoners have been, some of them Irish. This reassurance dismisses my constant worries over his safety as a result of the nonsense spoken in court.

Michael tells me that he got my first letter and those from my mum and brother Keith and from his own family but also a couple of dozen, he says, from well-wishers, including one from campaigning nun Sister Sarah Clarke – written in extra-large handwriting due to her near blindness – who has sent him a postal order for £50. He then details the relatives and friends I should contact to tell them he's okay and will write soon. He finishes with: 'I love and miss you so much. I sing Athenry for you. Keep strong, your Michael xxxx'.

As I reread the letters, I imagine his smiling face speaking the heartening words to me and think that I might get some sleep tonight.

Friday, 8 November, 3 a.m. – Mary

I wake in the night and reach across to the bedside table where I've left a half-written letter to DI Williams. I read through my explanation of how suspicion may have fallen on Michael because of his regular trips to Ireland. He often helps out the family in Donegal with their legal issues, such as land disputes, which sometimes requires visits to Dublin.

Thinking about our trips together, I remember one weekend visit to Glasgow when I went with Michael to Derry Treanor's pub in the Gorbals, late on a Saturday night. I overheard some customers at the bar discussing their active service with 'the lads'. It didn't take Hercule Poirot to work out that their talk, mostly from the sides of their mouths, was just alcohol-fuelled bragging. I add to the letter: 'He also goes to football matches in Glasgow. Although he might join with thousands of Celtic fans singing songs which support Irish reunification, it doesn't mean he agrees with the physical force beliefs of the Provisionals.'

On reflection, though, I tear up the page – Celtic supporters *do* sing pro-IRA songs and I don't wish to give DI Williams anything she could use against Michael.

Instead, I begin a new letter: 'Dear Michael, I got two of your letters from prison yesterday, and they were just so wonderful to receive.' I add some hopeful comments about the Irish peace process and general information about family and friends and end with:

I must go now because I want to try for the gym and work as normal today.

Love Mary xxxxx

P.S. Not long until we will meet on Monday. Keep singing Athenry for me.

I fall asleep again, wishing tomorrow was Monday.

Ten

The Lawyers' Ransom Demand

Friday, 8 November, 4.30 p.m. – Mary

'Tea, Mary?' Justin offers.

'Please.'

'Back in a minute. Make yourself comfortable,' his nod indicates a swivel chair in his office.

I sit down and put my briefcase on the floor.

I'm intrigued when I spot a folded copy of *An Phoblacht/Republican News*, partially hidden amongst the files untidily sprawled over the green faux-leather desk top but, before I can sneak a closer look, Justin comes back with two mugs of tea and settles in his chair.

'Bad news, I'm afraid,' he says.

I reach into my briefcase for a notebook and biro.

'Go on,' I say, my tone reflecting a calmness I don't feel.

'The police expert tested soil samples collected from the lock-up and the mortar sites and suggests similarities between them. Although he has not yet submitted his full report, even the promise of this new evidence is likely to persuade the judge to extend Michael's remand period.'

Justin pauses and waits until I catch up with my note-taking.

'It's not all bad news, though,' he adds. 'Stephen Kamlish has told me that, in his experience, soil comparison evidence of this type is not considered reliable.'

My positive predisposition is restored.

'The next area of concern,' Justin turns over a page, 'relates to your bugged conversations. The prosecution claims MI5 has provided more incriminatory quotes.'

'That's such nonsense, Justin,' I say. 'Those scraps of MI5 transcripts read like a second-rate film scriptwriter's imaginings of the conversations of a terrorist and his partner. We would never use such words or phrases as quoted.'

'I'm afraid, Mary, there's more,' Justin says, his voice softened, the change of tone perhaps to forestall a further rant from me. He picks up the copy of *AP/RN* and spreads the centre pages in front of me.

I lean forward to scrutinise the page. The heading reads, 'Prisoners of War Held in English Jails'. Included in a list of about ten names is 'Michael Gallagher'.

'They might as well put a "Guilty" sticker on his back,' I say, finding my voice. 'Where did this come from?'

'The prosecution included it in a note: they intend mentioning it at the hearing on Tuesday.'

'Does Michael know?'

Justin nodded. 'We spoke on the phone this morning. I then contacted the editor in Dublin. He was very apologetic, claiming crossed wires between his office and Sinn Féin's in Belfast.' Relaxing into his chair, the lawyer smiles across at me. 'It's quite an irony. Last week Michael was apparently in grave danger from the IRA, now they're being portrayed as best buddies.'

I can't empathise with his whimsical mood. Instead, I sense a helplessness creeping over me. 'So, there's no chance of bail on Tuesday, you think?'

'I'd say it's extremely unlikely. Michael has decided not to attend.'

'It would be a bloody waste of time for me too.' I put the notebook back in my briefcase.

'We need to attend, though, if only to confirm the next hearing date. On that point, I've just fetched this from our accounts people,' Justin says, passing me a sheet of paper. 'Now that Michael has gone from police custody to prison, his representation is no longer free. Under legal aid rules, the legal costs are means tested, and yours and your cohabitee's incomes are jointly assessed.'

'I'm sorry, I don't understand.'

'Well, it means you have to contribute towards Michael's legal expenses,' Justin says patiently.

'How much is it?' I ask, mentally totting up the hundreds Michael and I might have between us.

'Eight thousand five hundred pounds including VAT. Unfortunately, we can't represent Michael at court if you haven't settled your account.'

'But I won't even have an income until I find another job.' My voice is calm, although my insides are in upheaval. 'All our money has gone towards buying the cottage in Donegal.'

'You have credit cards, don't you? We don't have a facility to accept these, but you can get a cash advance from the bank across the road,' offers Justin. At least he has the decency to avoid eye contact as he says this.

I hesitate for a few seconds but have no choice. Michael has to be legally represented. 'Fine,' I say.

I exit Barclays bank and head back across the road, walking stiffly, with one hand pressed on an envelope containing £8,500 tucked firmly inside my blouse. I feel like the character in a B-movie, en route to a ransom drop. It would be just my luck to be mugged now, I think.

A short while later, on the Tube travelling back to Earl's Court, I examine the invoice. I resolve to spend less time chatting and drinking tea in the offices of Arbeid, Goldstein and Oshry. Their hourly rate is £60: it must be the most expensive cuppa in London.

Monday, 11 November, 11.05 a.m. – Mary

At the automatic glass-door entrance at Belmarsh Visitors' Centre, I rush past a couple of dawdling women with children. Once inside, I smile a greeting at Christine, who is once again behind the coffee counter. I presume she won't remember me, as the past seven days have felt like a year to me, but she returns my smile.

'You're out of breath, Mary. Are you okay?'

'Fine. I've been running. I had to go to Scotland Yard to retrieve my passport as ID. Then a mad dash for the train.'

'You could have waited. They're along every fifteen minutes.'

'I didn't want to miss any of the visit, I'm booked for 11.30.'

'Not even five minutes?' She glances at her watch. 'Well, I hope he's worthy of you.'

I smile. 'Oh yes. Of course, he is.'

She points to the far end of the room, where, beyond the cafeteria-like arrangement of chairs and tables, there's a 'Visitors' Reception' sign above a protective screen cubicle opening. 'You need to book in over there.'

Standing at the back of a queue of about twenty – mainly women and children – I remember my days as an Imperial College research student, when I was also a part-time maths tutor at Holloway Prison. Using the staff fast-track admission, I'd go past long lines of visitors, feeling sorry for them, true, but also feeling slightly superior. Perhaps this is karma?

It comes to my turn. 'Good morning,' I smile tentatively at the white-shirted, cropped-haired prison officer seated in the cubicle. 'I have a visit booked for 11.30 to see Michael Gallagher, XK1660, in the SSU.'

She looks at me, at her computer monitor and then back at me, now with an expression of disdain. She obviously knows who Michael is. There can't be many new prisoners inducted into the SSU, which is reserved for terrorist suspects and organised crime bosses.

I hand over my passport and bills. With hardly a glance, she returns them. 'I'm sorry,' she says, 'I can't see any visit booked for Michael Gallagher.'

'There must be.' Although beginning to panic, I keep my voice calm. 'It's a discretionary visit booked by his solicitor.'

'Sorry. No admission if not on my list.'

'Okay. Thanks,' I say. 'I'll ring the solicitor and get this mix-up sorted.'

Away from the desk, I phone Justin on my mobile. He promises to ring the governor right away to clear up the misunderstanding.

I go over to Christine.

'Having problems, Mary?'

'The official said there's no visit booked. But our solicitor arranged one directly through the governor's office.'

'Well, I wouldn't hold out much hope, today,' Christine says, then immediately softens her tone. 'They'll only be obstructive for twenty-four hours or so. Eventually they'll let you have your visit.'

She recounts how Irish prisoners' families have been treated over the years, including those with children. On frequent occasions, having arrived from Ireland for prebooked visits, they've been refused entry. On some occasions they've discovered their relative has been 'ghosted': transferred to a prison in another part of the country without warning.

Christine means well. Perhaps she thinks getting messed around is less problematic for me, who is childless and lives locally. I hope, however, that fighting my corner could help prison visitors generally be treated better in future.

Back in my seat, I can see a road through a large open double gate in the gloomy grey perimeter walls. A council cleansing lorry speeds from a distant cellblock, slowing only slightly as the driver waves at the gate's guard before careering through. I think how it's much easier for some to get out of prison than it is for me to get in. Does Michael imagine I've forgotten him? I try projecting my thoughts. I hope he senses I'm trying hard to see him.

It's approaching 2 o'clock and I'm near to despair when my name is called. I hand over my identification documents at reception and, without saying a word, the officer hands me my visitor's pass. I select a locker for my bag and fit the wristband attached to the metal key and its rubber numbered fob around my wrist. On my way out, Christine, despite being engaged talking to other visitors, makes a thumbs-up gesture and I return a cheery wave.

A female officer escorts me to a minibus and ushers me aboard. I take my seat and watch as the woman jumps nimbly into the driving seat.

Triumph! I'm going to see Michael at long last.

I'm the only passenger in the sixteen-seat vehicle and have a weird sense of privilege as we move off along the narrow road. The driver takes us through at least half a dozen high-security gates opening automatically on our approach and, after a couple of minutes, we arrive at a red-brick, two-storey building, where a sign above the entrance reads: 'Special Secure Unit, HMP Belmarsh'.

The officer escorts me into a room with an upright metal body scanner. As she turns to go, she returns my 'thanks for taking me' comment with a nod and a smile.

I'm confronted by a much larger officer, her blonde hair coiled above her head. She stands slightly crouched, rubbing her latex-covered hands like a vigilant hockey goalie. I leave my locker key on a tray and go through the body scanner. When I reach her, she pats me down, rubbing lightly over my arms, sides and down my legs.

'Thanks,' I say, although I wonder what exactly I'm thanking her for, and start to move away.

'Hang on a moment. Lift up your hair, please.'

I gather my hair into a bunch, baring the nape of my neck. I tense as I feel the woman's hand move up into my skull, probing all around the area at the back of my head.

'Mouth wide open.'

I comply and hold my breath as she looks into my mouth. 'And lift your tongue.' Again, I obey.

'Okay,' she says, peeling off her gloves. She takes my arm and leads me down a corridor and through a door. There, behind a glass screen, is Michael.

I pick up the handset to the left of the screen, and Michael does the same.

'Hello, my love,' I speak casually, as if we've just met for lunch.

Michael is grinning, his finger prodding his wrist. 'Mary! I thought you'd forgotten our big date.'

His voice sounds tinny over the intercom system, but the relief of seeing him after ten days is enormous. He's thinner, his beard is longer and stragglier but, still, he looks great, and he's wearing the new shirt and trousers I sent in.

Seated behind Michael is a red-faced, middle-aged prison officer. 'Don't mind me,' he says as I glance in his direction. 'I won't be listening. It's just standard practice.'

I nod my thanks but have no doubts we'll be listened to, not just by him but by remote monitors.

Sitting down, I place my hands on the underside of the seat and try to pull it forward. It won't budge. I try again and stare at Michael.

'Are you wondering the same as me?' He laughs and pats the worn arm of his chair. 'Why would anyone want to steal their crappy old furniture?'

I smile back, pleased he's been able to keep his silly sense of humour.

I'm resigned to our separation until after Christmas, so don't mention tomorrow's court hearing nor do I mention the lawyer's fees – which will be refunded once we take action for unlawful arrest, so no point in worrying him now. Instead, I talk about a planned trip to my parents and other news of family and friends. I feel like I'm in a bubble, alone with the same old Michael, unbroken by recent events.

But I'm desperate for some sort of explanation about the lock-up, so, despite a reluctance to spoil the mood, I eventually ask, 'Were you helping someone? Can't you tell me who it was?'

Michael leans forward in his seat. 'You know the family we visited last year after you'd given your overseas lecture?'

I think back and remember the occasion well. I'd given a talk on teaching mathematics to engineers at University College Dublin, and afterwards we went to a Traveller halting site to visit Michael's friend, also a recovering alcoholic, who Michael had helped when he moved from London. I understand now that the friend could have needed somewhere to store furniture left behind for the use of his extended family in London.

'Oh, it's okay now, I get it.'

'Yes,' said Michael, 'they would do the same to them as they did to us, only with lots of children involved; they could turn that whole community upside down.'

Hearing this, I can appreciate that Michael's reticence is laudable, if not sensible.

All too soon the female prison officer returns for me.

'Goodbye, my love,' I say quickly. 'I'll be back to see you at the weekend.'

'Stay strong,' he says. 'I'll keep singing Athenry for you.'

We both hang our phones back on their hooks and stand up. I lean forward and kiss the glass, and Michael does the same. I'm pleased at how uninhibitedly affectionate he's become.

Tuesday, 12 November, 10.30 a.m. – Michael

On the phone, Justin gave the expected 'bail refused' decision from the court. On the positive side, the judge had set another hearing for 2 January, saying the prosecution would need stronger evidence by then. I hoped that would cheer up Mary after she had put so much work into getting bail sureties.

I'd just hung up when I heard the mail delivery trustee. 'I've left your fan mail on the bed, squire,' he called across, as he moved down the spur.

Puzzled, I hurried to my cell and found dozens of letters scattered across the bedspread. The most I'd received previously was six in one day. I sat down and sifted through the envelopes: stamps from Ireland, the USA and UK mainly, with bolder correspondents adding POW alongside my name.

I recognised the handwriting on one envelope as that of Pegeen O'Sullivan. She had written once already, anxious to know if I was okay after reading the *Irish Times* report. In my reply I'd told her of that paper's omission of my barrister's court statement. This time she had enclosed a cheque for £25 and a copy of *Fuascailt*, the quarterly news-sheet supporting republican prisoners in England.

After wishing Mary and my family well, Pegeen had written: 'The *Irish Times* report is nothing new in suppressing truth. The Free State government banned my own father, Liam O'Flaherty, many times. His novel, *The House of Gold*, was the very first to fall foul of publication censorship laws in 1929 and many more of his works besides during the 1930s.'

I paused here, humbled that Pegeen would even compare my experience with her father's. She continued:

> You wrote of the pet budgies locked in cages in your exercise yard and likened these to the prisoners, torn from their natural habitat. You mentioned too the pied wagtail that lands on top of the razor wire roof every morning: a daily prison visitor to its incarcerated bird friends below. When I told Sister Sarah this, she laughed and laughed.

After finishing reading the other correspondence, I opened a small package and found the book *No Faith in the System*, sent by the writer herself, Sister Sarah Clarke, along with another postal order, this time for £20. In her scrawly handwriting she apologised for not visiting me, but she had been banned from English prisons since 1973.

I smile as I mentally congratulate this frail Irish nun on her ability to shake the mighty British prison system.

Eleven

Meeting the Glasgow 'IRA'

Friday, 15 November, 4.30 p.m. – Mary

I'm hoping official pressure from the Irish Ambassador could help improve Michael's treatment – he *is* an Irish citizen, after all. Having delivered my letter at the embassy's front desk, I ease along the pavement outside behind a line of protesters – their chanting voices competing to be heard above the roar of London's rush-hour traffic.

I drop some coins from my raincoat pocket into a collection tin, and the protester thanks me loudly in Irish as she leans in to my lapel to attach a metal badge bearing the same slogan as their decorated banner: 'Time for Peace, Time to Go'.

Nearing the end of the line, a young woman of about seventeen is grappling with a camera while a stack of newspapers she is holding is in danger of tumbling. I instinctively reach out and catch the papers, copies of *An Phoblacht*.

The teenager smiles her thanks. She aims her camera at an older woman, posing shyly under a streetlight.

'Make it quick, Sinéad,' urges the woman.

'Cheese, Nuala,' shouts a protester.

'C'mon, Nuala, give us a proper smile,' calls the woman with the collection can.

'Move your hair, Mum,' Sinéad says, 'I can't see Dad's face.'

Nuala, reaches down and moves strands of her red hair from the T-shirt under her open baggy linen jacket. Stamped on the white cotton front is the portrait image of a smiling man with prison bars superimposed on top.

The photography session finished, the girl joins her mother. I follow her and hand back the bundle. As she takes the papers, she gives me a quizzical look.

I smile at her. 'I'm not with your demo.'

Amused, she puts her hand over her mouth and turns to her mother. 'I assumed this lady was one of the replacements.'

'Excuse us. We only know a few of the local group,' the mother says. 'We're visiting from Belfast.'

I touch my badge. 'It's an easy mistake.'

Sinéad holds out a newspaper. 'Have one, anyway.'

I shake my head. 'I would, normally, but just don't have time to read it.'

'Why don't you make time?' The girl thrusts forward her chin. 'People should know what's happening.'

'Of course,' I say, bridling inside, 'but I'm devoting all my time to getting my partner released from Belmarsh's Special Secure Unit. He's been accused of helping the Heathrow mortar attack.'

'Holy Mother of God! Do you hear that, Mum?' Sinéad calls out. 'They've got this woman's man for the Heathrow mortars.'

The Belfast woman and her daughter are joined by the other protesters, who converge on us inside the lamplight arc shining on the pavement, muttering soothing words: 'How awful,' and 'Good luck' and 'Best of luck' and – from mostly male voices – 'Good man himself,' 'Fair play to him' and 'More power to him.'

I overhear Nuala say, 'Poor woman. Her man might end up like our Francie in the Kesh: it could be years before he sees the light of day again.'

Given that Michael should be out at the next bail hearing, the outpouring of goodwill engenders in me a fraudulent feeling not experienced since the time I was besieged by teammates after fluking the winning dart, a bullseye, for the Response team in the Earl's Court Charity Challenge.

'Michael should be released soon,' I tell Nuala and Sinéad. 'Compared to your Francie's situation, his is trivial.'

'There's nothing trivial about the SSU,' Sinéad says.

'But Michael's innocent.'

'They're all innocent.' Sinéad's quick-fire reply sounds like an invitation to debate the whole freedom fighter/terrorist question. Thankfully, her mother intervenes.

'What's your name, dear?'

'Mary.'

'Well, Mary, why don't you ask for help from this prisoners' rights group?' Nuala nods her head, indicating the line of protesters. 'They're good at highlighting anti-Irish abuses.'

'I doubt Michael would want the fuss.' Then, conscious of not being too hasty in dismissing her advice, I add, 'Then again, maybe it would be worth finding out more.'

'They've a function tonight at eight o'clock,' says Sinéad, 'in The King's Head, Crouch End. Do you know it?'

I nod. 'Yes, I lived in Crouch End for a few months.'

'We'll all be there,' says Nuala. 'Come along.'

Our conversation is interrupted by the shouted greetings of two men wearing combat trousers and jackets on the opposite pavement.

Nuala leans her head close to mine. 'Big Benny Mac and his mate Budgie, down from Glasgow.'

Benny, a heavy-set, balding man in his forties, steps onto the road followed by a small round chap who is clutching a bulging bag of beer cans to his chest. Dipped headlight beams catch Benny's swaggering gait as he weaves through the crawling rush-hour traffic, his hands raised in a salute to drivers they have obliged to slow down further.

Nuala takes a step back and looks at the two men as they arrive at our side of the road. ‘Starting early, lads,’ she says, nodding her head at Budgie’s bag. ‘The social isn’t till tonight.’

‘It’s thirsty work, this protest lark.’ Benny grins at Nuala. ‘Just a taster to keep us going.’

‘Well, as long as you know it’s a quiet affair and not the Wolfe Tones at the Barrowland.’

‘No worries, Nuala. Sure, we know our manners.’

Benny stands in front of the banner held up by the women, his eyes scrutinising the artful calligraphy. ‘So, this is where the money’s going,’ he says, his voiced raised, ‘while the lads on the front line are complaining to me they don’t have an ammunition clip between them.’

‘The kids in my school made this out of an old bed sheet,’ answers Nuala. ‘Cost us no more than a tenner for the crayons and pastels.’

Benny puts up his hands in a surrender pose. ‘Okay. The kids have done a great job.’ He takes a step towards Nuala. ‘But I’ll still be having a word with the leadership about where all the money’s going.’ In spite of his lowered voice, I still hear his final, ‘Because it’s not going to the war effort.’

I’m intrigued. This man might be worth talking to.

I back off from the group and on my way to the Underground station, I formulate a plan of action. From a phone kiosk, I dial Becky and leave a message on her answering machine: ‘Becky, it’s Mary. I’m going to an Irish event tonight at Crouch End. It’s in the King’s Head, not too far from you. I’m looking for a bit of support, and you might enjoy it.’

Friday, 15 November, 8 p.m. – Mary

We had arranged to meet fifteen minutes ago, and I’m standing outside the King’s Head, silently cursing. My mood changes when I see Becky hurrying round the nearby corner, vigorously waving and mouthing ‘sorry’.

We head straight to the ladies’ toilet, where we meet Nuala and Sinéad and another woman. I nearly didn’t recognise Nuala: she’s wearing smart jeans and a maroon cardigan over a matching tank top; her hair is up in a messy bun. Sinéad is rigged out in a red crop top and tartan mini kilt over black tights.

I introduce Becky, and Nuala introduces Helen, secretary of the local prisoners' support group, a small wiry woman I recognise from the embassy demo: she's still wearing the same green-and-white tracksuit.

Nuala offers to get us drinks and I accept, grateful to be spared the first round: previous experiences of crowded function bar hatches forever remind me of the exodus gridlocks after giving my maths lectures.

When the three women have left, Becky tops up her lipstick, combs her hair and then turns to scrutinise me. She puffs out her cheeks and shakes her head, eyes narrowing: her trademark look of disapproval. 'Couldn't you have worn something else?'

I examine myself in the mirror. My blue-and-white polka-dot shirt's collar is neatly folded over the neck of my blue mohair jumper, matched with nearly new car boot sale-purchased jeans.

'It's the best I could do. Most of my clothes are in my wardrobe at home, which the police won't let me get to.'

Becky's face clouds over. She reaches out and hugs me. 'Stupid me, I forgot!'

'Don't worry, Becky.' I give her a tight squeeze. 'You're here tonight: that's the main thing.'

High-pitched microphone squeals come from the pub's function room, followed by a man's voice: 'Testing one two three four.'

I check the two cubicles are empty and seize the moment to broach my plan.

'The thing is, Becky, I want to find a contact,' I say, talking rapidly. 'Someone who could ask the IRA to confirm they didn't use the garage that Michael had the key for.' My voice is lowered to just above a whisper. 'I was hoping you might help me seek out someone "connected".'

'Why me?' Becky asks, her eyebrows raised.

'You're a great networker, and you're half Irish.'

Becky smiles and winks at me. 'I'll mention the pike in the thatch at the ould granny's place,' she says, her last few words mimicking her mother's Irish accent.

'C'mon, Becky, be serious.'

'How about the Belfast women we've just met?'

'Nuala and Sinéad were guests at today's "Time for Peace" protest at the embassy: I should think they've distanced themselves from the Armalite lot.'

'Okay, we'll see,' Becky says quietly. 'Let's settle first.'

I'm pleased: she hasn't completely dismissed my proposition.

From the open doors of the function room, we have a view of the entire crowd of about 100, but our attempts to pick out Nuala and Sinéad are hampered by the subdued lighting and hanging clouds of cigarette smoke. Then I hear the Belfast women calling us from near the stage.

Sinéad stands aside and lets us into the sofa-bench seating. I sit down next to Nuala and gladly settle into the cushioned upholstery. She pushes our drinks along the low tabletop.

I pick up my sparkling water. 'Cheers, and well done for getting such a good place.'

On the stage, branch secretary Helen stands in front of the microphone. 'Now, without further ado,' she says. 'I ask you to give a rousing London-Irish welcome to The Three McGees.'

The audience responds with cheers and whistles as three lads, strumming and drumming with great gusto, launch into 'Sean South of Garryowen'.

After another few songs, Helen goes onto the stage with Sinéad. 'Attention, please,' she calls, and the hubbub around the tables and the bar hatch dies down. 'During this interval, I want you all to give generously to the prisoners' dependants' fund.'

Sinéad holds up a red plastic bucket.

'There should be a separate bucket for the front-line troops,' someone heckles. I recognise the voice as that of Benny from Glasgow. Scattered applause and shouts of approval greet his suggestion.

'Order, order,' Helen calls. She takes the microphone from its stand and, pulling the connecting wire behind, comes off the stage, 'Let's hear from a Belfast prisoner's wife.'

Standing, Nuala takes the mic. 'There wouldn't be a peace process today without the contribution of our prisoners. My husband's struggle didn't stop because he went inside. And it's not just Francie Diamond and our men and women in Irish jails,' she continues, 'we still have our prisoners in English jails. And this woman's man,' Nuala pauses and puts her hand on my shoulder, 'Michael Gallagher, who languishes in Belmarsh.' She raises her voice. 'Michael is our warrior too, so let's have a big hand for him … and for Mary, his partner.'

'Good God!' I sink down into my seat, but I'm unable to escape the applause and the sounds of banging on tables.

Nuala smiles at us, hands the mic back to Helen and sits down.

Becky leans across, glowering at Nuala. 'Mary came here to protest Michael's innocence; you didn't help there.'

Nuala looks at me abashed. 'I'm so sorry, Mary. I got carried away.'

'It's okay, Nuala.' I force a smile. 'I thought it was great what you said about your man.'

Speeches over, the band is back and almost everyone is dancing. I follow Becky's movements, her lemon top conspicuous as she flits in and out of view, but I lose her just as the music stops. I step between the straggle of dancers drifting breathlessly back to their seats and finally see her standing at the end of the bar talking to Benny and Budgie. Well done, Becky!

I stop alongside them.

'I was telling these guys about Michael.' Becky grips my sleeve, coaxing me nearer. 'Benny and Budgie.'

Benny returns my smile with an earnest nod of his head. 'Pleased to meet you.' We shake hands.

'Do you know Michael, by any chance?'

'Maybe yes, maybe no.' Benny gives me an earnest look. 'But I salute him as a comrade.' He makes it sound like he and Michael could have shared a foxhole in the past.

'Michael isn't involved,' I say quickly. 'They've picked on him for nothing.'

'If I had a pound for every time I got a tug from Glasgow's finest,' says Budgie, holding up his cigarette, 'these would be the best ever Havana cigars.'

'An armed raid on their flat isn't just a tug; they could have both been killed,' says Becky.

I'm really put off by the arrogance exuding from these two, but I know if I don't ask now, I'll regret it later.

'I was hoping you could help me make contact with someone in the know.'

Benny and Budgie don't answer, so I carry on, rushing my words, trying to remember to keep my voice down. 'You know, eh … somebody who would be close to the …' I feel my face flush as I search for the right words, '… the military side of things.'

Benny lets out a breathy, low, whistling sound; his hand raised, he mimics pulling a trigger at his head. 'People have been nutted off for asking things like that.'

Budgie takes a deep drag on his cigarette, then slowly exhales, his darting eyes taking in their surrounds. 'Loose talk costs lives.'

'I don't mean to cause trouble,' I mutter.

Benny ignores me and turns to Becky 'Any decent clubs around here?'

'Jumbalows, just around the corner,' I hear Becky say. 'They play mostly garage or house. The music is good, but drinks are costly.'

Benny leans down and says something into her ear.

'I'd love to, but my partner's waiting at home,' she says, delivering the oft-practised lie with her perfected tone of regret.

'We should be getting back to our table,' Becky says, squeezing my elbow and pushing me ahead while, at the same time, calling 'see you later' to the two men. They're not looking.

We reach our table. Sinéad is back also, her collection duties completed.

Becky picks up her lager, takes a mouthful and clatters the bottle back on the table.

Nuala looks across at us. 'Is something wrong?'

'We were talking to Benny and his mate,' says Becky. 'They treated us like coppers' narcs.'

'They were completely unhelpful,' I add.

'So,' Nuala says, leaning forward and folding her arms on the table, 'what took you to them in the first place?' I have a momentary image of standing in front of my teacher's desk at infant school.

'I thought Benny might be able to contact people, who might know things about the Heathrow attack,' Becky says, hesitantly.

Sinéad lets out a snort of disdain. 'You're wasting your time: those two, they collect money and sell papers, and that's the height of it, but they do like to big themselves up.'

Flashing lights silhouette the two guitarists, now wearing black berets. They point the necks of their instruments at the ceiling in time to gunfire simulation from the drummer and start 'Go on Home British Soldiers'.

Becky and Sinéad quickly move back to the dance floor and join hands to form a circle with the other revellers. I slide around the table and sit beside Nuala. She smiles and shakes her head. 'Somebody should have told those lads we're trying for peace with the Brits.'

'At least everyone's enjoying themselves.'

'But not you, Mary?'

'Does it show?'

'You're holding it together well.'

'How about you, Nuala? Was it an awful shock when you found out about your husband?'

'Yes and no. Both our families had been at it since before partition: generations of them.'

'So you knew he was involved?'

'Good God no.' She sinks further into the seat, her arms folded, hugging her chest. 'If Francie had been as careful covering his tracks from the Brits as he was with me …' she says, with a wistful sigh.

During a pause between songs, Nuala gets to her feet and reaches out her hand, beckoning me to join her. It feels like she's inviting me to run the London marathon. I smile and shake my head. She hurries towards the circle of people, and Sinéad and Becky unlink their hands to let her between them, just in time for the start of 'A Nation Once Again'.

I close my eyes for a moment and when I open them again all the lights are on and everyone is on their feet in response to the strains of 'Amhrán Na bhFiann'. A drunk man at the bar, arms pressed to his sides, sways in solemn reverence. I stand up, furious with myself. I haven't been caught out like this since my first visit to Donegal, when, last to stand, I was exposed as an outsider.

The national anthem finishes. When Nuala and I hug goodbye, she speaks quietly into my ear. 'If you want each other bad enough, you'll survive this, no matter what happens.'

Twelve

It's Beginning to Look a Lot Like Christmas

Friday, 6 December, 4.45 p.m. – Michael

Settling back in my cell after exercise, I switched on my pocket radio. Nothing.

'Shit! Dead batteries.' I cursed at the thought of a no-news weekend before I could buy replacements. On the hour, I pressed my ear against the dividing wall to Rachid's cell, straining to hear his radio. One item particularly resonated: John Gorst MP had resigned the Tory whip and, after seventeen years in power, the Conservatives would lose their majority. I was ecstatic.

Let out for evening recreation, I rushed to the TV, idle since the boycott by the ghosted IRA men. The BBC news detailed that Gorst had resigned over local hospital funding. This meant John Major's government was on its last legs and Tony Blair's Labour Party was the favourite to succeed.

While I sat savouring the potential loss of influence of the Unionist parties of David Trimble and Ian Paisley, and the prospect of the resumption of the stalled peace process, Baggot and Muir appeared, standing hunched over the armchairs on either side of me, their hairy forearms resting on top.

Fuck! Do I assert my rights, switch off the TV and leave? Frozen with indecision, I dithered through the weather forecast; then, when *Neighbours* began, the two guards came around, sat down on either side of me and remained rapt with attention throughout the soap opera. Afterwards, as they returned to their office, I switched off the TV feeling as wretched as I imagined I would after crossing a workers' picket line.

Monday, 16 December, 11 a.m. – Michael

Coming from the exercise yard, Rachid and Mustafa passed through the search process before me with just a pat-down. I expected Baggot's normal 'Pants off, Gallagher' instruction but not today: the four-foot wand with mirror attached lay idle under the static conveyor belt. The screw waved me on and then moved alongside me.

'I'm to let you know, Gallagher, the Irish Embassy has been in touch with our lot here,' he said gravely, the words undulating in his drawly West Midlands accent. 'Mirror searches have been stopped.'

'Fine,' I said, impassively. Justin had already told me this earlier, in a legal phone call.

In the previous weeks of close interactions, I'd grown used to Baggot's ways. When being officious he called me Gallagher but, when he was feeling less formal, he referred to me as Jock. Now, as we walked back into the spur, he scratched the shaven crown of his bull head and gave me a stony stare, as if my face might reveal the answer to the riddle of my nationality.

'The Irish embassy or the embassy of Timbuktu, Jock, it doesn't matter. Make no mistake,' he said, closing my cell door behind me, 'step out of line, and we'll be waiting.'

Mary had cautioned me against disputes with the prison staff, citing how they might affect my chance of bail. Warnings for minor offences, such as giving cheek to screws, all totted up towards a loss of privileges. 'I struggle to think what those privileges are,' she'd said when I'd mentioned this rule-breaking consequence.

After the hearing on 12 November, I'd pretty much accepted that getting bail was unlikely: there were too many details of bugged conversations and MI5's surveillance of my movements yet to be revealed. But Mary repeatedly pointed out the lack of incriminating evidence, and she had already collected guarantees amounting to £500,000 from our families and friends, influenced by her advocacy of my innocence and memories of the many 1980s miscarriages of justice. Achieving bail for her was not just to ensure my release but also to signal no confidence in the establishment's case.

Our differing perspectives bothered me greatly. I cringed inwardly each time she recounted her efforts to obtain bail sureties, dearly wishing I could explain the origins of that garage key.

Saturday, 21 December 12.30 p.m. – Mary

I feel a sense of desolation when looking at the double bed in my room at the Fairlawns Hotel, Aldridge. Over a month has passed since I'd been allowed to return to our lonely flat, but I've carried the longing for Michael's presence here with me, and I yearn for the mild irritation of seeing him switching on the TV for the Saturday football scores.

Downstairs, our annual Christmas party organisers, Mum and Dad, are at the drinks table just inside the function room door, greeting newcomers. Resplendent in a matching maroon velvet jacket and bow tie, Dad greets me with a wry smile and a glass of champagne. 'You're not quite last,' he says.

Mum gives me a warm hug, asking, 'Are you holding up okay, love?' She has a recent perm in her gold-blonde hair and is wearing a maroon checked-pattern suit – a special gift from us siblings for her seventieth birthday.

She asks about Michael and I tell her, 'He's holding up well.' Then I add, with quiet enthusiasm, 'I have a phone call arranged for 6 o'clock.'

'I thought he wasn't allowed to call a mobile phone.'

'He calls the home phone – I have it redirected,' I whisper, then add, 'Mum's the word.'

As I prepare to leave them to it, my mother leans forward and speaks conspiratorially into my ear. 'Your dad and I got a letter this week.'

'Oh yes? What about?'

'A blast from your past.'

'Oops,' I mutter.

'It's in my handbag: I'll give it to you later.'

'Who's it from?' I ask, but she's already turned away to greet the next guests.

According to the main table's seating plan, created on Dad's Amstrad computer, I'm to the left of Mum and Dad; my brother John is next to me, in the spot that should have been Michael's, but John's partner, Barbara, has been seated further along, nearer the children's table. Keith and Jean, with their teenage children, David and Lindsay, are alongside Uncle Bill and Auntie Olga. About a dozen other neighbours and friends have name labels.

Just as the first course is being served, John and Barbara arrive with Hayley, a stylish late-teen, Hannah, only eleven but already a sultry sophisticate, and Joel, who, although nearly six, still receives 'Isn't he a lovely looking boy?' accolades when introduced to grown-ups.

'I told you we'd be late,' John, his face reddened with the drama of the journey, complains loudly. Barbara smiles at us all, and I hope the wan smile I return conveys a sisterly empathy.

'Roadworks,' John continues, as he takes his seat. 'Why do they leave all the lane closures in place at the weekend when no work is going on?'

'It wouldn't happen in a planned socialist economy,' I say, tongue in cheek, hoping to distract him. It works; he pulls in his chair and elaborates on recent Chinese economic reforms – introducing more market forces and their justification in Marxist theory. 'Capitalism must precede socialism,' he explains. 'The Soviet Union got it wrong by trying to jump from an agrarian society directly to socialism.'

I wonder if an authoritarian society like China can be on the road towards socialism. However, not having my usual appetite for a lively debate, I simply nod.

A troupe of carol singers arrive: middle-aged and older, and mainly women. At the opening bars of 'God Rest Ye, Merry Gentlemen', Keith joins them. As the jolly choir absorbs its new chorister, I'm impressed by Keith's ability to remember, or perhaps improvise, the bass harmony so perfectly.

We greet the final notes with exaggerated applause. After two more songs, a basket is passed around for charity. The singers then stream out of the room and the partygoers start moving around, getting extra drinks and forming transient groupings. As I'm considering whether this liquid mixing is a party version of Brownian motion, Mum shunts the erstwhile mentioned letter across the table to me. 'From Mike Laverty,' she whispers.

Vague curiosity is mixed with a feeling of 'don't I have enough to deal with just now'.

'What did he write?'

'He reminded us of your old friendship and wanted your address and phone number.'

As I look at the distinctive handwriting, I recollect the love poem Mike gave me comparing Sisyphus pushing the massive rock uphill to his efforts to express feelings towards me. I was impressed, only discovering later that he'd plagiarised the work. A timelier eye-opener would have saved months of my teen years – although failed relationships, in retrospect, probably seem worse than they actually were. I take the folded single sheet from the envelope and read its few lines. No thank you, Mike, I think, but I'm pleased he presumably has positive thoughts of me after all these years.

Saturday, 21 December, 2 p.m. – Michael

Signs of the approach of Christmas Day began to show in the spur. Past hit favourites like 'It's Beginning to Look a Lot Like Christmas' spilled from the officers' bubble, and decorations had been hung along the back wall, with strands of tinsel draped around the duty roster board. Hilarity among the staff was commonplace and disposable paper cups were nursed carefully by officers, leaving the coffee pot and teapot almost neglected on the corner table. Each day, as Christmas approached, we were let out of our cells for a little longer, body-searched less often, and our five-minute phone calls were extended to six and sometimes seven.

I was sitting slouched in my usual armchair in the TV area at the start of the Saturday afternoon recreation period. Glancing over the top of the newspaper I was reading, I caught Baggot and Muir, the only two officers on duty, eyeing me from the bubble and then walking over to me.

'We've a treat for you Jock,' said Baggot. 'Got our hands on a copy of *RoboCop*.' He held up the video cassette.

'Nice of you to offer,' I said, 'but no thanks.'

'It's okay. We know the rules.' Baggot put his index finger to his lips and winked at me. 'We won't tell if you won't.'

Muir earnestly nodded his head in agreement.

'I'm sorry, I don't really fancy it.'

Baggot smiled and bent towards me. I caught from his breath a strong whiff of alcohol mixed with peppermint. 'Seen it a dozen times already, have you?'

'Never. I don't like violence and sci-fi horror stuff,' I answered truthfully. I straightened up from my slouch.

The two men exchanged a 'he's got to be kidding' look.

Baggot moved to stand close to the TV. 'You don't mind us then?'

I held up my newspaper. 'I'm sorry, the noise would be a distraction,' I said. 'Besides, you know the rules,' I added, unable to help myself.

Baggot walked away from the TV and rejoined Muir, the two men casting longing glances towards the darkened screen. Strangely, having been responsible for the loss of their afternoon's entertainment, I felt a twinge of sympathy as I watched them trudge back to their office – the expected satisfaction at exercising my power to overrule the screws had failed to materialise.

Saturday, 21 December, 6 p.m. – Mary

At five minutes to six, I go upstairs to the bedroom. As I get to the door, my mobile rings. It's Michael. I tell him about the party over bursts of static interference.

'Have you had to make excuses for me?' he asks.

'Bad case of the sniffles.'

'Couldn't you have thought of something more serious? You make me sound like a real wimp.'

He's right, but I didn't want to make up an over-elaborate excuse as they may have caught wind of our problems from the TV or the papers.

I try to brighten his mood. 'My parents have just given me a note from an ex-boyfriend from my school days, Mike Laverty, wanting to contact me.'

'What's that got to do with anything?' asks Michael, sounding stressed.

'Just making light conversation,' I say, annoyed at the communication difficulties. Another static burst prevents further talk.

I hear, 'Your time's up, Gallagher, you've messed us around long enough.' This loud, jarring, hostile voice sears through my brain, yet, confusingly, the speaker's Black Country accent bears melodic similarities to the cheerful resonance of the friends and neighbours I've been listening to this afternoon.

'What's going on?' I call into the phone.

'What the fuck are you playing at …' I hear Michael say, the rest of his words lost.

'Michael, Michael, can you hear me?' Unable to help myself, I call repeatedly until I hear the hum of the disengaged line.

Wandering outside, I join my nieces and nephews in admiring the Fairlawns' gardens, which are lit up with Christmas fairy lights. The sky is deep blue, chequered by moonlight-silhouetted clouds. Weighed down with my current worries, my mood fails to yield to the mid-winter charm of the scene.

Though I'm devastated by the phone call, it could be another year before I see some of these friends and family again, and I don't want to appear morose. I stand at the hotel front, waving goodbye to Uncle Bill and Auntie Olga travelling home to Leeds, shortly followed by my mum's oldest friend Joyce and her husband Martin, travelling to Nottingham, as well as local neighbours and friends. The rest of the partygoers have rooms for the night. Back in the foyer, the beat of Los del Río's 'Macarena' blasts out from the ballroom and, through its open double doors, I see revellers forming into lines for the latest dance craze.

I find an armchair and lower myself onto its plush cushions. It's just far enough away for the music not to be too intrusive. I sit back and close my eyes.

Seconds later it seems, Hayley and Lindsay are tugging at my arms; they've changed out of their chic teen clothing into silky slip dresses and cross-strap Latin dance shoes. I look at the clock above the reception desk and realise I've been sleeping for half an hour.

'Party time,' they call out in unison.

'Not for me,' I say and sink farther into the spongy comfort of the armchair.

They reach down to me and we hug. I then watch them rush through the doors towards the music and worry about sixteen-year-old Lindsay's ankles as her high heels jiggle precariously on the shiny dance floor. It strikes me then: my niece is the same age I was when I fell for Mike Laverty.

Saturday, 21 December, 6 p.m. – Michael

I stood dialling Mary's phone for our arranged six o'clock call. No more than ten feet away, the office door had been left ajar and, for the first time, I could see inside. Baggot and Muir, both in shirtsleeves and wearing earphones, sat on swivel chairs, two disposable cups on the floor between them. Muir, eyes closed, was tapping his feet, while Baggot's fingers pressed rapidly on the buttons of his Game Boy console.

Mary answered on the eighth ring. From the start, irregular bursts of static had us talking over each other. Nearing the end of my five minutes – but confident I'd be allowed one or two extra – Mary mentioned Mike Laverty, something about him looking for her address. At the same time as she finished her sentence, I heard a call of 'time's up'.

I moved the receiver from my ear and looked across at Baggot, now standing, holding up his hand, signifying five. I ignored him but, before I could resume my conversation, the screw threw down his earphones and hurried through the doorway with Muir at his back.

'Your time's up Gallagher, you've messed us around for long enough,' said Baggot.

I realised this was payback for stymieing their *RoboCop* viewing earlier. 'What the fuck are you playing at? You can fuck off,' I said. 'I'm still talking.'

Baggot reached out and wrested the phone from my hand, leaving it dangling by its cord. He and Muir then grabbed me by the elbows and pushed me inside the office.

'That's it, Gallagher,' Muir said, letting go of my arm, 'you've gone too far this time.'

Disoriented at the screws' reaction, I became further distracted by the sound of interference coming from the headphones on Baggot's chair. Surreally, I heard Mary's voice faintly sounding, through the crackling static: 'Michael, Michael, can you hear me?' and then the line went dead.

The truth struck me like a bolt of lightning. Baggot had been listening to our call. 'You nosy fucker,' I roared.

I picked up the earphones, connecting wire and all, and threw them at Baggot, narrowly missing his head.

Immediately, I felt Muir's hand grab my wrist, forcing the arm up my back. With Baggot gripping the other arm, the two screws shunted me to my cell, pushed me inside and locked the door.

I sat down, trying to calm myself, cursing: up until the very moment when I heard Mary's voice through Baggot's headphones, I'd assumed the monitoring of prisoners' phone calls was carried out by a distant civil servant hunched in a Whitehall Home Office building. Now I knew the eavesdropper on my most private conversations could be the screw who locked me in my cell, I could never again look forward to a personal call. It felt ten times worse than the remote MI5 audio surveillance.

And who the fuck was Mike Laverty? I'd a vague memory of Mary mentioning him, a boyfriend from her teenage years who pretended he had written a book. Poor Mary. She had enough problems with one Michael without having to deal with two.

Saturday, 21 December, 10.30 p.m. – Mary

Heavy drumbeats wake me again, the earlier pleasing music having now developed into a headache-inducing racket.

Returning to the function room, I find it deserted except for my parents. After sharing their satisfaction that the party has gone so smoothly, they listen while I spill out the dramatic details of my phone call.

'I don't know if it was me or his guard who made Michael angry.'

'Don't be too hard on yourself, love,' my mother says, 'it would have been the awful warder.'

'His behaviour in prison could affect his bail chances,' says my dad, ever the realist, if not the diplomat.

After saying goodnight, I return to my room, still scolding myself for stupidly mentioning the Laverty letter and ruefully reflecting on how that brief teenage episode may have, a generation later, caused a commotion in, of all places, the SSU in Belmarsh. On the other hand, Michael knows all about his namesake, and we'd spoken light-heartedly about my former boyfriend's predilection for tall stories.

I tell myself that, like Mum said, Michael's 'what the fuck' shout was probably a reaction to the guard's time-up order, but a niggle of doubt still lingers in my head. I feel completely useless. Michael could now be worried I'm considering reigniting my friendship with Mike Laverty. He's trapped in the ideal breeding ground for negative thinking, and I've no means to reassure him.

When teaching in Holloway, I had observed that, whatever small personal choices the women were able to exercise inside the jail, they were powerless to control events outside and this could cause them to resort to drugs or illicit hooch to numb their feelings of helplessness. With Michael's history this was a particular concern for me.

I change into my pyjamas and climb into bed, automatically leaving space on the left side.

Thirteen

Mass in the SSU

Wednesday, 25 December, 10 a.m. – Michael

'Padre's here,' said Baggot, standing with Muir and a priest draped in a white and gold-coloured chasuble outside the open door of my cell.

'Father Ambrose,' he said, as we shook hands. 'I'm the new prison chaplain. Happy Christmas.'

Word had got around about this appointment. His steel-grey hair, a contrast to his boyish face, was, I concluded, from premature ageing caused by the soul-searching involved in his decision to abandon his Church of England ministry and become a Roman Catholic priest.

'Happy Christmas, Father.' I glanced at my watch. 'But it's only ten o'clock. Mass isn't till eleven.'

'That's for the chapel service,' answered the priest. 'I'm afraid they're not letting you attend, Michael.'

I turned to the two screws. 'My application was granted by your governor.'

'That was before your disturbance last Saturday,' said Baggot.

'You're not being denied your rights,' added Muir. 'We've had the Padre call on you personally.'

'But the Mass is for communal worship,' I said outwardly calm but inwardly furious. My hopes of a chance meeting with Irish prisoners from the other spurs in the SSU now lay in tatters.

'Why not have it in your cell?' suggested Muir.

'Where you couldn't swing a cat.'

Baggot pointed towards the washroom. 'How about there?'

'The toilets?' I said and began undoing the top buttons on the new shirt I'd put on for the occasion. 'Just lock me up again.'

'Give the Padre a break, Michael,' pleaded Muir. 'He's left his missus and kids on Christmas Day.'

Muir, the staunch Scottish Protestant, I suddenly realised, was showing more concern for the priest than I was. I recalled that I'd never missed a Mass at Christmas, not even during the nihilistic dalliances of my vagrancy days.

'Okay,' I said. 'Let's do it.'

In the washroom, Father Ambrose went straight to a wooden changing bench and dragged it in front of the doorless toilet and shower cubicle. From his black leather Mass kit, he took out a silver chalice and paten, water and wine cruets, a candle and candleholder, every sacred piece in miniature but all familiar from my altar-boy days. He lined them up along the bench and lit the candle with his Zippo lighter. Lastly, he brought out a pocket CD player, which he set down on the floor.

A trustee prisoner, the white bobble of his Santa Claus hat bouncing off his muscle-bound shoulders, interrupted us through the doorway.

'Post for Gallagher,' he announced breathlessly and handed me a thick bundle of letters.

I gave an impatient sigh as I put the letters down next to the CD player. 'The trustees let the mail pile up to avoid daily deliveries.'

'Some prisoners don't get mail at all, Michael,' said the priest, quietly.

'I'm sorry, Father, I don't mean to sound ungrateful.'

'Do you answer every letter?'

'It's the least I can do, when they've gone to the trouble of writing.'

'Of course,' said the priest. 'One should make time to do just that.' I was relieved he didn't add, 'For when God made time, he made plenty of it': the old Irish saying would not be appropriate in here.

From the CD player, a children's choir sang 'In the Bleak Midwinter', their rendition accompanied by gushing water sounds from the urinal. We made the sign of the cross and the Mass began. After Communion, I stood head bowed, hands joined, while Father Ambrose said his concluding prayers. Soon I was lost in the litany of whispered entreaties to His divine power.

My eyes were drawn to the bunch of envelopes under the bench, and I scolded myself for my churlish reaction on their delivery. The letters and cards came from writers around the world, from those who believed in my innocence or my guilt, using pens, typewriters or word processors, under late-night lamps at kitchen tables, or tea-breaks at the work bench, during lunch in staff rooms, after coming home from the field, the pub, the political meeting or the fundraising dance, telling me about good or bad harvests, and football and hurling and camogie triumphs and disasters. Going to all that effort just for me! And when they reached the end of their task, some would spend so much time fretting about how they should sign off.

'Oh, don't worry about that,' I assured them, almost saying the words aloud before I was torn from my distraction by the priest's raised voice: 'The Mass is ended. Go forth and serve the Lord.'

I waited while Father Ambrose packed his sacred items back into their pockets in the red velvet lining.

'That's a lovely case, Father.'

'A Christmas present from my wife,' he said, his face beaming. 'It's the first time it's been used.'

I sniffed the air around the toilet: the cocktail of cleaning fluid, altar wine and incense smells hadn't completely eliminated that of sewage. 'Not a very nice place for its first outing.'

'God is everywhere, Michael,' said Fr Ambrose, smiling. 'The stable in Bethlehem may not have been so sweet-smelling either.'

Tuesday, 31 December, 4 p.m. – Mary

Returning from a job interview, amongst my mail I find a bulging white envelope with Justin's law firm's stamp on the front. Skimming over the cover letter, I stop at the sentence, 'The prosecution does not intend to submit any material from covert recordings of your conversations at the upcoming bail hearing on Thursday 2 January.'

I'm elated. At the end of the last hearing, the judge had warned the prosecution that more substantial evidence was needed to avoid bail being granted. Although I knew the covert recordings could not be incriminating, who knows what devious misinterpretations the prosecution might have concocted, just as they had done at the first bail hearing, which forced the magistrate to lock Michael up 'for his own safety'.

Also in the envelope is the report from our defence soil expert, Professor Pye. The report from Dr Bull, the prosecution's soil expert, received a couple of weeks ago, claimed a strong correspondence between soil samples found in the lock-up garage and the mortar sites. Our expert should easily be able to discount such a conclusion, given Stephen Kamlish's reassurance that soil evidence is unreliable.

However, after reading Professor Pye's report, I'm left profoundly disappointed. Written in dry scientific language and without visual displays of the data, the report finishes with: 'There is no definitive evidence of a connection between the garage and the mortar sites.' Given the strength of Dr Bull's statement and the less categorical one from Professor Pye, could the judge decide there is *some* evidence – perhaps enough to keep Michael on remand?

Returning to my desk, after making a cup of tea, I'm contemplating what methodology the expert could have used to strengthen his conclusion. I notice, among our family pictures on the facing wall, an old photo of

Michael with his son Anthony, then aged about twelve. Their physical similarities intrigue me: although Anthony is much shorter, anyone would recognise them as father and son. But if the length of Michael's nose was measured and compared to Anthony's, it would undoubtedly be different, as would their ears: the width and length of Anthony's would differ from Michael's. I think to myself, *There must be a way of summing up the strength of association between two data sets*?

I move to the sofa, lean back and close my eyes. I imagine the faces of Michael and Anthony from the photo superimposed on each other, with Anthony's magnified to compare the two shapes easily. In a eureka moment, I realise a similar method can be used to cross-compare sets of soil data.

Back at my desk, I copy Professor Pye's data into an Excel spreadsheet and employ the correlation coefficient function. This provides me with a number close to one for a good match and near zero for a poor match. Unlike Professor Pye's conclusion, my calculations are definitive: the soil inside the garage is clearly dissimilar to the soil from the mortar sites.

Shortly after my triumph, Michael phones. Before he has time to speak, I yell into the phone, 'You're coming home: the garage is innocent, I've got the proof.'

Tuesday, 31 December, 5 p.m. – Michael

After pretending to understand Mary's soil analysis theory, patiently explained through crackling interference on the phone line, I felt vaguely hopeful, rather than confident, about my bail prospects.

'It's time something was done about that phone static,' I complained to Baggot as he led me back to my cell.

'It's not getting fixed anytime soon,' said the screw, 'so get used to it.'

'I might not have to,' I said, unable to resist. 'There's a chance I could make bail.'

'Pull the other one, Jock!' he spluttered, waving me briskly into my cell. 'Your lot have been bombing the fuck out of this country for years, and you think they'll give you bail?'

He was still laughing as he closed the door and walked away.

Fourteen

Bail Judge

Thursday, 2 January 1997, 9 a.m. – Mary

I go to the side of the concourse at Belmarsh Court and into an anteroom for a prearranged meeting with Justin Kopelowitz and Stephen Kamlish. Sitting around a small table, I offer round my cigarettes. 'Have you spoken to Michael this morning?'

'He's in good spirits,' says Justin.

'Did you pass on the correlation analysis I sent to Professor Pye?'

Justin nods. 'I faxed everything and got back an acknowledgement.'

'So, he should include this in his report. It clinches the issue.'

'Even so,' says Justin. 'Michael's already been disappointed once. It's best not to raise his hopes about bail.'

I'd been looking forward to Justin commenting favourably on my soil evidence work. Instead, I'm getting negativity.

'I've collected over half a million pounds of pledges for bail money, and several of the guarantors are here today: Michael's cousin, John O'Donnell, and my brother Keith, and my parents are standing by the phone, waiting for a call.'

'Stephen will make the bail application,' says Justin, his tone this time placatory.

'And call me as a witness?'

'Yes, Mary. Just stick to simple replies to any questions,' Stephen says.

'We don't want to risk your answers coming back to bite you when the covert surveillance evidence is supplied.'

'On the other hand,' Justin adds, 'Walters is the judge again and he won't be pleased the prosecution haven't produced any of the fresh tape evidence he requested.'

'Yea,' says Stephen, smiling. '"Put up or shut up", he warned them.'

Our barrister's reasoned optimism in the face of my sagging spirits may just be soothing lawyer bedside-manner speak, but it works and I cheer up.

Justin and Stephen are seated near the front of the courtroom, with the prosecution table to their left, separated only by a narrow passageway. I choose a seat at the end of an empty row at the back.

When a middle-aged man carrying a thin folder marked HM Court Services is about to stride past, I catch his eye.

'Do you know when the hearing will start?'

'We're just waiting for the judge, madam,' he says and goes to turn away but pauses again. 'And for the accused, of course,' he adds with a dry chuckle, before carrying on with his walk down the side of the room.

The accused? Really? Unbelievable! As I think that, Michael enters the dock, just twenty feet along from where I'm sitting and directly facing the judge's bench. He's wearing his pale green suit again and I wonder whether it's socially unacceptable to attend several court appearances with the same apparel, like always wearing the same party dress. He lifts his hand and gives a subdued wave, and I wave back excitedly.

We stand when the judge enters through a doorway at the side of his bench. Judge Walters is wearing the same two-piece charcoal grey suit, and collar and tie of matching blues. I've no worries now that Michael's repeated attire might not be up to scratch.

On the judge's hand signal, we sit.

'*Regina v Michael Gallagher*,' announces the court clerk, the official

I'd spoken to earlier. This time there's no trace of humour in his voice. 'Conspiracy to cause explosions and two other charges, sir.'

'I believe you wish to repeat the bail application, Mr Kamlish,' asks the judge.

Stephen half rises, murmurs his assent, nods his head and sits again.

The prosecution barrister, Mr Horwell, stands and addresses the judge's bench. 'We have a full report from Dr Bull, our soil expert, who I'd like to call as a witness. You will have before you a copy of his report and that of the defence's expert witness.'

Dr Bull expounds on his comparison between soil from the garage and the mortar sites, elaborating on the similarity of grain sizes and foliage.

Professor Pye now takes the stand. At Stephen's prompting, he outlines his credentials: extensive consultancy and expert witness experience relating to sediments, soils and dust, and current Professor of Sedimentology at Reading University. He then refers to the conclusions of his written report.

The judge is looking down at the document on his bench. 'So, you cannot definitively state the soil found in the garage is dissimilar to the mortar sites soil.'

'Correct: the results are not definitive, but neither are the samples indicative of a strong connection.'

Why has Pye not updated his report after reviewing my correlation analysis? Justin is staring pointedly ahead, and I wonder if he's avoiding my eye contact. I try to maintain an even temper. Glancing at Michael, I detect an almost imperceptible shrug of his shoulders, as though resigned to yet another defeat.

Stephen now refers to the long list of people prepared to stand surety to Michael's previous good character, the flimsy nature of the evidence to support the prosecution case and then, just when I think our barrister has decided against calling me, he says, 'Finally, we would like to invite Dr Mary Attenborough to give evidence.'

As I read out the words of the affirmation to tell the truth, I feel Michael's and my future depends on expressing myself clearly.

'What is your relationship to the defendant, Michael Gallagher?' Stephen asks.

'He's my partner; we've been together for eleven years.'

'What has been your reaction to these charges?'

'Absolute shock. I'm certain he's innocent.'

Although I've been advised to address my comments to the judge, I forget and look over to the defendant's dock, hoping for a smile from Michael. I'm not disappointed.

'And what makes you so sure?'

'We were always together and have hardly spent a night apart since we started our relationship, and I know Michael is a peace-loving man.'

'Are you aware of the evidence presented by the prosecution?'

Now I wonder whether Stephen is deliberately giving me a chance to strengthen the case against the soil evidence.

'Yes, certainly I'm aware. The minute traces of explosives found in the garage, I believe, are the result of environmental contamination or cross-contamination in the police laboratory. I examined the soil reports from the two expert witnesses and performed some statistical correlation analysis, with the conclusion there is definitively no connection between the soil found in the garage and the mortar site soil.'

The judge interrupts. 'Mr Kamlish, you must know Dr Attenborough is not being called as an expert witness. I cannot consider her opinion on forensic evidence.'

Although he can legally only consider expert witness evidence on this issue, he would know of occasions when flaws have been uncovered in such scientists' work. So, he might take note of my opinion subconsciously, I think to myself.

'Of course, sir.' Stephen nods apologetically towards the judge and turns back to me. 'In these hearings the prosecution is known to argue the accused may abscond if granted bail. Do you think Mr Gallagher would be a flight risk?'

'Our families and friends have pledged their hard-earned property equity or savings for his bail. Like me, they are convinced of his innocence and trust him to honour conditions for bail. And could I just add something else? My partner has a degenerative spine condition, he's also a recovering alcoholic and the additional strain on his well-being is a worry to me. He's a writer and not able to pursue this work under such draconian prison conditions as in the SSU. It is inhuman to keep him in jail when there is no real evidence.'

'Thank you, Dr Attenborough,' says Stephen and sits down.

The prosecution lawyer flourishes the bat wings of his barrister's cloak around his shoulders as he stands. I hope he doesn't detect my involuntary shudder as his sombre gaze rests on me.

'Dr Attenborough, did you know Mr Gallagher had hired a lock-up garage in 1994?'

'He didn't hire a lock-up garage; he was merely photographed outside the garage holding a key.'

'Were you surprised by these photographs?'

'No.'

'Would you expect Mr Gallagher to have had regular dealings with lock-up garages?'

'No. But it wouldn't me surprise either: as I said in my statement, he could have been helping out a friend.'

'So, you didn't know he had the key to a lock-up garage. Couldn't there easily be other related activities you also didn't know about?'

'Michael wouldn't be involved in any activity which could possibly result in a loss of life. He's a caring man. If he is guilty of anything it would be of being too ready to help others.'

'Thank you. I have no further questions.'

'Thank you, Dr Attenborough, you may be seated,' says the judge.

'We will have a short recess while I consider this motion.'

The judge exits, and Michael is being led away from the dock by a police guard before I have a chance to show any gesture of encouragement to him.

After ten minutes, everyone is back in place and the magistrate speaks.

'In my deliberations, I've taken into account the seriousness of the charges; this alone could mean Mr Gallagher presents a flight risk. However, if this were the only factor then bail would never be granted with serious charges, which would be against the spirit of the Bail Act. Dr Attenborough presented a compelling case that Mr Gallagher will submit to custody as required and, therefore, I have decided to grant bail with a surety bond of £250,000. A requirement would be that Mr Gallagher surrenders his passport and stays at the residence of one of the guarantors twenty-four hours a day, the only exceptions being to meet with his legal representatives or to attend court.'

Stephen stands up.

'Thank you, sir. We just need a few moments to confer with Mr Gallagher and his bail guarantors.'

I temper my excitement. Michael has this offer of bail, but who would be prepared to let him stay in their house twenty-four hours a day? He can't stay with me as I had no assets to offer for surety, our new cottage being outside the UK.

Stephen Kamlish and John O'Donnell go into the corridor outside the courtroom and, through the open door, I can see them chatting. After a few moments they return.

'Mr John O'Donnell, one of the bail guarantors, has agreed Michael can stay in his house in South London,' says Stephen. 'He has a large house and a spare room as their eldest son is away studying in Cardiff and will be gone for three months.'

'Thank you, Mr Kamlish. I'm therefore granting bail with the conditions as specified.'

I'm jubilant. Michael has bail!

Horwell is immediately on his feet.

'The prosecution wishes to appeal.'

After spending a few seconds writing on a notepad, the judge raises his head and looks towards the prosecutor's table. 'Very well, Mr Horwell,' he says. 'If everyone agrees I'll apply for the appeal to be heard tomorrow morning in the Old Bailey.'

Justin comes up the side aisle to where I'm seated.

'Can't they just concede when they lose a fair fight?' I say, trying to remain calm.

'Don't give up, Mary. We can get all the bail guarantors to attest to their sureties today so, if the appeal does fail, Michael can be released without delay.'

'Good idea. I'll go to my parents' place in Aldridge now and help them with the documentation for their part of the bail.'

I watch as Michael is led away. One minute I think he's coming home and the next I'm having to accept he's back in the SSU. He gives me a thumbs up and I smile back with renewed hope – if we can win in this magistrates' court, we can win again in the Old Bailey.

Thursday, 2 January, 2 p.m. – Mary

Dad holds up his briefcase. 'All present and correct.' As he lowers his arm, the leather-bound case knocks against his hip and he puts out his hand on the wall to steady himself.

Despite his attempt to appear at ease, the shock of the arrest clearly haunts him. Mum and Dad are the most conservative of people where money is concerned. Being prepared to pledge their home for Michael's freedom is a mark of how much they've been touched by the horrific events of the last few months.

'Thanks, Dad, for doing this. It means so much to me and to Michael of course.'

'Well, I was lucky to avoid problems in the past myself.'

'How do you mean?'

'During the war, when stationed in India, I delivered messages from R. Palme Dutt, an executive of the British Communist Party, to his opposite number in the Communist Party of India, who were campaigning for independence against the British. I could have been dismissed from the Air Force and charged with treason.'

I'm horrified. The MI5 bugging of our London flat has me convinced that listening devices could have been planted anywhere, even here in the house in Walmer Meadow. Could they still charge my dad with treason? I'm prepared to believe anything is possible.

'Dad, don't say things like that. They might be recording your every word.'

Dad doesn't respond to my paranoia but returns to the matter in hand.

'It's bright enough to walk,' he says, and when he turns to Mum and me with a steely eyed expression, I'm reminded of childhood excursions past. Holding aloft his *Ordnance Survey Route Planning Map of Great Britain*, he would lead Mum and us three children out to his Robin Reliant three-wheeler and we would all squeeze in. But this will be no trip to the seaside – I should warn him but don't have the heart.

The public waiting room of Aldridge Police Station is deserted, except for a young constable sitting with his head lowered over a newspaper spread out on the counter.

Dad approaches. 'My name is Frank Attenborough. My wife and I have called to sign a bail surety affidavit in respect of Michael Gallagher – I believe his solicitor has faxed the necessary papers.'

'I wouldn't know about that,' the constable says, his voice a flat monotone tinged with irritation. He keeps his gaze fixed on his *Daily Express*.

'Okay,' says Dad, 'but could you please find out for me.'

'It's urgent,' I add. 'We have a bail hearing tomorrow at the Old Bailey in London.'

The constable raises his head and holds up both hands defensively, as if besieged. 'No need to speak all at once!' He closes his newspaper and gets to his feet. 'Just wait here. I'll see if anyone knows about this.' He heads off down an adjacent corridor.

We wait on a bench near the front of the room in what feels like Arctic temperatures until the constable returns accompanied by an officer bearing sergeant's stripes. The sergeant's gaunt appearance reminds me of DS Greasley, although he is slightly taller and has greying hair around the temples. He calls out, 'Mr Attenborough.'

Dad puts his hand on the back of the chair in front, eases to his feet and walks steadily over to the counter. I'm just about close enough to hear the conversation.

'Hello, Mr Attenborough, I'm Sergeant Baker. We've received a fax from Mr Gallagher's solicitor with a document for you and your wife to sign, but it's my job to ensure you're aware of the risks involved.'

'Yes, thank you. I'm fully aware of the situation.'

'This man is detained on terrorist charges. Do you really want to see him let loose on the streets, where he could present a public danger?'

'Thank you for your thoughts, sergeant. He's my daughter's partner. We've every faith he's innocent of these accusations.'

'This man is facing up to thirty years in jail,' the sergeant says, his voice now raised. 'Yet you think he doesn't represent a flight risk? These characters are ruthless; he's not going to care about your daughter. You could lose your house, your savings, everything.'

'Could we just sign the document please?'

'Okay, but don't say I didn't warn you. Before you sign, I need to examine the proof of funds.'

'Yes, our house is worth £70,000. I've the house deeds here and a statement from the mortgage company showing the mortgage as paid in full. We also have a building society account statement showing £5,034 in savings.'

'So, you're offering to stand surety for the amount of £50,000, is this correct?'

'Yes.'

'I'll have to contact the court to see if these documents are sufficient. It could take some time. You could come back tomorrow.'

'We need it done today. Can't you hurry this up, please?'

'Things take the time they take.'

Dad turns away from the desk and I'm proud of him for keeping his cool. I get out my mobile phone.

'You in the blue jumper,' booms the sergeant's voice.

'Yes,' I say.

'Phones aren't allowed in here.'

I send a half smile, half glower in the direction of the officer and head for the exit. If my dad can remain calm in the face of hostile treatment, so can I.

Outside, the wind has picked up and I curse my decision to wear my grey wrap coat, which I'm trying to hold closed. My beret only covers one ear, and I can't wear my gloves because I have to key in Justin's number. I'm hoping the phone heats up quickly to provide sufficient ear warmth without frying my brain.

Justin answers, and I explain our problem. 'I can give the police station a ring, Mary, but I'm not sure they will react positively,' he says.

'In which case, you could contact the court and ask them to confirm to Aldridge Police that they will accept my parents' surety.'

'Okay, and I'll phone the police station afterwards.'

I catch the last bus back from Aldridge to Birmingham at 10 p.m. to get the train to Euston. The ordeal of the three-hour wait in the police station had left my parents cold and tired. However, now all the sureties are in place; the only remaining step is to convince the judge not to accede to the appeal.

Friday, 3 January, 6 a.m. – Mary

I've set the alarm for 6 a.m. to allow me time to walk to the Old Bailey, just in case they shut down the entire London Transport network in their attempts to thwart us. A rational part of my brain tells me this is unlikely, impossible even, but there's no point in taking the risk when we're so close to victory.

I get to Blackfriars Underground station by 7.30 a.m. The Old Bailey, where I've arranged to meet Anthony, doesn't open to the public until 9 a.m. and is only ten minutes away, so I walk for a while along the river before turning towards the courthouse. I don't remember ever being here before, yet it's very near the Farringdon Street offices of the *Morning Star*, where I'd often go, particularly in my wannabe journalist days of the late 1970s, to hand in articles, mainly concerning motions at shareholder meetings calling for disinvestments from Apartheid, promoted by the End Loans to South Africa Campaign.

Still fifteen minutes early, I approach the Old Bailey and spot Anthony outside the court. I do a double take at the increased resemblance between him, just in his early twenties, and his father. We hug and exchange small talk about his journey from Bournemouth as we go inside the building. After climbing the main stairs, we pause at a small plaque on the wall below an embedded shard of glass and read its inscription. It explains how in 1973 the Belfast Brigade of the Provisional IRA exploded a car bomb in the street outside, killing one and injuring 200 people. The shard of glass is preserved as a reminder.

I turn to Anthony. 'I appreciate this is a bit of history, but I'm not sure how this information placed outside the courtroom is going to help with impartiality if someone is up on IRA charges.'

'Some people get more impartial justice than others,' says Anthony drily.

The hearing is scheduled for 9.30 a.m. The public gallery overlooking the wood-panelled courtroom is empty apart from Anthony and me. The judge's bench is directly opposite at the far end. Stephen Kamlish and Justin Kopelowitz are sitting at a table on the right, and the prosecution barrister is on the left. Michael won't be present, so I can concentrate on holding my nerve.

After ten minutes sitting on the edge of the bench seat wishing there was someone to pray to, I hear the announcement from the court clerk: 'All rise for the Common Sergeant of London, Judge Neil Denison.' We all stand as the judge enters.

The clerk announces the subject of the appeal, and the judge requests opening statements. Horwell argues that Michael represents a flight risk – nothing he hasn't claimed before, but this time it's being made to a High Court judge. Stephen makes a counter statement, pointing to the experience and legal qualifications of the district judge who granted the bail, the weakness of the evidence and Michael's strong family ties. Here he makes reference to Anthony's and my presence in the public gallery. The judge looks towards us. Anthony's head is lowered, but I smile solemnly, projecting the image of an academic concerned about her wrongly accused partner.

At the end of the presentations, the judge thanks the barristers. 'Now for my decision,' he says but, instead of telling us, he begins writing in a foolscap notebook. Seconds pass, and I realise I'm holding my breath. I let it go just as the judge speaks.

'I have reviewed yesterday's proceedings at the magistrates' court and listened carefully to the statement presented here on behalf of the appellant, the Crown Prosecution Service. I can see no reason, however, to overturn the decision of the court, and I will grant bail.'

I repeat his words in my head. *I will grant bail.* My sense of relief is so great it almost overwhelms me. They really mean it this time.

'I therefore rule Michael Gallagher should be granted bail under the strict conditions as specified. Mr Gallagher must reside at his relative's address in south London, twenty-four hours a day, and not leave this address until next attending court on January 10th. His passport is to be held by police, who shall be granted access to the south London address at any time.'

I want to grab hold of Anthony in celebration but compose myself sufficiently to simply shake his hand vigorously and nod my thanks in the direction of the judge.

Downstairs in the foyer, Justin explains that it will take time for Michael's release paperwork to be processed, and he probably won't get out until around teatime.

Friday, 3 January, 5.20 p.m. – Mary

Floodlights illuminate the portcullis-shaped metal inserts of the Belmarsh prison gates as we wait inside the taxi, ten minutes early for Michael's expected release.

Finally, he steps out, clutching a transparent plastic sack with 'HM Prison Service' printed on it in prominent blue lettering. He brushes strands of his red hair away from his forehead and pulls his jacket closer as he looks vacantly around, confused perhaps by this sudden transition to liberty. Worried that he won't see us, I push open the taxi door. He spots me and smiles. I run over, clasp my arms around his shoulders and, as he drops his bag to the ground to return my embrace, whisper in his ear, 'You're out, Michael. We did it.'

The sound of passing footsteps break into our private world. 'Anthony is waiting with the taxi,' I remember.

'Yes, we should go anyway before they change their minds,' Michael laughs.

Anthony and Michael hug before we head off on the new phase of this odyssey, with Michael now transformed from prisoner to house-arrest detainee.

Friday, 3 January, 6.30 p.m. – Mary

The awaiting family members applaud as Michael goes into the house and then there are hugs all round. Michael's sister Margaret and brother Eddie are here, along with John, his wife, Vera, and their two teenage sons, Martin and Michael. The O'Donnell's have prepared a 'welcome home' meal.

Before dinner, I lead Michael into the back garden, to allow us to talk without being overheard. I ask him straight out about the garage key – the root cause of all of this trouble. He puts his arms around my shoulder and draws me closer. 'I don't want to talk about it now – the less you know the better. Even if the police did have another suspect, they wouldn't let me go. They'd just have the other stooge to keep me company in the dock.'

Despite some reservations about this explanation for his reticence, I don't pursue it, not wanting to disturb our euphoric mood.

After the meal we move to the sitting room, and John puts on music and offers drinks. Michael is soon occupied in conversation with family curious to know about the horrors of the SSU. It's after eleven when we finally manage to take our leave and, for the first time since the awful Monday morning in October, are able to relax.

Friday, 10 January, 9 a.m. – Mary

As we arrive at Belmarsh Magistrates' Court to renew the bail, there's no armed police presence and no helicopters circling above. I suppose it would seem a little ridiculous when Michael has just travelled here on a double-decker bus.

Justin meets us as we finish going through security.

'It's a different judge,' he says.

'But there shouldn't be a problem,' I say, taking hold of Michael's arm. 'Michael has passed the time writing and helping with cleaning and gardening: an exemplary bailee.'

'I'm sure everything will be fine,' says Justin.

But it wasn't. The judge moved the goalposts by insisting all the bail guarantors must be present in court and before I knew it, Michael was in handcuffs and heading back to Belmarsh.

I'm proud of Michael for not countenancing putting my parents through the ordeal of travelling to London but am terrified he could now be left in jail.

I contact Becky, who had offered £50,000 surety and is able to attend a sitting of the court tomorrow. It's going to be alright I tell myself, but it's hard to keep my spirits up.

Saturday, 11 January, noon – Mary

With a sense of déjà vu, I stare expectantly at the prison gates until Michael appears. Still in his court suit he mouths 'phew' and fans his face with his hands as I walk towards him. 'We have to stop meeting like this,' I say as I playfully grab his arm and pull him towards the taxi.

'So, Becky saved the day,' he says.

'Yes, she had to rearrange a meeting with a client and was slightly late. I nearly had a heart attack waiting. Luckily, there was an earlier court case that overran, so her tardiness went unnoticed and she was able to pledge her surety. She says you owe her a bottle of Baileys.'

Fifteen

Coppers and Cuppas

Wednesday, 2 April, 9.45 p.m. – Michael

As the train slowed at Leighton Buzzard, I stood gripping tightly the leather straps of my travel bag. I watched Mary on the deserted platform, her eyes searching each carriage exit door until they came to mine. I waited for her face to light up, then the enthusiastic wave. I wasn't disappointed.

In the interminable age it took for the door to slide open, I wondered what I'd do if that fervour ever waned, perhaps worn down by her constant work on the case and frequent court attendances, the latest today. Did Mary have a breaking point? I prayed I'd never have to find out.

I set down my holdall, and we hugged.

Mary broke off first. 'I've a taxi waiting.'

We both reached for my bag, but I got there first and grabbed the straps. 'I'll manage, thanks.'

'What about your sore back?'

'What about my self-respect?' I took a backward glance at the train as it moved away.

'Sorry I'm so late,' I said to Mary, my voice just above a whisper, even though the Indian music coming from the cab driver's radio would have made it impossible for him to hear our back-seat conversation. 'I waited for John and Vera to get in from work.'

'It would have been very rude not to, they've been so good to us.'

'I hope I haven't kept Keith and Jean up.'

'They'll have gone to bed: work in the morning.'

'How was court?' I asked.

'It took longer than we thought.'

'Applying for the bail address-change should be just a formality.'

'That had been straightforward,' said Mary, matching my low tones. 'But after an agreement between our side and the prosecutor's, the judge set the date for the Old-style Committal hearing: from 25 June, over three days.'

Mary paused as the taxi took a sudden lurch while turning into Keith and Jean's cul-de-sac. She then added, 'We've been pushing for this hearing: it will test the evidence to see if the prosecution has a strong-enough case to proceed.'

'So, that should result in a "no case to answer" decision, ending the whole business,' I replied with feigned confidence – no point in spoiling Mary's optimistic mood.

The house lay in darkness apart from a dim light upstairs. A sudden unease came over me. We'd visited Keith and Jean's many times but mostly just overnight; now I was to stay under house arrest there for the foreseeable future. I had to trust our good-natured friendship would survive the necessary impositions within the Attenborough daily household routine. Not to mention the mandatory police check-up visits, not likely to go unnoticed in the quiet cul-de-sac.

I made it almost noiselessly upstairs to our bedroom, thanks to the thick stair carpet. Mary followed after locking the door.

'Thank God for Lindsay,' I said in homage to Mary's niece, who had recently embarked on a performing arts diploma course in London, leaving her bedroom vacant.

Thursday, 3 April, 6.45 p.m. – Michael

On hearing Mary's voice, I closed *No Faith in the System* and got up from the writing desk.

Mary put down her briefcase and we hugged. 'Why are you here? It's your turn to cook.'

'I swapped with Keith.'

'Shame. I was looking forward to carbonara.'

'So now you can look forward to rakott krumpli.'

I sat down again. 'I wanted to speak to you before we eat: it's important.'

'Quick,' she said, taking off her jacket. 'My breath's bated.'

'I want to change my lawyer.'

'Whoa!' Mary looked at me open-mouthed. 'What's brought this on? Aren't we happy with Justin?'

'Yes. As a duty solicitor he's been great but ...'

'He and Stephen got you bail, after all,' said Mary interrupting.

'Not without your great work.'

'Thanks.' Mary kicked off her shoes. 'That was my genius legal mind.' She laughed as she sank down on the bed and lay back against the pillows. 'But seriously, Stephen and Justin have worked very well as a team.'

'They've been great, Mary, but I've been reading Sister Sarah's book. She says defendants can stay too long with lawyers inexperienced in this type of case and then, when things go wrong, end up appealing to solicitors like Neil O'May, Mike Fisher, Alastair Logan or Gareth Peirce, expecting them to work miracles.'

'We can't really say things have gone wrong.'

'Not yet,' I said. 'But we should act now, rather than at the last minute.'

'Gareth Peirce is the obvious one.'

'No chance, she's so famous after the *Name of the Father* movie and she's dealing with at least a dozen IRA cases at the moment.'

'So who of the others?'

'Maybe Neil O'May: he got an acquittal verdict recently for an IRA-accused man at the Old Bailey.'

'Well, if you think it best, you should contact him,' said Mary. 'It's sad about Justin, but hopefully he'll understand. As a duty solicitor, he's almost certainly never had such a high-profile case before you came along. Stephen is very experienced though; can't we keep him on?'

'I think solicitors have relationships with specific chambers, so it mightn't be possible. I'll phone Neil O'May's office tomorrow to arrange a meeting and definitely ask about keeping Stephen on board.'

Friday, 4 April, 8 a.m. – Michael

Down on one knee, I waved my trowel and lurched theatrically backwards into the hedge as Jean drove out of the garage. She waved and laughed, revved up the engine and turned onto the road. The sticker emblazoned across the back windscreen, with a large red heart and the words 'I love my Skoda', would persuade even the win-at-all-costs Malachy, protagonist of my abandoned writing project, to lose any notion of jumping bail: the Skoda's resale value, £4,500, represented the makeweight equity needed, along with three houses, to reach the aggregate amount of my £250,000 surety bond.

I went back to my geraniums, lobelias and alyssums, making ready to replant them along the bottom of the driveway hedge.

When putting the empty pots back into the shed, I found a Size 5 Mitre ball. It was marked with a felt-tip pen: 'David Attenborough, Class 5A.' As David, Mary's nephew, was now at Nottingham University, I treated the find as a serendipitous reward for my labour.

I'd started playing keepie-up in the back garden when I heard a car engine. Through a gap in the hedge, I saw a squad car park in the driveway. Fuck. Less than two days, and the police were already here.

I went to the front where I met a burly young copper with a mop of bushy brown hair in his short-sleeved uniform. I ushered him inside, where he introduced himself as Constable Ben Brown. 'No need for formalities,' he said, putting away his ID badge. 'I've been briefed on your background.'

PC Brown followed me into the kitchen, talking non-stop about the good weather and well-kept gardens in the cul-de-sac, and he accepted my offer of tea and biscuits. While I prepared the tea, he gave me his solution for sorting out the local weekend rowdyism: 'Give them a good kick up the arse and send them on their way.'

The half-hour visit ended with PC Brown gloomily speculating on his relegation-threatened team Coventry City's prospects for Sunday's away match at Liverpool as we walked to the squad car.

'Okay, Mr Gallagher,' he said. 'Thanks for your time and the refreshments.'

'You're welcome. Maybe you'll call again.' In saying this I hoped he wouldn't take me too literally.

'Yes. But there's just the two of us in the bail remand sub-section: we don't get out much.' The constable then told me about his colleague, PC Franklin, saying she was the only woman in the station but just like one of the lads.

Our parting small talk was interrupted by the heavy droning of a neighbour's lawnmower, which caused us to look across to the corner house. An elderly man raised his arm and saluted in our direction. After waving back, I reached out, grabbed the constable's hand and shook it vigorously.

'Have no fear,' I said brightly. 'I'm sure Coventry will beat Liverpool on Sunday.'

PC Brown looked surprised but managed a smile.

Both my ostentatious handshake and my football prophecy were equally absurd: Liverpool, four times past European Champions, sat second in the league, while Coventry languished near the bottom.

Thursday, 10 April, 2 p.m. – Michael

I opened the door to a big woman wearing a police uniform and blocking out the sunshine on the porch.

'Michael Gallagher?' she asked with the semblance of a smile.

'That's me.'

From the pocket of her tunic, she brought out the bail conditions form and glanced at it.

'PC Tess Franklin. I've called to visit you under the Criminal Justice and Public Order Act 1994.'

We walked along the hall and stopped at the kitchen. 'We can go in the sitting room if you prefer?'

'The kitchen's fine, sir.'

'Tea, coffee, juice?'

'Tea please,' she said, climbing on the kitchen bar stool and causing me to fear for the safety of its spindly wooden frame.

'Milk? Sugar?

There was no reply, so I turned and saw PC Franklin examining the bail conditions form.

'Milk? Sugar?' I repeated.

'I'm sorry. Milk please, no sugar,' she said, lifting her head. 'I was just checking your details.' Folding the paper, she slotted it back into her tunic pocket. 'You don't exactly fit the usual profile for home-detention orders.'

'In what way?' I asked.

She tipped her head and looked at me. 'It's usually young tearaways on banning orders from weekend night-club bust-ups.'

I laughed. 'Maybe you're talking to the oldest swinger in town.'

'But we've also got you marked down as a flight risk.'

'So they say.'

'Flight to where though? Scottish accent would indicate somewhere like Cowdenbeath or Stenhousemuir. They're my two football teams in the station's weekly pools' syndicate.' She guffawed at her quip.

I brought the tea tray and took my seat opposite her.

'I'm a pushover for a good cuppa,' she said, taking up the cup and saucer. 'You could be an axe murderer for all I know.' A questioning smile then spread across her face. 'You're not, are you?'

'What?'

'An axe murderer?

'Try again,' I said, surprised by her lack of knowledge about me and my case.

'Tax evasion?' She took a bite from a chocolate biscuit and sedately sipped her tea.

'No.'

'Doing a runner with the company's funds?'

I shook my head. 'They claim I was involved in the IRA mortar bombing at Heathrow Airport.'

The big woman clattered the cup down on the saucer.

'For fuck's sake,' she exclaimed, clearly startled at finding out she was sharing a cuppa with a supposedly dangerous terrorist.

I tried not to laugh. 'I'm innocent. At least finish your tea. Please.'

After some hesitation, she picked up her cup, caressing the fine china with her fingers as if checking for damage.

'Constable Brown was here last week,' I said. 'Didn't he mention my background to you?'

PC Franklin smiled. 'All he said was, "Ask him to pick your Lotto numbers."'

'I don't understand.'

'You told him Coventry would beat Liverpool.'

I laughed, recollecting my fluky forecast. By some miracle, Coventry had won 2–1.

As we were walking to the squad car, the neighbour in the corner house came hobbling across the road.

'Watch out for old nosy,' I said. 'He'll wonder why you're here.'

PC Franklin got into the car, started up the engine and rolled down her window.

'Good afternoon, sir,' she said, as the neighbour came alongside. She then turned to me. 'And thank you for your help, Michael.'

'It's no bother, Tess,' I said, as she drove slowly away from the kerbside.

I waved at the car's rear window and the neighbour waved too.

'So, you're with the police?' he asked.

'Well, not exactly,' I said. 'They call sometimes for advice on security.'

Friday, 2 May, 1 p.m. – Michael

The thudding metallic sound of the outside knocker jarred against the serene flute melody coming from Keith's study. I rushed to the door and pulled it open. Two men stood in the porch; an unmarked car parked behind them in the driveway. 'We've called about the Heathrow business,' one man said.

'Come on in,' I said, stepping aside. Unlike my usual police visitors, they weren't in uniform. Aged around fifty, they were older than other detectives I'd met; the speaker wore a tweed deerstalker cap. *How pretentious*, I thought.

I showed them into the sitting room, giving a nod at the study door. 'My brother-in-law, Keith, is practising. We should try not to disturb him.'

'It's him we want to see,' said the man wearing the Sherlock Holmes hat.

As he finished speaking, Keith, flute in hand, came to the entrance to his study. 'It's okay, Michael. Come in gentlemen.'

The men walked into the study, and Keith closed the door.

Typical Keith, unruffiable.

I moved nearer, straining to listen: among the faint words I heard Keith say, 'Heathrow Airport' and another voice mention 'runway'.

I thought, Keith's in there being grilled and doesn't have a lawyer.

I knocked softly on the door. Keith came out.

'What is it, Michael?'

'Are those police giving you a hard time?' I whispered.

Keith first looked at me quizzically, then smiled. 'They represent a residents' protest group,' he said quietly. 'I've been commissioned to do a noise report opposing the Heathrow third runway proposal.'

Sixteen

Case to Answer?

Friday, 2 May, 11.30 p.m. – Mary

When I get back from the Leighton Buzzard Labour Party election victory event, I find Michael sitting up in bed but wide awake, anxious for news. I change and join him, and we talk about our hopes for the new government and the future for the stalled Irish peace process. I tell him about the emotional singing of 'Nkosi Sikelel' iAfrika', reminiscing about the minor support I provided to the ANC's military wing, uMkhonto weSizwe, when I was just a young teacher in Mozambique.

'I'm sure your support wasn't so minor,' Michael says, 'nor were you that young. I started my undercover career at the age of fifteen with the Irish Anti-Partition League branch in Glasgow.'

He then carries on, explaining about his father taking him to weekly meetings in the Gorbals and how he loved listening to the guest speakers, many of them old men, veterans of 1916 and the Civil War. 'At one meeting, bundles of picture cards were distributed showing a soldier in Dublin in a bright green uniform hoisting a tricolour over the GPO alight with flames,' he added. 'On the walk home, my da gave me a hundred and said, "Don't go telling your mother."'

I laugh. 'Does not telling your mother count as being undercover?'

'There's more. I distributed most of the cards inside newspapers and magazines in local newsagents' shops, but then I was caught at school, leaving them inside books in the library. The headmaster wrote to my parents and claimed I was sowing sedition within the school.'

'On that occasion, you and your dad were guilty as charged. I bet Mamie wasn't happy.'

'She gave my father an awful tongue-lashing when he got in from work, and my seditious career was put on hold.'

'No house arrest, though,' I add, before turning over and falling asleep.

Monday, 16 June, 7 p.m. – Mary

'Hello, it's me,' I call.

'In here, Mary.'

I go into the sitting room. Jean sits watching the *Channel 4 News*.

'No Michael,' I say, 'and no cup of tea.'

'Maybe he's exhausted, poor soul.' Jean smiles and uses the mute button on her TV remote. 'A box of legal documents arrived and he's been studying them upstairs ever since.'

'They're probably for next week's Old-style Committal.' I head for the stairs.

'Dinner in half an hour,' Jean calls after me. 'Roast chicken.'

I climb two steps at a time. Michael is waiting at the bedroom door. As we hug, I see, over his shoulder, four red-coloured ring binders on the desktop.

'Sorry about no tea. The bundle arrived and I lost track of time.'

I get onto the bed and prop myself up with the pillows.

'Anything of interest?' My tone is calm and disguises feelings of optimism but also trepidation.

'Well, so far there's no silver bullet, if that's what you mean,' he says, as if he has just read my mind. 'But MI5 were very interested in your rollerblading activities.'

'When? Where?' I sit up from my slouch.

'It's here, in the surveillance log. Your code name is Wood Map.' He undoes the binder locking mechanism and removes a page.

'Let's see then.' Ego and curiosity get the better of me. I take the paper from him and read about 'Operation Useless' on Sunday, 18 October 1994, when an MI5 operative reported that I rollerbladed in a circle around Philbeach Gardens approximately twenty times.

'Operation Useless!' I laugh. 'The MI5 mobile unit team show more nous in naming the operation than their bosses who assigned the work.'

Michael glances at his watch. 'I'd better get downstairs: the table won't set itself.'

Monday, 16 June, 8 p.m. – Mary

Michael and I work together, side by side, sifting through numerous outdoor surveillance logs, MI5 transcripts of our conversations, and police and forensic scientist witness statements.

After two hours, Michael stops reading and turns to me. 'Can we take a legal case against MI5 for misrepresentation?'

'Misrepresenting who?'

'A trainee alto for the Really Big Chorus in the Albert Hall.'

He reads aloud from the log containing our transcripts from the bugging of the flat: '8 March Agent Pin 217 19.45 hours: MA is making croaking noises.'

'Give me a break,' I say. 'I'd only just started to practise!'

Michael laughs and his hands briefly cover his ears. 'How could I forget?'

He puts his arm around my shoulder and gives me a hug. 'Agent 217 didn't need to be so unkind.'

We move apart, and he turns back to another page earmarked with a yellow Post-it note.

'If you've had enough of the singing critique, let's see what you make of this.'

He begins to read aloud.

> 28 April Agent Pin 223 00.15 hours: Moaning increases, and frantic shouts means rumbustious coupling taking place between MA and MG.

> 3 June Agent Pin 424 23.40 hours: It has gone silent, apart from faint sounds of moaning suggest Mary and Michael are united in amorous congress.

We laugh. 'Pin 424,' I say. 'Now, that's the agent who should have commented on my singing!'

Michael sighs and begins to recite:

O wad some Pow'r the giftie gie us
To see oursels as others see us!
It wad frae monie a blunder free us
An' foolish notion

'At this rate we'll never get finished.' I get to my feet. 'I'm going to make us tea.'

When I come back upstairs, Michael is at his desk, the 'Witness Statements' folder open in front of him.

'Have you found anything?'

'They're just like the others,' he says, quickly leafing through the ring-binder pages. 'Nothing to get excited about.'

I sit down on the bed and reach out for the 'No Further Action' file. There are police statements from people who owned garages and flats, and details of short-term renters at the time of the attacks. The more I read, the more ridiculous it seems that just because a resident, Colin Garneys of Elmcroft Mews, witnessed some men with a Ford Sierra one evening, it's been picked on as the definitive location for an IRA gang. God knows what would have been spotted elsewhere if there had been more nosy neighbours at the ready.

The constant rustling sound of Michael leafing through the 'Witness Statements' folder stops and, for about a minute, his eyes are fixed on one page that he eventually removes from the binder.

'This might be something,' he says and hands the page to me. 'See what you make of it.' The slightly hoarse inflection in the tone of voice I recognise as restrained excitement.

I read aloud:

> Witness Statement of NIMA DEVONSHIRE
>
> This statement (consisting of 2 pages each signed by me) is true to the best of my knowledge and belief and I make it knowing that, if tendered in evidence, I shall be liable to prosecution if I have wilfully stated in it anything which I know to be false or do not believe to be true.
>
> Dated 19th Day of March 1994
> Signature Nima Devonshire
>
> I am a director of Ashley Devonshire Properties, the company which owns garages at Elmcroft Mews. On Thursday 17th February 1994 I received a telephone call from a man who said his name was Fraser and he wanted to rent one of the Elmcroft garages. I asked what he wanted the garage for. He said for storage of machine equipment. He had an uneducated working class 'market trader' London accent.
>
> We arranged to meet the next day at the garages at 2:15pm. When I arrived at the garages the man was already there. He did not have a car with him. He was aged between 30 and 40 years, about 6ft 2ins tall, thin build, dark brown wavy hair which was collar length – a

> little bit longer than collar at the back and about 2 days growth of facial hair. He was wearing a white/cream casual shirt which looked like he had slept in it for a few days, faded well-worn blue denim jeans, a faded dark navy anorak with a zip at the front and no rings or jewellery. I showed him garage no. 26 which he said was okay. He paid me for 13 weeks in advance. This was £300. He also paid the £50 deposit. I counted out the cash and it was correct. I handed him a rental agreement for the garage which he signed at the bottom left-hand corner. I asked him to write his name and address in the top left-hand corner which he did. He wrote 'John Fraser, 198 Uxbridge Road, London W12'. I signed the agreement and kept it. I gave him a key for the padlock on the door. I left and the man remained at the garage. I did not see Mr Fraser after that.

'What do you think?' I ask calmly, but I've already worked out the significance.

'This witness has described the man, John Fraser as over six feet, with facial stubble, not a beard, and a London accent – so it's clearly not me. And what's more, she did an E-FIT.'

Michael flipped the pages of the ring binder and showed me the photofit picture of a man with a thin triangular face and collar-length shaggy hair, bearing absolutely no resemblance to Michael.

He laughs delightedly. 'We have our silver bullet.'

'Yes,' I exclaim, as I put my arms around him, 'Absolute proof you didn't hire that garage.'

Tuesday, 24 June, 10 p.m. – Mary

Michael, allowed back in our Earl's Court flat for the duration of the Old-style Committal, is asleep when the phone rings. I grab the handset.

'It's your dad here. Just calling to make sure everything is in place before the hearing.'

Although unsurprised by Dad's abruptness – it saves on phone bills – I attempt a standard conversation preamble. 'Hello, Dad, how are you?'

'Fine, thanks. How are the new legal team? On the ball, I hope.'

'Oh, yes. Neil O'May is definitely an expert in the field. We had to go along with his preference and change barrister, but Ken Macdonald is a very experienced QC and very personable.'

'Good. Just to recap the evidence: we've the lock-up with minute traces of explosives and your expert has identified this as probably lab contamination; the witnesses to the buying and selling of the Ford Sierra car seen outside the garage did not pick out Michael at the ID parade.'

'Yea,' I say, wondering where this is going.

'No evidence in the Sierra?'

'Nothing, and the car itself was destroyed by the police, although they conserved some contents from it.'

'So, Michael only became a suspect when he dropped off the key for the garage deposit.'

'Right, Dad. No connection to the lock-up prior to or during the Heathrow attacks.

'It's just occurred to me, Mary, the prosecution needs to link Michael to the garage before the attacks took place and the lock-up owner would probably have met the man who hired the garage in the first place.'

'You're correct. We've Mrs Devonshire's statement – her description of the hirer, John Fraser, and the artist's impression bear no resemblance to Michael. She said Fraser had a "market trader accent".'

'Well, why was this Devonshire woman never invited to the ID parade?' Dad asks before answering his own question. 'Because, they knew, if she failed to pick out Michael, it would destroy the only strand holding their case together. They must be hoping that she'll change her description.'

'Dad, I thought you were calling to give us a pre-court boost.'

'It's always best to be on your guard. Fail to prepare, prepare to fail,' he says, chuckling, as he hangs up the phone.

Wednesday, 25 June, 9 a.m. – Mary

Entering the witnesses' waiting room at Woolwich Crown Court, I'm closely followed by a woman. Aged in her early forties, she's in a smart trouser suit, with a handbag tucked under her left arm. We nod cordially as we sit at opposite ends of the table.

While looking over some documents, the sound of rummaging distracts me. I raise my head slightly and see the woman has placed a soft leather glasses case, a set of car keys on a BMW fob, a scrunched-up receipt and a small packet of tissues on the table alongside a sheet of paper. When my eye catches hers, she gives an exasperated sigh.

'You wouldn't happen to have a pen?' She holds up the paper. 'I need to fill in this witness expenses form.'

I reach across with my biro. Her hand trembles slightly as she takes it.

'Thanks,' she says, handing back my pen after a couple of minutes. 'Are you here on legal business?' she adds, indicating my briefcase.

'I'm the same as you. I'm here to give evidence.'

'Oh, good. You'll know what to do, then.'

'Just answer the questions from the barristers.'

'That may be a problem. It was a long time ago.'

'Well, just say when you don't remember.'

'I'm just worried he might wriggle out of it. You never can tell with those sorts. The police don't have the machine guns here for nothing. It's not every day the chance comes up to put one of them away.'

'Hang on a minute.' I stand up. 'Are you giving evidence in the Gallagher case?'

Before she can answer, the prosecution barrister, Richard Horwell, appears in the doorway and calls over to her. 'Ah! There you are, we've been searching for you.'

The relieved expression on his face changes to a frown when he recognises me. He indicates a path for his witness to follow to the door without passing me. 'You'll have more privacy in our own witness room.'

Once they've gone, I replay the conversation with the woman in my head. She must be the lock-up owner, Nima Devonshire.

About to go into the courtroom, I'm met by Neil at the door. He seems even thinner than the last time I met him, and I hope it's an optical effect of the dark suit he is wearing and not appetite suppression caused by concerns over Michael's case.

'Neil, I'm worried about the lock-up owner. I was just talking to her in the witness waiting room.'

'You shouldn't be speaking to the prosecution witnesses. What were you thinking? You could be accused of witness tampering.'

Before I have time to explain she followed me and I had no idea who she was, Neil is ushering me into the courtroom.

Too late now – we're in the hands of fate.

Nima Devonshire, takes the stand.

'And can you describe the accent of Mr Fraser?' asks the prosecution barrister.

'Irish or Scottish.'

I'm astonished. She has changed the description from working-class London 'market trader' to Irish or Scottish. Surely that can't be allowed?

'And can you describe Mr Fraser?'

A small woman, she raises an arm above her head. 'About five foot nine or ten.'

I recall that evening in Leighton Buzzard, how jubilant we'd been when we found this woman's statement in the evidence, where she had described the person who had hired the lock-up as 'about six feet two inches tall'.

Ken Macdonald, cross-examining, addresses Mrs Devonshire. 'Do you agree that you made a statement on 19th March 1994 in which you described Mr Fraser as having an uneducated working class "market trader" London accent.'

'Yes, but now I remember more clearly the man in question. He certainly had an Irish or Scottish accent.'

'And what makes you so sure on reflection?'

'I am a British citizen but originally from Iran. I have been director and manager of Ashley Devonshire Properties for longer now and meeting with our customers has helped me to distinguish between different accents.'

'You also said in that statement Mr Fraser was about 6ft 2ins tall, but now you remember him as about 5ft 10ins'

'Yes, taller than me, about 5ft 10ins would be correct.'

She delivered this statement with a slight quiver in her voice but, despite further probing as to why her account has changed so dramatically, Ken is unable to get her to vary her latest description.

The cross-examination over, Nima Devonshire is led away by DI Williams.

Friday, 27 June, 3 p.m. – Mary

Ken Macdonald, summing up for the defence, points out the contradictions between Devonshire's written statement, plus her identikit picture, with the evidence she gave verbally at this committal hearing, and asks the judge to dismiss the case against Michael.

Judge Cooper leaves the room for just twenty minutes and on returning states there is a case to answer, citing plausible evidence that Michael had hired the lock-up. He then revokes bail.

Shocked, I look across the courtroom to Michael and give him a wave. He raises his hand to wave back, but two prison officers grab his arms and escort him from the dock.

Michael had driven the car to the court this morning. We'd planned a five-day break in the Lake District, leaving today after the case was dropped. I've not driven the car for over six months, not having quite recovered my concentration since Michael's initial arrest.

Now I have no choice. In spite of a whirlpool of distracting thoughts, I resolutely approach our red Fiesta, summoning all my powers of attention. Then I see, through the hatchback window, the luggage packed up for our break. I lean against the car door and my resolution vanishes – the tears drip down my face.

Seventeen

Reunited With Old 'Fiends'

Friday, 27 June, 4 p.m. – Michael

'Bail is revoked.' Judge Cooper bowed and left. The clerk handed me a sheet of paper, and two stern-faced prison officers came bustling in. Mary, her face expressionless, waved from the public gallery. Before I could respond, the screws grabbed an arm each and shunted me away.

In the corridor outside, we walked along the tunnel leading to the prison.

'Is it straight to a cell or sweatbox first?' I asked like any unfazed veteran of the system, not a jelly-legged weakling who wanted to cry.

'A holding cell for now,' said one guard, as he led me up a flight of stairs. 'Then it's a house block.'

No SSU! My first good news all day.

We stopped at a desk, where an officer sat lip-synching 'If you wanna be my lover' from the Spice Girls' song blaring from his transistor radio. He punched a number into a keypad at the wall and the cell's gate slid open.

Around forty prisoners were crammed into an area about three times the size of a normal cell, most of them laughing, shouting or holding animated conversations. I wanted to put my hands to my ears and keep them there. Nostalgia for the SSU's quiet solitude was soon overtaken by my sense of grievance: as a Category A prisoner I should have had my own sweatbox.

The radio weather report gave the London temperature as 24 degrees Celsius. Cigarette smoke hung in the dead air, while the smell of marijuana fused with sweat and deodorant. Many of the men had shaved heads and big-muscled, tattooed arms, their skimpy vests failing to conceal mounds of rolling belly flesh.

Visions of sharing twenty-two-hour daily lock-ups with one of them brought back the nightmarish forebodings of Sergeant Snaith at Canon Row: I could get paired with anyone. This morning, I woke snuggled into Mary. Who will share with me tomorrow morning?

No one looked my way except for a tall black lad standing at the edge of a huddle of youths wearing colourful T-shirts and high-waisted baggy pants. As my eyes searched for a place to sit, his hand indicated an empty space on the bench behind him.

Mouthing my thanks, I sat down, pressing my back hard against the cool wall tiles. I skimmed through the court document – the gist being that bail was revoked and past bail conditions had been satisfied. The full names of my sureties were listed: John and Vera, Becky, and Keith and Jean.

My first thought was one of irony. With the loss of my freedom and any prospect of absconding gone – not that I would have – they were now free from the threat of forfeiture of a quarter of a million pounds. I also realised, with alarm, that their sense of relief at the lifting of the 'Michael millstone' from their necks might also apply to Mary. Might she now consider a future without me?

She had waved as I was taken away but maybe as a symbolic gesture: the last wave goodbye. I desperately needed some contact, though a letter, phone call or visit could take days.

On the gate supervisor's radio, an announcer read the evening news. 'Michael Gallagher, accused of taking part in mortar attacks on Heathrow Airport, had his bail revoked this afternoon at Woolwich Crown Court.' The woman went on to describe, in some detail, the events of 9, 11 and

13 March 1994. As I sat listening with my head bowed, I also heard the exchanges of the young lads beside me.

'Proper heavy-duty man.'

'He's a freedom fighter.'

'No, he ain't. He's a fucking terrorist.'

'This dude fucked it to them proper, he did.'

'I saw him in the court. A ringer for our governor at the YO.'

'The motherfucker should be hung.'

'Yea … hung, drawn and quartered, should our old guv.'

An outbreak of laughter followed, and the group, still in jerky rapper mode, went on to berate other staff from the Young Offenders unit.

The lad who'd helped me locate my seat, moved slightly sideways, lowered his eyes and pointed his finger at me.

I nodded.

He gave a short, quiet laugh and leant towards me. 'You're the man,' he whispered, reaching out his hand which I shook. 'Jaden's the name,' he added as he turned to rejoin his mates.

I'd been no more than twenty minutes in the holding cell when I heard the familiar Scottish accent. 'Okay, Gallagher, let's be having you.' PO Muir stood at the opened security gate. I stood up. My old adversary from the SSU stepped aside to let me pass.

I wasn't surprised to encounter Muir: his transfer to the house blocks would have been due to the prison's staff rotation policy. When, six months previously, he had escorted me from the SSU to the outside gate for my release on bail, we exchanged light-hearted chat. Now, there were no words spoken, and the rhythmic jingle of the cell keys at Muir's waistband gave me a stomach-churning reminder of our resumed captive–captor relationship.

We walked along a concrete pathway towards a three-storey cell-block building. Inside it was like a vast arena, the sun's rays flooding through its high glass roof. In contrast to the dark, crypt-like SSU, this place was as airy as a cathedral. About sixty cells in all, their doors closed, lined both sides of the three landings, with steel-meshed netting to prevent suicides stretched across the two upper levels.

While walking towards the officers' station at the far end of the ground floor, we passed a dozen or so empty chairs situated around a large TV emitting a low drone. Neatly dealt sets of playing cards lay face down on a nearby table, adding to the *Marie Celeste* atmosphere of the landing.

Once inside the office, Muir nodded acknowledgement to a man aged around fifty – much older than the average Belmarsh warder. A fringe of ginger-coloured whiskers framed his lower face, giving him a kindly appearance.

'What size tracksuit are you, Gallagher?' Muir asked, taking a step back, measuring me with his eyes. Before I could reply he hurried from the room.

The other officer whistled under his breath as he filed some leaflets inside a buff-coloured folder, then looked at me. 'I'm Officer Priddy. Just doing the paperwork for your accommodation in House Block Four.'

'What type of …?' I asked unable to finish the sentence.

'Being a Category A prisoner, you've been allocated a single cell.'

'Thanks,' I said, greatly relieved.

'It just remains for you to change out of your clothes.'

'I'd rather keep on my suit, if you don't mind.'

Priddy shook his head. 'Afraid you're only allowed leisure wear.'

In spite of his refusal, Priddy's attitude, aided by his softly lilting Cornish accent, seemed more amenable than the obdurate Muir.

'I left a Tacchini tracksuit behind in the SSU: it might be still in the store.'

Priddy flipped some pages, 'Afraid there's nothing left of your property, apart from six phone credits.'

'What? Mine?'

Priddy nodded.

My heart leapt. Six units! Enough for a three-minute call.

'So, can I make a phone call?'

'I don't see why not, as long as it's to an authorised person.'

'Of course. It's my partner and she's authorised. Definitely.'

Just as I was about to state qualifications for Mary's suitability, Muir came marching back into the office, a light-grey tracksuit draped over his arm.

I stepped across to a doorless cubicle at the wall, slipped off my shoes and stripped to my underpants. The tracksuit fitted reasonably well, though the whiff of disinfectant only partially dispelled the odours of sweat and tobacco from the worn polyester.

Muir put my court clothes into a prison-issue property bag but not the shoes. 'We're out of trainers,' he said. 'You'll need those.'

I put them on; the shiny, black leather slip-ons stuck out like kayak paddles from beneath the tracksuit's elasticated bottoms.

Muir patted the keys at his belt. 'We'll get you settled in.'

'I'd like to make a phone call first,' I said, speaking matter-of-factly.

Muir glanced at his watch. 'What? Not now, surely?'

'Yes, now,' I answered forcefully. 'Officer Priddy says it's okay.'

'You've just been admitted, Gallagher, you need to apply for phone credits,' said Muir.

'I've six units remaining from my time in the SSU.'

'You've been released since then,' shot back Muir, his voice now raised. 'Those credits aren't valid.'

Priddy looked again at the property page. 'You may be correct.'

I cursed Priddy inwardly for conceding to the domineering Muir, but then the older man spoke again. 'There's no harm checking the regulations.' He leafed through the ring binder, stopping at a page near the back, which the two men read intently.

Priddy eventually lifted his head. 'It says here, Mr Gallagher, being remanded on bail means technically you've never been freed.' The Cornishman then closed the binder, making it clear who had the last word.

I was elated. This middle-aged, mild-mannered officer had used the rule book to assert himself over the younger, swaggering Muir.

While standing under the phone hood, the receiver practically stuck to my ear. I prayed Mary would be at home and not caught up in crawling commuter traffic. Maybe she hadn't even driven home but decided to go on her own to the Lake District or take someone in my place.

She answered on the eighth ring.

'I've just come upstairs with some of our luggage from the car,' she said breathlessly, then explained that the dire traffic situation had forced her to park outside our residents' zone.

She told me she'd already phoned our parents. When I sought reassurance about my mother's reaction, Mary snapped back, 'I'd tell you if she wasn't okay.' Her next few words, all about traffic, were interrupted by crackling static.

'I've got to go,' she said, during a brief lull in the noise. 'I've still to fetch our walking boots and poles.'

'Yes. You'll need those for the trek back to the flat.' She didn't laugh, and I knew right away it was a silly remark. While I waited for some response, there was a renewed outbreak of static, then the line went dead.

'Mary. Are you still there?' I called repeatedly, my thumb pressing randomly on the square metallic number buttons on the payphone casing.

'Time's up, Gallagher: you've had your call,' Muir said, coming alongside me and holding out my induction folder.

'That wasn't even two minutes,' I started to complain but stopped, fearing my voice would reveal the utter dismay I felt.

It had been a day full of arguments, legal and otherwise, and I'd come off second best, except for this last one – only to win the worst phone call of my life.

Muir ushered me along the line of cells to the left-hand side of the ground floor and stopped at the last one, which he locked me inside. I stood with my back against the door and closed my eyes. Not since the rock-bottom days of my drinking had I felt so alone.

Peering through the bright sunshine streaming from the small, barred window, I studied my new surroundings. The bed along the right-hand wall dominated more than half the floor space and the bedside cabinet and chair were secured by iron bolts to the floor, so no difference there to the SSU. However, the bed had only one pillow, and the mattress, partially hidden by an off-white sheet and crumpled grey coverlet, was only half as thick as in the unit.

A bath towel folded on the bed, its edges frayed and original red colour fading to pink, was a drastic comedown from the unit's fluffy cotton offerings with their matching facecloths. I sat on the bed, removed my shoes and socks, lay down and pulled the coverlet over my head.

Friday, 27 June, 5.50 p.m. – Mary

The phone call from Michael took me by surprise, and my feelings of desolation at the court decision and disorientation in the face of Earl's Court parking mayhem have now changed to utter dejection, having been cut off before I could say something positive. But how many words of comfort could I now muster with the return of this nightmare, and Michael again imprisoned?

I have to send in more clothes and money, arrange for him to get newspapers, and ring the prison to book visits and complain about that phone call being cut short, but a terrible lethargy takes hold of me: I want to lie on the settee, close my eyes and hope it all goes away. I'm not due at work until 7 July as I had booked time off for our planned break, so no need to rush back.

I turn on the TV and discover that the bail withdrawal wasn't a big enough event to make the news. Now I force myself into action: packing away items from our holiday baggage and making a list of things to send in. As Michael is a Category A prisoner I'm not allowed to hand in items –

everything has to be posted, which can be an exhausting process. In one bag I place some clothes including shoes, nightclothes and gym stuff. Then I gather up some writing paper and stamps for a smaller parcel, thinking it might get through to him quicker so he can write straight away. From the bookshelf, I take his little book: *Keep It Simple: Daily Meditations for Twelve-Step Beginnings and Renewal*. I decide to send it in to him along with his St Christopher medal. We need to be lifted by meditation and prayer, even if only one of us is doing it.

After wrapping up the items, I begin a letter to Michael:

> What can I say but that I am devastated. I can't imagine how they can sleep at night knowing the work that we put into getting you bail. But this setback will not deter us; in the end we must win because we have truth and justice on our side.

I finish by telling him how much I love him and look forward more than ever to our next prison visit.

Friday, 27 June, 7.30 p.m. – Michael

I was awakened from a disturbed half-sleep by the slamming of cell doors, the bangs becoming louder.

I went to the sink and stuck my head into the shallow tin basin, splashing cold water around my face and neck. After vigorously drying off, I draped the towel around my shoulders, imitating the keen gym buff rather than the haggard first-night prisoner readily identifiable as bully fodder.

A warder opened the cell door then stepped back to let his trusted-prisoner companion, a young chap of about thirty with a boyband haircut, push a steam-engulfed metal trolley closer to the entrance.

I thought of the old lag's adage, 'never trust a trustee'. This particular one eyed me up and down. 'Yer Mug,' he said, in a local twang.

Who was he calling a mug!

'How djee mean?' I said back, adding a thickness to my Glasgow accent.

'For your tea, squire.' Head tilted to one side, his eyes searched the cell floor behind me, then he gave an exasperated sigh. 'What d'you think I meant?'

Turning my head, I saw, just kicking distance away underneath the bed, a plastic mug along with a plate, knife and fork on a tray.

I bent down, grabbed the mug and the trustee tossed in a tea bag, poured boiling water and added milk.

'Thanks.' I took the tea, inwardly cursing my stupidity, my edginess laid bare. The mouthy cockney probably surmised I'd been locked up for tax evasion or something similarly tame. Before any more words could be exchanged, the screw slammed the door and locked me in.

I sat down on the bed and took a mouthful of tea.

Fuck! I'd forgotten to ask for sugar.

The exchange with the arrogant trustee had energised me. From the induction folder, I took a prison-shop order form, visiting application and lined writing paper, and placed them inside the bedside cupboard. Dealing first with the tick-box shop requisition and assuming I'd get money sent in, I took out a form and ordered bananas, lemonade, mints, toothpaste, toilet roll and phone cards.

I then picked up a visiting-order application form but put it straight back again, reminded instantly of stories I'd heard about visiting room 'Dear Johns'. The prisoner, wearing aftershave, hair gel and best tracksuit, goes to meet his visitor and then, having waited alone in a crowded room throughout the entire hour-long period, realises his absentee loved one would never come again. Mary, I hoped, would let me know in a more humane way if we had no future together.

My eyes kept being drawn to the envelopes in the cupboard, as I weighed up the risks of writing to her. Apart from morosely deliberating on a forthcoming trial, there wasn't really a lot to say, and if I asked her to give herself a break from working on the case, she might think me presumptuous – having decided she had already done her duty.

My attempts at further sleep were disturbed by music, mainly hip hop or rap or garage, coming from different cells, then, later, as the evening was drawing to a close, replaced by more traditional pop, such as from the Bee Gees and Simply Red. Around the time the cell's overhead light was switched off from outside, the rhythm of Cyndi Lauper's 'Girls Just Wanna Have Fun' slowly fused into my memory.

Friday, 8 November 1985, 8.30 p.m. – Michael

Leaving my flat already half an hour late, it took another fifteen minutes to walk the 200 metres to the Response Community Project centre for the Earl's Court Anti-Apartheid Group's get-together. Once inside, after negotiating the semi-darkness of the upper floor, I took the stairs, wincing with pain at every downward step, while the music came crashing up to assault my ears.

On reaching the basement, I stopped in front of two empty chairs at the admissions desk and looked through the function room's half open door. Just inside, Greta Donnelly, wearing a black satiny trouser suit, her long arms reaching up to the low ceiling, bobbed up and down in time to the beat. Facing Greta was her flatmate, Mary Attenborough, whose gyrating figure, short blonde hair and deep red dress, flitted frantically in and out of the strobe lights. Beyond them, other women dancers took up most of the small floor space, while around the room, groups sat at low tables laden with drinks.

When Greta saw me, she came through the doorway, Mary following behind.

'It's Michael! He's come to boogie,' called Greta, Scouse accent exaggerated by having to raise her voice above the music.

'Sorry Greta.' I patted the small of my back. 'No can do since my mishap on yon balance-beam pirouette.'

Both women laughed, though they'd heard it before.

I brought out two one-pound coins from my parka jacket and dropped them through the slot of the collection tin on the admissions table.

Mary sat down in one of the empty chairs. 'But you'll stay for a while, won't you?'

'Not in there.' I glanced through to the function room. The music's volume, to say nothing of the boozing company, had stricken me with a heightened awareness of my fragility.

'In that case, could you mind the table while we get another dance?' asked Greta.

'What will I do with myself?'

Greta laughed. 'Just sit there and look pretty.'

Mary held up a coloured leaflet which read 'Free Nelson Mandela'. 'And hand these out.'

'That's all?'

'Yea, that's it.' She stepped across to a desk used by the day-time volunteers and picked up a discarded *Guardian*, opened at the crossword. She laid it down on the table. 'You can occupy yourself with this if you get bored.'

'Girls Just Wanna Have Fun' blared out suddenly from the loud-speakers. Greta took Mary's wrist, tugging her towards the music. I gingerly lowered myself into a seat.

As the track ended, Mary and Greta caught my eye, their hands clasped in fake prayer for more dance time.

I nodded my agreement – the crossword was proving to be a diversion.

The music halted abruptly. Prompting groans from his audience, the DJ called out, 'We've a temporary problem, folks.'

Mary stepped up onto the low stage and, after a brief exchange of words with the DJ, reached her hand behind a speaker and the music started up again. To loud cheers, Mary gave a mock curtsy – as much as she could in her tight-fitting dress – then stepped off the stage. Approaching me, she said, 'I need a break now, after my public appearance.'

I raised my hands above my head and clapped with exaggerated rapidity. 'Well done, Mary.'

'It was nothing. A wire was loose.'

'That's my duty done. It's time to be off.' I pushed *The Guardian* along the table.

'You're going already?' Mary sat down beside me.

'I only turned up to show solidarity. Wouldn't have left my sick bed otherwise.'

'Sick bed?' Mary smiled. 'When we spoke last month, you told me you didn't have a bed.'

'Okay. I was being pretentious – it was my sick mattress I left this evening. The back pain has me confused. And sore.'

Mary laughed. 'You don't have to explain, Michael. Your groan when you sat down earlier was louder than the music.' Then, as if to make amends for her flippancy, she added, 'I remember everything you told me about your awful condition.'

'Really?'

'A trapped sciatic nerve pressing against the spongy part between your discs 3 and 4, which you think originated while playing football during access time with your twelve-year-old son Barry. And you need surgery,' she said, without a pause.

Surprised but pleased she had remembered so much, I wondered what else I'd told her at the last function.

'Wow!'

Mary's exclamation broke into my thoughts. She had her eyes fixed on the puzzles page of *The Guardian*.

'What?'

She pointed at the paper. 'You've completed the cryptic crossword.'

'It was quite easy, actually; helped pass the time.'

Mary shot me a look suggesting she'd engaged her bullshit detector. 'But you only had a few minutes.'

Getting to my feet, I moved off and turned at the foot of the stairs.

'Okay, confession time,' I said, 'I'd already nearly finished the same crossword at home, in my own copy.'

She laughed. 'You rotter! And here was I, struck by what a clever wordsmith you were.'

'It hadn't been touched, so I assumed none of the volunteers were interested in crosswords,' I said, before beginning to climb the stairs.

'Me neither,' called Mary and, after a short pause, added, 'I enjoy a game of Scrabble, though.'

'Me too,' I replied, lying.

Seconds later when I'd reached the outside door, I heard her voice again. 'In that case, I may pop round to yours for a game sometime.'

I exited onto the street wondering if I'd heard right: did Mary Attenborough really say that?

Two days later, on Sunday afternoon, the buzzer on my intercom sounded.

Friday, 27 June 1997, 10 p.m. – Michael

The music had stopped, and the midsummer sun had gone, leaving the cell window a black mirror with four vertical bars. I had tried to sleep but couldn't, kept awake by the nagging memory of that awful phone call and still hearing Mary's stilted sentences and her tone of resigned dejection.

Getting onto the floor at the side of the bed, directly under the night light, I smoothed out a letter page. Determined to be upbeat, I used the first few lines to ask about our families and friends. I sympathised about our abandoned Lake District trip and, suspending reality, promised we'd soon have our mountain walks again. I reminded her of how, many years ago, she had converted me from a TV couch slob to a walking enthusiast and of her patient indulgence, in those early days, of my smoking breaks and stops to recover my breath.

I wrote: 'Do you remember the first time I went with you on your long treks up to Cashelnagor and around Dunlewey? It was a sunny Donegal day. We had walked about eight miles and I had stopped, lagging behind you by about fifty yards. Errigal Mountain was straight ahead and Dunlewey Lake to the right. You came back to give me a drink or an orange or something. The mountain was at your back as you came down the path. You were wearing your bluey-green vest and shorts. When you came up beside me, I just reached out and held your face in my hands. Do you remember? I just looked at you. You were the most beautiful sight I've ever seen.'

Saturday, 28 June, 9 a.m. – Michael

When my cell door was unlocked, I went straight to the office. The duty screw, a big woman with frizzy fair hair, introduced herself as PO Armstrong. I handed her Mary's letter and nodded my thanks but, as I turned to leave, she spoke again.

'Our governor got a call first thing this morning from your brief, Mr O'May. Your missus had demanded she be allowed a prison visit, an urgent one, no less. On her high horse about our payphone not working properly, claiming you were denied your rights.'

Never had I heard such good news delivered in such a negative manner. I could have kissed this woman.

After breakfast, while lying on top of my bed, the door opened and Armstrong stepped inside. 'We're a defender short for five-a-sides, Gallagher. Are you up for it?'

'I've only got these.' I pointed to my shiny shoes on the floor.

'No worries. We've plenty of trainers and, if you find ones to fit, you can hang onto them.'

Instantly I got off the bed and followed Armstrong out of the cell to the gym.

From a pile of trainers inside a wicker hamper near the gym entrance, I managed to find a pair: well-used, cheap and scruffy, like the others, but they fitted perfectly. So much for Muir's claim at my induction that they had no trainers.

The full-sized gym had goals with nets and marked-out lines on the wooden floor. Of the ten players, two stood in front picking out their respective teams – the yellows and the reds. I recognised one of the selectors – the tea-server from the night before. Some of the others referred to him as Sparky. Wearing a yellow bib, he stood like an Irish gaffer at a Monday morning casual labour queue, revelling in the selection process, his eyes going along the line of prospects before an almost imperceptible nod of his head beckoned forward his choice.

The gawps I got from the others came as no surprise: I was easily the oldest player and the only one in prison-issue tracksuit and trainers. The others all wore the latest fashion – bubble-soled shoes and brightly coloured tracksuits, Kappa, Adidas and the like. After Sparky had picked his last player, I was given, almost as an afterthought, a bib by the red team's captain.

Armstrong, who was the referee, blew her whistle and the game got underway to a steady stampede of thudding feet, with the ball being passed around at speed and no little skill from some of the players. Due to my lack of fitness, I'd opted to play goalie/sweeper and, during the first ten minutes, I managed a couple of decent saves and reasonably accurate passes to teammates.

Sparky, in the opposition defence, constantly called out tactical instructions. His voluble commentary exemplified the maxim 'do as I say, not as I do': he lacked skill and positional awareness, allowing our strikers, two skinny black kids, to regularly outrun him. One of them, after he'd scored a goal set up by my long pass, gave me a closed-fist salute and called out, 'Nice one, pops.'

When his team went two goals down, Sparky decided to play up front. Shortly afterwards, when I'd saved his tame shot, he followed through and barged me. Seconds later, after I prevented another goal, he responded like a petulant child, scowling as he shoulder-charged me. I retaliated by pushing him backwards. Then, with both hands clutching the ball, I mimicked shoving it into his face – I'd seen professional goalkeepers do this to harassing forwards on TV. However, unlike the disciplined restraint of a Gary Lineker, Sparky swung his fist and hit me full on the forehead. I staggered backward, though – maybe in a soccer goal-prevention version of autonomic reflex – I managed to throw the ball to one of my teammates just before I fell across our goal line.

Sparky stood over me, snarling, calling me a Scotch fucker, but he didn't follow up his attack. Seizing the moment, I clambered to my feet and launched myself at him. We grappled for a few seconds, with his fists flailing around my head while I grabbed at lumps of his hair, causing havoc with his middle parting. Then I heard the welcome shrill of the prison's alarm bells and, from my hunched stance, jelly-legged and hanging onto Sparky like a battered boxer, I saw the flurry of white-shirted screws approaching, the clatter of their boots pounding on the wooden floor getting mercifully louder.

As Sparky was led away by a posse of screws, I tottered breathless and shaking out of the gym, Armstrong at my back, the game abandoned.

Saturday, 28 June, 11 a.m. – Michael

Opting at exercise time to stay behind while most inmates went outdoors, I'd settled comfortably into an armchair under the iron stairs. My name being called interrupted the quietness.

Sparky, now wearing a trustee's maroon bib and trailing a stout brush, came towards me. 'Are you the Mick Gallagher on the news?' He stopped about ten feet from where I sat. 'I've been told you were on MI5's most wanted list.'

'That's stretching it,' I said, though not quite denying his informant's totally exaggerated claim. 'So what?'

Sparky clasped his hands around the stout brush shaft, wringing them like a beseeching petitioner. 'I'd like to apologise for this morning's misunderstanding.'

I nodded my head towards the empty armchair opposite. 'Can you come a bit closer?'

Sparky propped his brush against the stair's railing, stepped tentatively towards me and perched himself uncomfortably on the edge of the armchair.

'Stupid fucking me,' he blurted, his tousle-haired middle parting and petted lip made him look like a small boy.

'Relax, these things happen,' I said, evenly.

'I'll do anything you ask, Mick, everything!'

I didn't answer. I didn't know whether to laugh or cry. Sparky would have obeyed my every wish at the snap of my fingers – stood on his head, anything. It was a terrifying thought.

Eighteen

Hanging by a Thread

Wednesday, 7 January 1998, 4.20 p.m. – Mary

I reach the offices of Bindman & Co. on Gray's Inn Road ten minutes early, hoping to catch Neil O'May before our meeting with Dr Russell Stockdale, the defence's fibre expert.

As I push open the foyer door, Neil appears at the entrance to the adjacent corridor. Jacketless, his white shirt open-necked, it's the first time I've seen him dressed so informally. He ushers me to a small conference room and we sit down on either side of a table, facing each other.

'I expect Dr Stockdale to arrive shortly with his preliminary report,' he says, 'Have you read the prosecution expert's report?'

'Yes,' I say. 'But it seems to represent an act of desperation, given the police have tried, unsuccessfully, to link fibres from our flat and Michael's clothing to the scene of the attack.'

'It is certainly more normal to compare fibres from the alleged perpetrator and the scene of the crime,' answers Neil, 'but in this case it could still work for them: establishing matches, as claimed in Dr Priston's report, between fibres found at three places – the lock-up, the mortar sites and the Ford Sierra – could show that the lock-up is "guilty", i.e. that it had been used for the preparation of the mortar bombs. If the jury believe the prosecution's assertion that Michael had hired the premises, while also knowing what it was to be used for, that would point to his guilt too.'

I extract Dr Priston's report with my notes from my briefcase. 'Are you hopeful then that Dr Stockdale can counter Dr Priston's contention of the rarity of those four fibres found at the mortar sites and in the Sierra, and another, supposedly very rare pink one, found at the mortar site and in the lock-up garage?' I say, talking non-stop. 'Surely, without hard statistical backing, Priston's description of these fibres as "rare" can't be sustained.'

'We'll hear soon enough,' says Neil. 'A professional witness is duty-bound to use their expertise to present an impartial opinion to the court on matters which are in dispute. We're not able to direct how they will act. Dr Stockdale comes highly recommended, as a former Home Office forensic scientist now with his own independent practice.'

I nod agreeably but dearly wish I could add, 'Thanks Neil, but aren't you duty-bound to find an expert who can counter an opinion based on dodgy scientific grounds?' I keep my irritation in check: there's no point in lecturing Michael about his occasional irascible outbursts if I can't control my own.

At exactly 4.30 p.m. the receptionist shows Dr Stockdale into the room. Neil greets him with a handshake and introduces me. Our expert is about fifty, with grey, slightly receding hair, and is dressed formally but quite stylishly. I lean across the table and shake his hand.

Dr Stockdale sits down next to Neil. During the precis of his report, he continually refers to Michael as 'Gallagher'. Surely 'Mr Gallagher' would be more appropriate? It appears to me that Dr Stockdale has already formed the opinion that Michael is guilty.

While I muse about how to make a point about the use of a title, Dr Stockdale explains he is in agreement with Dr Priston about the rarity of the five fibres found that appear to connect the garage, the Sierra and the mortar sites.

'But where is the statistical analysis which might lead to such a conclusion?' The strain in my voice causes a pathetic squeak at the end of the sentence.

'As fibres forensic scientists, we use our expertise and the data we have – this is sufficient to draw the necessary conclusions.'

'Is there a fibre database with representative samples which can be used to authenticate this rarity, or otherwise, of various types?'

'The only database in existence dates from 1984 and, even then, it was considered to be unreliable,' says Dr Stockdale.

I'm infuriated: the opposing experts agree about the uncommonness of the five identified fibres, and we just have to accept their word for it, without any corroborative data.

'Aren't you concerned about the police destroying the Sierra after taking the fibre samples, making it impossible for the defence to check the presence or otherwise of those supposedly rare fibres which have been identified?'

'This situation alone doesn't mean the prosecution's fibre evidence has been nullified.' Dr Stockdale's surefootedness in dismissing my questions doesn't falter. He continues, 'The manner in which the samples were handled is a classic forensic scientist's nightmare. Fundamental principles of forensic science have been breached. There is, at least in theory, the possibility for compromise of the samples and I believe Dr Priston would probably agree the working conditions were not ideal. There may be a reservoir of contaminating fibres provided either by the scenes of crime officer, DC Field, or by a source in Scotland Yard. Though to propose this hypothesis it might be better to have some indication of what this reservoir might be.'

I'm exasperated. Dr Stockdale thinks there could have been contamination by DC Field's evidence collection team, but he isn't prepared to say so unless he can propose a possible source. Surely the point of our defence expert is to cast doubt on the evidence though not necessarily to definitively disprove it? Dr Stockdale's reasoning seems deliberately perverse.

'The police also collected items from our flat and my brother's home, where Michael was staying. No matches with the mortar sites, the garage or the car were found. Surely this should carry some weight?'

'We can't draw conclusions from those analyses. That would represent an attempt to establish negative evidence.' There is a tone of growing irritation in our expert's latest rebuttal.

Negative evidence, I feel certain, could be used in establishing doubt. For instance, if Michael is covered in a type of fibre from location A, which is very transferable, and yet this fibre isn't present in location B, then its absence is indicative of the fact Michael has probably not been in location B. I don't bother to voice my opinion, as I already suspect the issue is a lost cause with Dr Stockdale.

Thursday, 8 January, 1.45 p.m. – Michael

Escorted by Muir and Baggot, I saw, through one of the square windows along the corridor, two minibuses carrying visitors drawing up at the entrance.

As I approached the security gate leading to the visits area, Baggot put out his hand and barred my way.

'Not so quick, Gallagher,' he said.

Muir tore open a cellophane-wrapped package and unravelled a roll of cloth, revealing a bright yellow and green jumpsuit. 'You've to wear this over your clothes,' he said.

I laughed. 'Those patches are for escape-risk prisoners.'

'And for prisoners like yourself deemed a risk to the staff, after last week's indiscipline.'

I didn't need a reminder: I still had a week-long dull headache from the Minimum Use of Force Tactical Intervention (MUFTI) squad's 'affirmative action' for refusing a squat search.

'You can't force me,' I said.

'True,' answered Muir. He began to fold up the suit again. 'But no patches, no visit.'

Through the window beyond Muir, I could see Mary at the dispensing machine, emerging from the melee of visitors, holding a can in each hand. She walked, bright-eyed and smiling, towards the visitors' admission door.

The muscles in my throat tightened. I reached across and took the jumpsuit from Muir.

Thursday, 8 January, 2 p.m. – Mary

The massive green and yellow squares of a jumpsuit reach my eyes a split second before I see it's being worn by Michael. After my shock comes the urge to laugh, but I manage not to.

When he is a couple of yards away, I get to my feet. Quickly his arms are around me. As he goes to pull back, I hold onto him and close my eyes. 'A little more time.' Michael draws me tight against him for a few seconds longer, then we sit down facing each other.

I study his face. Only the soft brown eyes seem familiar, the rest of his features almost lost inside his full red beard. He tugs at the round, elasticised neck of the jumpsuit. 'Sorry about the fancy dress.' He leans back in the chair. 'They said I had to wear the suit: otherwise no visit.'

'You could be dressed like Daphne Duck for all I care.'

'I am,' he says.

But no way is this Disneyland I think, as I look at the rows of red-bibbed prisoners sitting in bolted-down bucket seats, facing their visitors, while white-shirted guards stationed around the room watch vigilantly.

We catch up on news from the family, but I'm anxious to discuss the bundle of evidence for the trial, delivered to us last week.

'Have you read the M4 tape transcript? It claims you say you want to fire bullets at the major.'

Michael laughs. 'If you listen hard, you can make out what was really said.'

'Which was?'

He puts his finger to his lips.

Michael's reticence is not surprising given our paranoia about being overheard.

I move on. 'Exhibit M7: your Malachy writing story, we know there's no problem with, but you'll need to tell me about Exhibit M9, where you tell me you were followed.'

'Don't worry. I've a rational explanation for the witness box,' says Michael.

'Normal people wouldn't even notice if they were being followed.'

'I'll explain why another time.' Michael leans back in his chair, his arms folded. 'What's the latest on the fibres?' he asks, his sudden switch of subject a tactic I recognise from whenever he wants to move to safer ground. 'How did the meeting go yesterday?'

'Not good. Stockdale wanted mostly to accept Priston's analysis without question.'

'Don't forget, they worked with one another,' says Michael.

'Yes, but he has to act professionally. I've his report now and he has at least sent a few forensic-science-paper references concerning fibre frequency. I'm finalising a statistical model showing that, given the number of fibres in the car, the likelihood of at least six matches with another unrelated location is nearly one, i.e. a certainty. This would nullify the fibre evidence, as a strong comparison between fibres would not indicate they came from the same source. However, I'm not an expert witness, so I've asked Neil to engage a statistician and see if they can work with Dr Stockdale and get him to amend his report.'

'You've done great work, Mary,' Michael says as he leans across to give me a quick kiss on the lips.

'How's your writing doing?' I ask, turning to the last topic on my mental list.

'I'm working on a scene where I'm lying skint in the doss house on Christmas Eve and my mother turns up unexpectedly from Ireland.'

'Hasn't that scenario been … overdone?'

'But it happened.' Michael's expression is sombre, the sparkle gone from his eyes.

I've upset him: I should have kept quiet.

'Because it's true, doesn't mean it works in a narrative,' he says imitating my voice when I critiqued his storylines. We both laugh.

'Discussing your stories – it was great back then, wasn't it?'

'Was it really?' says Michael. 'We always ended up arguing.'

'And making up.' I reach out and hold his hands. 'We'll have it back again, for sure.'

Monday, 12 January, 9.30 a.m. – Michael

From my seat in the dock, I watched the courtroom gradually filling up. Ken and Neil, their backs to me, sat at the defence team's table separated by a narrow passageway from the prosecution staff to their left. Benches reserved for the media were already full, but the public gallery above their heads was nearly empty: I'd asked family and friends not to come until the closing days of the trial, and there were no victims of the attacks on Heathrow, so no impacted relatives.

People began filing into the jury box. A man with a clipped grey moustache, his dark-red face matching the colours in his regimental tie, hurriedly led the way into the front row. Ken, closely observing the jurors, leaned towards Neil and said something.

The clerk stood up: 'All rise for the Honourable Justice Tucker.'

The judge emerged through a door at the side of his bench, gave a brief bow and sat down. His pronounced florid features, framed by his wig's grey curls and a double chin, suggested fine dining.

When everyone had settled, Ken approached the judge's bench. Justice Tucker beckoned the clerk and, after a consultation which included Ken, moved to speak mutedly to the regimental tie wearer. The man shuffled off. I offered up a grateful prayer at being spared this ex-Para as a likely jury foreman.

The usher then brought an old man wearing a tweed suit to the jury box. This replacement would likely have recollections not only of the IRA pub bombing at nearby Woolwich in 1974 but memories, too, of the German Luftwaffe's blitz of his local docks during the Second World War. As I watched this gent taking the oath, I speculated on why he hadn't exempted himself because of his age: to actually volunteer for jury duty suggested a zeal for law and order, and also that he might regard himself as ideally suited to be jury foreman.

It wasn't a good start.

In Justice Tucker's opening speech, he set out the parameters for the jury deliberations and said that if they had doubts after hearing the evidence their verdict should be 'not guilty'.

Richard Horwell stood at his table, tall and pale-faced. 'My Lord, I appear for the Crown and my learned friend Mr Ken Macdonald appears for the defendant Michael Gallagher.' The prosecutor stopped then and, with his hands at his chest, clutching the edges of his barrister's gown, peered over the top of his glasses straight at me.

Since being led into the dock by my guards, not more than twenty minutes earlier, I'd been ignoring random furtive glances from around the court. Horwell's unabashed stare now seemed to give licence for others – press reporters, jurors and police observers – all to gawk at me.

I forced my eyes to wander nonchalantly around the courtroom, assuming the demeanour of any other audience member waiting for the curtain's rise. Letting my hands rest on the dock's wooden ledge, I prayed they wouldn't shake.

'Members of the jury. You have access to the evidence bundle. The court officer,' he continued, indicating a woman at a table filled with recording equipment to the back of the courtroom just below my position in the dock, 'will provide you with all relevant documents, statements of witnesses and transcripts from tapes. The Crown's case is based on a triangle of objects forming a chain of evidence – a metal frame used for launching mortars at Heathrow Airport, a lock-up garage and a Ford Sierra car – matching fibres link all three. The accused has not denied his possession of a key to the lock-up, in which traces of RDX and PETN – constituents of Semtex, an explosive regularly employed by the IRA – were found.

'In addition to this evidence, we will introduce transcripts from excerpts of conversations between the accused and his partner, Mary Attenborough, secretly recorded by the security service, in the two years following the Heathrow bombings. Ladies and gentlemen, when viewing all of the facts I have outlined objectively, the vital role Michael Gallagher played in the transmission of these attacks will become apparent.'

Horwell then added with dramatic emphasis, 'You will hear from the security service, MI5, their belief that Michael Gallagher had been highly trained in counter-surveillance techniques.'

While he had been speaking, I'd been taking sneaky looks at the two rows of jurors, trying to figure out from their demeanour, their potential for sympathy or, more likely, hostility. I also tried to guess who they'd appointed to be their foreperson.

No one made eye contact with me except a woman seated in the back row, at the end nearest to me. In her late twenties, with spiky orange hair and wearing purple lipstick, she had shaken her head disapprovingly when Horwell described the more heinous aspects of my alleged behaviour.

'I will now hand over to my learned friend,' the prosecutor said, giving a nod towards Ken.

'I thank Mr Horwell for his opening statement,' said Ken, getting to his feet. 'He has set out very clearly the case for the Crown. It is my intention, however, as defence counsel representing Michael Gallagher, to present to you a quite different version of events. I have every confidence when you've heard this, you will come to see the evidence as extremely weak, and it in no way proves the Crown's case.'

His eyes totally focused on the jury box, Ken continued. 'The traces of explosives apparently found in the garage will be shown by our expert witness, Dr Keith Borer, to be consistent with contamination from the police forensic laboratory at Aldermaston.

'The prosecution claims matching fibres have been found at three different locations: the lock-up garage, the car and the mortar plates. We will be presenting the evidence of an expert fibres witness who will cast doubt on the reliability of these findings.

'My client did not hire the aforementioned garage but merely returned the key to retrieve the deposit. Similarly, he did not make available a Ford Sierra car: Mr Gallagher willingly participated in an identification parade in which neither the buyer nor seller of the Ford Sierra car identified him.

'We then have the secretly recorded conversations of my client and his partner, Dr Mary Attenborough, the transcripts of which you've been provided with. The prosecution has claimed Michael Gallagher incriminated himself several times. The defence will call both parties as witnesses to fully put their meanings and words in their proper context, thus showing a complete absence of ill-will towards anyone.'

At the other end of the jury box, next to the replacement juror, sat a young lad. A metal ear stud glinting through loose blond hair matched rows of shiny studs embedded on the sleeves of his leather biker's jacket. The youth and the spiky-haired woman aside, I decided the jurors might select anyone from the six men and four women dressed more conservatively to be foreperson. As Ken finished speaking, the biker used his elbow to nudge his older neighbour awake.

Wednesday, 18 February, 10.30 a.m. – Michael

Over the weeks of the trial, the succession of witnesses had come and gone causing me little excitement. Some jurors had been studiously making notes but most had simply referred occasionally to their evidence bundle during witness testimony. There had been a string of police witnesses describing the location and the damage at the mortar sites, and from

Special Operations branches SO13 and SO19 who had been present at my arrest. The garage owner, Nima Devonshire, was also called, and she repeated her amended description of John Fraser. During the proceedings, whenever my name was mentioned, some jurors would glance in my direction, so I had tried to look attentive, despite the monotonous predictability of the witness statements. The old replacement juror kept falling asleep, and I wished I could do the same. Today promised to be livelier though.

Horwell addressed the judge. 'The Crown is calling a member of the security services to give evidence relating to the events of 15 November 1995. In order to protect her identity, we're employing the use of a screen, as arranged, My Lord.'

The judge nodded his agreement as court officials wheeled a large curtain screen around the witness box, prompting a frisson of animated chatter in the room.

Only the judge, jury and the two opposing barristers now had a view of the witness box. I had seen enough of spooks on the day in question to last me a lifetime – so the lack of visuals was no loss.

Once the agent was in situ, Horwell stood up: 'Could you introduce yourself, please?'

'My Personal Identification Number is 138 and I work for the security services in the counter-terrorist mobile operations unit,' came a woman's voice from behind the screen. 'I have done so for the past eighteen years.'

Horwell indicated a sheet of paper he had extracted from his file. 'Please describe some details of the operation, as detailed in the operators' log dated 15 November 1995.'

'I was in charge of a team of fifty-three operatives deployed in the pursuit, both on foot and by car, of Key Tin – the designated code name for Michael Gallagher – who was suspected of Provisional IRA membership.'

'Did you form any opinions about the behaviour of Key Tin?' asked Horwell.

'I did. Key Tin employed several sophisticated manoeuvres,' she said. 'He had clearly been highly trained in the use of counter-surveillance techniques.'

Horwell greeted this statement with a self-satisfied swoop of his gown and sat down.

Ken indicated that no cross-examination was required and the MI5 officer made a hurried exit as the screen was wheeled away.

'Did you give the prisoner your reason for his arrest and detention?' asked Horwell after DS Fisher was sworn in.

'I told him we were investigating a very serious matter, and we hoped he could be of help.'

'And how did the prisoner react?'

'He told us we were wasting our time.'

'Thank you, DS Fisher,' said Horwell as he took his seat and handed over to Ken.

'DS Fisher, in my copy of the tape transcript, there is a question preceding my client's comment concerning wasting your time,' said Ken. 'Could you tell the court what this was?'

Fisher's eyes searched his document for a few seconds before answering. 'Have I got a terrorist sitting in front of me? That's the question. Or am I wasting my time?'

'And what was the reply?'

'The suspect said, "Aye, you're wasting your time."'

'In fact, Mr Gallagher was merely replying to what you put to him, isn't that so?'

'Yes.'

'Can you read the next sentence please.'

'We didn't think you would be an easy nut to crack. You've undergone intensive training as to how to react to this kind of situation, haven't you, Mr Gallagher?' Fisher read.

'Were these comments based on evidence you had about my client?' asked Ken.

'No, but he had been under suspicion for some time.'

'Thank you, Detective Sergeant Fisher.'

Horwell announced Dr Ann Priston as the prosecution's last expert witness. She described herself as a specialist in fibre analysis with over twenty-five years' experience working for the Metropolitan Police Forensic Science Laboratory. Giving a summary of her report, she stated that matching fibres found in the garage, the car and on the mortar plates were so uncommon that she was able to conclude the three sites were almost certainly connected. Cross-examined by Ken, the scientist conceded the only database available to her was over twelve years old, and she therefore relied upon her personal expertise.

'Thank you, Dr Priston. No further questions.'

Nineteen

Taking the Stand

Thursday, 19 February, 10.30 a.m. – Michael

I took my seat in the witness box and, as directed by the clerk, recited the oath.

'Can you describe for us, Michael, how you spend your time?' asked Ken.

'I work with addiction recovery groups and on my creative writing. I watch some TV, play Scrabble with my partner and discuss interesting things about life in general.'

'How long have you been involved with addiction recovery groups?' he asked.

'Since I had my last drink in 1984 – giving back is part of the process of making amends.'

Ken read out a statement from the woman in charge of the local addiction centre expressing her high regard for my voluntary work with her clients.

'How else have you made amends for your past behaviour?'

I was pleased Ken was giving me the opportunity to counter media reports portraying me as a wife- and family-deserting, benefits-cheating scoundrel.

'I've been supporting my ex-wife and our three children, including financial help for my middle son Anthony to get through his English degree at Oxford University, where he got first-class honours, and I was responsible, also, for the monthly mortgage payments for their family home.'

'Can you please explain for the court how you came to be in possession of the key to the lock-up at Elmcroft Mews?'

I had rehearsed my statement for days and could recite it almost word for word. 'During coffee after an addiction recovery meeting in Hammersmith, I mentioned I was driving to Glasgow the following morning and if anyone wanted a lift en route, they were welcome. John, a recovering addict, who I'd met for the first time at the meeting, asked if I could give him a lift – anywhere near Manchester would do.

'I suggested to meet at Shepherd's Bush Green at 9 o'clock, but he asked to wait until 10, as he wanted to go to a lock-up garage he'd been renting to give back the key in return for the deposit. I told him I couldn't leave any later than 9 as I had a doctor's appointment in Glasgow in the afternoon. On hearing this, John decided to forget about the deposit.

'When we arrived at the motorway services station nearest to Manchester, John wanted to give me a "thank you" gift but had no money. He therefore left the garage key on the passenger seat, along with the rental company's agreement, suggesting when I got back to London, I could claim the £50 deposit.'

'Had this man a surname?' asked Ken.

'It said "Fraser" on the deposit docket, but they don't do surnames at recovery meetings.'

'Didn't you find it unusual he had no money?'

'Not really. I've been in the same situation myself and know of plenty more who have.'

'What was he using the lock-up for?'

'I didn't ask.'

'Can you describe this man, John Fraser?'

'6 feet 2 inches tall, with dark, untidy hair,' I said, matching the description given by the lock-up owner, Mrs Devonshire, in her first statement.

'While being detained in Canon Row did you attend an identity parade?'

'Yes. I volunteered, to show I'd nothing to hide.'

'And what witnesses took part?'

'The seller of the Ford Sierra and the dealer who later bought it.'

'Did either identify you as being the person involved in those transactions?'

'No.'

'Going back to the events of 15 November 1995, I would like to remind the jury of the statement of the security officer number 138 who described you as being highly trained in the use of counter-surveillance techniques. Have you been trained in counter-surveillance?'

'No, not at all.'

'Can I ask you to read the transcript of Tape M18, in your bundle of evidence please.'

I looked at my copy of the transcript.

KEY

..	Natural pause
….	Indecipherable
( )	Sounds like
[ ]	Descriptive text/non-speech sound

M Male voice – Michael Gallagher

F Female voice – Mary Attenborough

M …. eastbound …. deserted but …. middle-aged …. Red anorak and headscarf …. she saw me …. disappeared …. connection ….

westbound line. I hung around looking …. ads …. wall …. walked along …. wee tunnel …. a mirror up at the ceiling …. great view …. platform …. empty except the same wee woman …. never believe me, Mary …. the workman …. down the escalator behind me …. big burly …. saw …. phone box …. The train came in …. no one …. off …. I got on …. stood waiting …. pair came rushing through the tunnel and jumped …. next carriage …. doors were closing …. I managed to jump off onto the platform. I watched it leaving …. and woman looking out …. I should have waved at them …. [laughter]

F But, why would they bother …. follow you

M Not got a clue. It could be something …. writing …. the IRA after all.

F But, you're not in the IRA, are you?

M Course not. But …. a lot about it.

Ken raised his eyes from his ring binder.

'Okay, Michael. Now we've read the transcript, can I ask you to recollect for the court your movements on the morning of 15 November 1995?'

I cleared my throat.

'On the way to Holland Park Tube station, I stopped at the bottle bank where I dropped off our empties. Walking on along the deserted pavement, I saw a man wearing a council worker's yellow vest leave his brush and dustcart and step inside a doorless telephone box at the roadside. As I went past, I could see the man was holding the phone handset. He had big shoulders and, although he had his back to me and his face was partially hidden by the turned-up collar on his jacket, I could see him speaking and nodding his head as if involved in conversation. On the road, next to the kiosk, a man operated a pneumatic drill, breaking up the surface, while other workmen noisily shovelled lumps of tar. I thought it odd.'

'In what way?' asked Ken.

'How could the man in the phone box hear the speaker at the other end with all the din outside? Later, when I got to Holland Park, I thought there was something not quite right. Here, I would sometimes make small talk with young blokes who carried out garden maintenance work like sweeping up leaves. They were mostly from a West Indian background, and sometimes we exchanged banter about cricket and football.'

I stopped speaking then. I was worried I sounded racist or patronising.

'Please go on, Michael,' urged Ken.

'On this particular day, all the youngsters were gone. Instead, four much older white men were engaged around the shrubbery and flower-beds. Two of this lot, working with yard brushes and wheelbarrows, wore shiny new boots, and they all seemed much more industrious than the young lads, who had probably been press-ganged into taking on the work.

'At Holland Park Underground station, I took the escalator to the Central Line's east- and westbound platforms. When I got near the bottom, I looked up and saw a man near to the top. He was big and burly, and wearing a green wax jacket.

'On reaching the landing separating the two platforms, I went to the eastbound one. It was deserted except for a middle-aged woman wearing a red anorak and tartan headscarf, carrying a rucksack, about twenty yards away. When she saw me, she took a few steps and turned left into a passageway to the westbound platform.'

The judge fidgeted, his eyes wandering, looking nowhere in particular. I didn't know if I was making any sense, especially with my eastbound and westbound platform directions. My voice, the accent more Glasgow than usual, seemed to bounce off the courtroom walls. Only the fear of coming to a stuttering stop kept me talking. My tie needed loosening, but I didn't dare.

'Stopping just a few feet from where this woman had turned, I saw a convex mirror, half-way along and near the top of the wall, allowing me to see onto the westbound platform. She was huddled close in and talking to the man I'd seen behind me on the escalator. I recognised him then, for sure, as the same heavy-built bloke I'd seen in the phone box.'

At this point I sensed the demeanour of some jury members had changed: gone was the latent hostility in their eyes; they leant forward in their seats as if in eager anticipation of my story's denouement.

'A nearly empty eastbound train drew up at my platform. I stepped aboard and, as I waited for the doors to close, the man and woman rushed through from the other platform and jumped aboard the next carriage. When the doors began to slide closed, I jumped off the train, then watched as it pulled away.'

The judge stopped me. 'You just want to tell us how you gave your pursuers the slip,' he said, his fingers tapping impatiently on the top of his bench. 'You can stop there: we don't have to be mind-readers to know what's coming next.'

Had he been a mind-reader, Justice Tucker would have learned that as I travelled on the escalator taking me back onto the street, irrespective of who was following me, this was the end of a chapter in my life, with no going back to old ways.

'I have no further questions, My Lord,' said Ken.

'When you took this key from a total stranger, weren't you concerned at what might have been inside?' asked Horwell, beginning his cross-examination.

'No, I didn't think about it. I just left the key and rental contract in the glove compartment. One day I was in the Hampstead area, I remembered I had it and thought: where's the harm? So, I phoned the rental people and arranged to hand it in.'

'And what name did you give?' asked Horwell.

'John Fraser – the name on the agreement.'

The prosecutor shook his head in disbelief and came to the end of his table, just a few feet from the witness box. Seeing him close up for the first time, I felt a rush of smugness at the specks of dandruff on the shoulders of his black gown. The mood passed instantly though, overtaken by a terrible urge to inspect my own shoulders.

'Can you tell the court please, who you intended meeting on the morning of November 15th 1995?'

'No one; I was going to Oxford Street for clothes.'

'Why did you take counter-surveillance measures?'

'Curiosity. I couldn't understand why anyone would be following me. So I was just checking I wasn't imagining things.'

'In your earlier testimony, you said these men were more industrious than the young lads. Are you implying here that middle-aged white men have a greater work ethic than the young men they replaced?' Horwell looked towards the jury box, where the three black jurors sat in the back row.

'Of course not. They told me they'd joined a Youth Training Scheme but were then forced to do menial tasks that weren't very fulfilling or beneficial towards future employment.'

Horwell turned towards the jury. 'Could I ask you, please, to go to Exhibit M7 in your bundle of evidence?'

The prosecutor then inserted a cassette into a tape recorder in front of him and switched on the recording:

M Maybe the sirens are goin'

F .... (shopped you)

M Er no no .... you don't know

M There are not many people like that, Mary

F That do what?

M I mean there's plenty MI5 people …. and prisoners and politicians …. plenty IRA

F But …. you're not in the IRA

M No but ….

F More Parmesan

M Please …. .. for characters like mine

F That do what?

M That er have been involved …. been involved in er putting their neck on the line …. depend on other people .. er …. not in his own hands if you like .. and them .. er whatever they came to do was done …. not being able to go back …. a couple of (cars) with them .. …. compare notes how it was in England

F Yeah …. get the feet up

M A very isolating business …. valued not quite accepted

F Mm

M And if you …. (sussed) out …. they drop …. a shot

F Mm ....

M .... no use anymore .... busted flush ....

F .... put .... graze ....

M I mean there's a real story in that .. there's a story there

F (I know) .... for people .... left behind cleaning up

M You .. more pasta.

F No but it was really good

M Ah but a struggle to finish .... no pun intended

F [Laughs]

After apologising for the many unintelligible words, Horwell turned to me.

'When you talk to your partner about this IRA character, are you not, in fact, referring to yourself?'

'No. It's fiction, completely made up.'

'You're frightened when you hear sirens. Left behind to clean up after your friends, who have come over and, as you say, "done what they had to do". Have I correctly got your meaning, Mr Gallagher?'

'No. What I said was, I regretted not being able to go back and have a couple of jars with the rest of the lads and compare notes as to how it was in London.'

'Hmm.' Horwell bent his head, his eyes scanning his transcript. 'It's very much the same thing, is it not?'

'I don't drink, haven't done so for fourteen years, so I'm not talking about myself.'

'I have no further questions,' Horwell said abruptly and nodded across to the defence team's table. 'Thank you.'

Ken, looked pleased, giving me hope my answers had gone down well. He stood up again.

'Your creative writing tutor at Birkbeck University has made a statement describing you as having a natural aptitude and showing great promise. Can you say if any of your writing has been based on personal experience?'

'I've nearly completed one novel based on my time as a homeless alcoholic, but my other writings are entirely fictional.'

'Again, you tutor has referred to your outlook as completely pacifist. Would you agree with his observation?'

'Absolutely.'

I left the witness box pleased that Horwell's scratching for racist tendencies, in an attempt to influence the three black jurors, had failed.

I was amused at how the opposing counsels had variously portrayed me. Horwell's questioning had inferences of nefarious plotting in a seedy Earl's Court bedsit. Ken's questions, on the other hand, had aimed to show my day packed with good works and evenings spent with Mary, our cosy bijou dwelling an after-dinner hive of creative ideas and philosophical discussions.

Friday, 20 February, 9 a.m. – Michael

Standing in the holding cell, I stared in disbelief at the newspaper. It had a photo of Mary, her head highlighted with a red circle, crossing the finishing line at the Windsor half-marathon, with an article underneath: 'In the sixth week of the Heathrow mortar bombing trial, Mr Justice Tucker will consider a request from jury members to be shielded from the view of witness Mary Attenborough, girlfriend of accused Michael Gallagher.' I try to curb my anger as I consider the implications of the supposedly unbiased jury signalling that they are scared of Mary.

The key rattled in the door and Neil was ushered in by the turnkey. He sat down on the bench; I backed off to stand against the wall.

We did not exchange our usual morning pleasantries nor did he ask how many times I'd been strip-searched – always at least six – on the journey through the tunnel from my cell. Instead, he took out two sheets of paper from his briefcase, handing one to me.

The document, dated 20 February 1998, on Neil's law firm's stationery, listed the order of proceedings:

> Mary Attenborough witness testimony
>
> Dr Stockdale – to counter fibre analysis report of Dr Ann Priston for DPP
>
> Prosecution and Defence summing-up
>
> Judge's direction to Jury
>
> Jury retires
>
> Verdict

I held up the newspaper open at Mary's picture. 'You've left this out. If some of the jurors are frightened of Mary, it means they've already made up their minds. Let them be screened.'

'Come on Michael. Not challenging it would reduce the entire proceedings to a farce.'

'But that's what it is,' I said, my voice raised. 'We should just blindfold Mary and lead her into the witness box.'

'There's no need to get funny. The judge couldn't possibly agree to such a request,' Neil said, his face red. 'Mary's all set to take the stand. She really believes she can convince the jury.'

'Why encourage her in a sham?' I said, my voice now lowered. 'She's been through enough already.'

Neil leaned forward in his seat and looked at me. 'The Mary I know would face that jury blindfolded if she thought it would help your case.'

I had no answer – a feeling of remorse began to gnaw at my insides.

'We have to concentrate on what matters,' said Neil, calmly. 'She wants to tell the court about the real you.'

The real me! Who was that?

I looked again at Mary's photo: her face, pink and glossy, hair tied back in a ponytail, grimacing with determination, her stare fixed on a distant point beyond the finishing line.

'Okay, let her go ahead.'

Friday, 20 February, 7.30 a.m. – Mary

On the landing outside my flat, I hear a buzz on my mobile. The screen reads *Home*; I stop and answer.

'Have you seen this morning's newspapers?' asks my mother.

'Not yet, I'm just leaving for court.'

'There's a photo of you. It says, "jury requests screening from chief defence witness in IRA trial."'

I put my briefcase on the ground and lean against the wooden banister rail. 'The lawyer phoned last night and told me. But can you blame them? Armed guards every time they turn a corner in the court building and a helicopter never far away. It's not surprising they're prejudiced against us. We've knocked out most of the prosecution's evidence, so they'll now hear from me personally: I'll show they've nothing to fear,' I say calmly.

My mother then starts questioning the integrity of lawyers and judges, and I let her carry on, only half listening.

'A reporter phoned from the local paper last night. He spoke to your dad and was trying to get the low-down on you.'

I smile at my properly spoken mother's descent into slick B movie actor talk. 'And did he give them any … low-down?'

'Your father said he'd never heard of you.'

'Well done, Dad.' I smother a burst of laughter. 'That'll throw them off the scent.'

'Don't you want to know about the photo?'

'Not really.'

'It's at the end of your half-marathon last summer,' Mum says, undeterred. 'You've got that stubborn "nothing will stop me" stare.'

This jokey chatter is her way of trying to steady my nerves.

I glance at my watch. 'I'll be late for the court, Mum.'

'What have you on?'

'My black and cream suit. I bought it in Chelsea, especially for today.'

'Perhaps a good choice …'

'I'll phone this evening,' I say, ending the call. A clothing-related discussion is the last thing I need after recent hours spent checking my fibres' analysis submission.

As I reach the sanctuary of a small waiting room reserved for Court 10's defence witnesses, Ken Macdonald, wearing his wig and long gown, comes striding through the doorway with Neil at his back. We exchange greetings and Neil leaves his briefcase down on the armchair next to mine and goes to the vending machine. He calls across, 'You having a drink, Mary?'

'Sparkling water, please.'

'And the usual for me,' Ken says, gathering the voluminous skirts of his gown around him and taking a seat facing me.

Neil lifts out a bottle of lemonade and a packet of KP nuts from the dispenser and gives them to Ken. He then comes over to me with my bottle of water and his Diet Coke.

Ken pours some nuts into his hand. 'The judge will be anxious to crack on and have the trial finished – you shouldn't have to hang around for long before taking the stand, Mary.'

I take a sip from my bottle. 'I know we can't discuss evidence, but has Stockdale got back with an amended report? Or brought in a statistician expert?'

'Hmm,' Ken and Neil look at each other.

'Not yet,' says Neil, 'but he's aware of the urgency.'

'You know about the jury's wish to be screened?' says Ken. 'The judge will rule shortly.'

'Surely he won't allow it?'

'Not a cat in hell's chance,' adds Neil.

'Have you told Michael?'

'He was upset,' says Neil, 'but I managed to placate him.'

I'm diverted to worrying about the potential fate of Ken's starched white shirt as he shovels oily peanuts into his mouth. Before my anxiety properly takes hold, the room door swings open and the prosecutor, Horwell, calls Ken. 'The judge wants us in chambers.'

'Thanks, Richard.'

Ken excuses himself with a nod and drops the empty peanut packet into a bin at the door.

'Back to basics after last night's feast, eh?' I hear Horwell say, as they leave.

'What's with their matey exchanges?' I ask Neil. 'And what feast?'

Neil shuffles uncomfortably on the edge of his seat. 'Traditionally, on the last week of the trial, the judge hosts a meal for the opposing barristers.'

'I'm sorry, Neil, I find that tradition seriously unethical.'

'Believe me, they won't have discussed the trial.'

I stare at Neil. 'So, they share a meal, probably lasting two or three hours, and not one word's spoken about the case they've worked on for six weeks?'

'Obviously, they may have touched on generalities but on no account would they have discussed the evidence,' says Neil. He fails to disperse my sense of unease.

Twenty

Verdict

Friday, 20 February, 10 a.m. – Mary

While waiting to go through the upright security scanner in the court building, I see Michael's sons, Damian, Anthony and Barry, talking and laughing on their way upstairs to the public gallery and I'm encouraged by their clearly upbeat mood. Once in the courtroom, I make my way to the witness box. It's the first time I've seen Michael in two weeks – having been advised by Neil that we shouldn't communicate until after my evidence. I'm relieved he looks healthy. I give him a wave and get a smile back from the dock.

I quickly glance at the jury, being careful not to stare. An Old Bailey jury selected from a Central London population would have been comprised of a better community mix, but at least there are five women jurors – three white and two black.

Justice Tucker walks to his bench and lowers himself into his chair. 'Members of the jury,' he says. 'I wish to explain the ruling I made earlier. In our democracy, we pride ourselves on the openness of our justice system; the cornerstone of our rule of law. It is for this reason I have not acceded to your request to be screened from the view of the witness, Mary Attenborough.'

He joins his hands together to form a steeple shape, like a bishop about to bestow a blessing. 'No effort will be spared in ensuring your safety and to guarantee you carry out your democratic duty free from any potential threat of violence.' As if on cue, two armed policemen enter the courtroom through the double doors and take up position on either side. 'Mr Macdonald, you may proceed with your witness.'

A court official hands me a card. I state my name, my occupation and read the oath affirming to tell the truth.

Ken eases his face into a kindly smile and looks across at me. He asks about my relationship to Michael, my professional life – from doctoral student, senior lecturer to IT consultant – and includes my recently published book, *Engineering Mathematics Exposed*. He then questions my attitude to IRA violence, and I confirm that I support only non-violent civil disobedience.

Ken turns then towards the jury. 'Can I refer you to your transcript copies of Exhibit M/4. The distorted sound reproduction in these tapes has led to many misunderstandings, but I'm confident Dr Attenborough can help correctly interpret this excerpt.'

After months of sifting through screeds of manuscripts I can remember almost every word and its context; also, the frequent misinterpretations of their meanings by our covert listeners. Neil, not given to compliments, in an uncharacteristic lapse, has told me that in all of our bugged conversations he's not heard us say a bad word about anybody, except between our two selves of course, although our personal arguments never lasted very long.

Ken switches on the recording. I rest the transcript copy on my lap. No matter how many times I read this, I'm still annoyed at the caricatured misrepresentation of Michael's accent and expressions.

M/4 EXHIBIT
[Television news on – report on announcement of North/South Ireland Joint Authority]

M The Government now .... the IRA

F .... Dublin and the IRA

M I know

F like there's nothing really between Dublin and the IRA ..

M Yeah

[Partly intelligible conversation about time and news items]
[Movement and background noise]
[Some brief sections of low level, unintelligible speech against background of TV news]

M That's true .. och aye .... we have to decide on a (peace dividend)

M We'll *gie him a hand .... you know ..

M should be firing bullets at yon major's seat .... attempts at progress

F of course

M Prime Minister's been (like) speaking to the Nation .... woo the backbenchers .. tail wagging the Tory dog .. they've .... got any cohesion the Ulster workers (kinda freed) .. you know what I mean .... I mean the IRA .. might not be happy you know .. I think they've just done enough to keep them (indoors) ..

F The joint North South Authority declarations of (birth right) .... if the Ulster Unionists don't (do it) they've turned already.

M just you know they've (*girned) hard but I mean direct rule free

Dublin's just unpalatable for them you know so I mean they'll just .... we'll accept .... by any other name you know ....

[Mostly unintelligible conversation then silence]

END OF TAPE
* to gie (Scots – to give)
**to girn (Scots – to complain repeatedly)

'Can you explain please what your partner meant by, "we should be firing bullets at yon major's seat"?'

'Michael didn't say, "yon major".'

'No?'

'He said, John Major.'

There's an outbreak of scattered murmurings around the courtroom.

'It wasn't firing bullets at his seat, it was at his feet.' My correction is met with more hushed exclamations.

Ken waits until the noise has abated. 'You'll have noticed the effect these words had around this courtroom. What was your own reaction, Mary?'

'This is a well-known figure of speech – meaning someone needs to be speeded up to act decisively. The Unionist parties held the balance of power in the Tory government. Michael was expressing his frustration at John Major for allowing the parties of David Trimble and Ian Paisley to hold up the peace process.'

'Thank you, Mary. That will be all for now.'

Horwell stands, stares at the transcript on the table for a few seconds, then picks it up and turns to me.

'Michael Gallagher has used the personal pronoun "we" in his comment and presumably means more people than just himself. Can you please tell the court, Dr Attenborough, about whom your partner is referring?'

'Michael meant the peace negotiators. Michael is a strong republican supporter.'

'A strong supporter?' Horwell asks, taking a quick look towards the jury benches. 'But in your statement to the police you said Mr Gallagher had no extreme political opinions.'

'I said Michael had no *extreme* views. Of course he has strong political opinions,' I say.

'Strong enough to help the IRA in its campaign of violence?'

'Absolutely not! There's no way he would resort to such actions.'

'So, what would you have done if you had found out Mr Gallagher was involved in violence?'

'Michael is entitled to his political opinions and shares the same with many others, including people here in England. I know of plenty of innocent Irish prisoners wrongly convicted, such as the Birmingham Six. What I'm trying to say is, Michael Gallagher will join in a struggle against injustice wherever he finds it.'

'Struggle against injustice?' asks Horwell, throwing my words right back at me. 'Could this struggle have extended to helping the Provisional IRA carry out its wanton attacks on Heathrow Airport?'

'Michael Gallagher would not engage in violence which could threaten life or injury.'

'So you would have left him if you had discovered such involvement?'

'I wouldn't be in the relationship unless I knew his character.'

'So you would have left him?' Horwell turns and looks across at the jury benches. 'And reported him to the authorities?'

'In general terms I would report anyone who I thought was about to cause injury or death.'

'You would have reported him to the authorities had you known.'

It wasn't a question, so I didn't answer.

'And if you were to discover he was indeed involved, you would leave him?'

'He's not guilty, so it's not something I'd have to consider.'

'I will ask you again. Would you end your relationship with Michael Gallagher if you found out he had been involved?'

'And I will repeat to you what I've already said. Michael has done nothing wrong.'

'Thank you, Ms Attenborough, I have no further questions.'

Thank you too, I think. It now only remains for Dr Stockdale to combat the evidence of the Crown's scientist Dr Priston. One last push should get us over the line.

I leave the witness box and almost get to the exit at the rear of the court when, behind me, I hear Ken say, 'And, in view of this, Your Honour, it will not now be necessary to call our fibres expert.'

Though barely taking in those words, I can still hear in my head Stockdale's comment at our meeting. 'As fibres forensic scientists, we use our expertise and the data we have – this is sufficient to draw the necessary conclusions.'

Friday, 20 February, 3 p.m. – Michael

Back in the holding cell, I was left only with my thoughts. My admiration for Mary's steadfast assurance in the face of Horwell's hostile and relentless cross-examination – at no stage had she faltered – was overshadowed by Stockdale's absence, resulting in Ken's concession to Dr Priston's fibres evidence.

The turnkey unlocked the door and Neil came in.

'Stockdale's faxed report arrived at the lunchtime break. It hadn't changed in substance from the original.'

'He ignored Mary's mathematical model?'

'He said it didn't alter his earlier position. We told him then we wouldn't call him.'

'Mary could have testified. Her analysis contradicted Dr Priston's conclusions.'

'Mary wouldn't be recognised as an expert; her opinion wouldn't carry weight in the court.'

'Why didn't Stockdale engage with a statistician?'

'Only he knows the answer.'

I felt sorry for Neil. He'd recommended Stockdale and had been let down. But I was annoyed too. The self-restraint and diplomacy he had practised throughout had got him nowhere: why, now, just this once, could he not shout, swear and stamp his feet?

For his summing-up, Horwell stood at his desk facing the jury.

'You have to ask yourselves, if a passing traveller in straitened circumstances offered you a key to a garage lock-up of unknown contents, what would your reaction have been? Then, we turn to the audio surveillance. Here there are several circumstantial indicators.'

Horwell's eyes moved slowly along, pausing momentarily at each juror. 'For example, ladies and gentlemen, how many of you have addressed your partner across the dinner table and asked, "You're not in the IRA, are you?"'

Some jurors smiled, while others laughed, adding to the guffaws around the courtroom.

'I would also ask you to think carefully about what the accused said himself from the witness box: the reason he first knew he was being followed was because of the illogical behaviour of one man in a phone box. He then did a racial profiling exercise where he decided no middle-aged white men could be landscape gardeners or park attendants in Holland Park and no black youths would be gainfully employed there.

'Members of the jury, I will now relate the events of November 15, 1995, as described by the security officer. Following a tip-off that Michael Gallagher was to meet with a PIRA contact, her team mounted an undercover surveillance exercise in which a total of fifty-three personnel were deployed.

'During the operation, the accused used techniques such as double-back manoeuvres, jumping on and off Underground trains, before aborting the rendezvous without any obvious signal to his contact. The actions proved beyond any doubt that Gallagher was trained in highly sophisticated, anti-surveillance practices. He had been too clever by half.

'In the final analysis, ladies and gentlemen of the jury, your decision on whether or not you return guilty verdicts, will rely on a common-sense analysis of this clear evidence.

'This concludes the summing up for the prosecution, My Lord.'

Ken took up position nearer the end of his table, 'Members of the jury, there isn't a shred of evidence with which to convict Michael Gallagher. The forensic experts have pointed to the possibility of accidental contamination of the explosives and fibre evidence. The contents of the three audio surveillance tapes produced have been shown to have been either misunderstood or misinterpreted.

'At an identification parade, the two witnesses so crucial to the police's case failed to identify my client, in spite of the fact they stood a mere fifteen feet from him, the same distance as I am standing from you now. As for being followed, Mr Gallagher explained that the actions he took to avoid his pursuers were born purely out of curiosity.

'You heard DS Fisher and his "tough nut to crack" comment. Really! Does this reformed alcoholic, dearly loved by his partner and his family, and constantly on hand to help those in difficulty through awful addictions, strike you as a tough nut to crack? Mr Horwell also emphasised the heinous outrages of PIRA, and here he may be correct. But what has this got to do with my client?

'You might ask, and you would be entitled to, how on earth Michael came by that lock-up key,' said Ken. 'Even if you doubt my client's account, there could be many reasons for this, but none make him guilty of these charges: he's not on trial for his naiveté. The fateful morning when he took possession of the key, who could have imagined the dreadful consequences to follow?

'Let us not forget, also, my client has led an unconventional life, both when in the throes of his own addiction or later when contributing as a valued part of the recovery community, helping such people, who, as he put it, "come and go all the time".

'The reason Michael stands in the dock today is based on a tragic convergence of events that have engulfed not just himself but Mary Attenborough, his partner, who has worked tirelessly to prove his innocence.

'This man,' said Ken, nodding his head towards me, 'doesn't take lives. On the contrary: many lives have been enhanced by Michael Gallagher's unfailing readiness to give of his time for those suffering from the ravishes of addiction.'

I felt my face go red at Ken's exaggerated claims, but I knew he had to improvise, to focus on the personal and to try to make up for the ground we'd lost by not having Stockdale. We shouldn't even have had to argue about the garage key if the fibres expert had used Mary's statistical modelling: the garage would be innocent and so would I.

Ken then stood in front of the jury box, his eyes searching along the lines of faces. The old man at the end, having fallen asleep on the first day, had been nudged awake regularly ever since by the young biker with the ear-stud, who was now wearing a suit. The spiky orange-haired woman had her head bowed, biro in hand, busily writing in a notebook.

'I have nothing but admiration for your conduct and the respectful attention you've shown throughout these proceedings. I trust this will lead you to find Michael Gallagher not guilty on both charges.' And with those words Ken sat down.

The judge began his summing up and instructions to the jury and, after about ten minutes, ended with the words: 'Please be minded, also, in coming to your verdict, you should banish from your minds any notions of antagonism against Irish people in general and act in the best traditions of English justice.'

Tuesday, 24 February, 3.30 p.m. – Michael

After a day and three-quarters deliberating on the evidence, the jury members filed back into the courtroom. Their faces gave no hint as to what had been decided, though the young woman with the spiky orange hair shot a glance towards me through red-rimmed eyes. Their earlier report to the judge that they were unable to reach a unanimous decision surely meant they were veering towards an innocent verdict? Or was I clutching at straws?

I played guessing games as to who had been appointed their foreperson, but no one stood out: the old man I had as favourite at the beginning had fallen asleep too often during the trial.

Justice Tucker called out. 'Will the accused please stand.'

Remembering Mary's constant warnings not to slouch, I stood straight, clasped my hands together behind my back and said a silent Serenity Prayer.

The judge called out: 'Members of the jury, have you reached a majority verdict with no less than eleven out of twelve in agreement?'

The biker got to his feet. 'Yes, we have, My Lord.'

I thought the young bloke had misunderstood and would sit down again. But he reached into the side pocket of his baggy fawn jacket and brought out a piece of paper.

The court clerk read out the charges, pausing after each sentence.

'How do you find the defendant on count number one?'

The foreman looked down at his piece of paper.

'Guilty.'

'How do you find the defendant on count number two?'

'Guilty.'

Trying to act normally, I waved up to the public gallery in a gesture of thanks for the support shown by my family and friends. Mary, looking shocked, stared woodenly back at me. My sons Damian, Anthony and Barry wore forlorn, crestfallen expressions, reminiscent of when they were small and were about to cry. I wanted to hug them.

Horwell and his staff mouthed sedate congratulations between them. Ken and Neil, their heads lowered, started to gather together their files.

Unlike the other jury members, who were smiling and talking animatedly amongst themselves, the spiky-haired juror bowed her head and wept quietly. The woman beside her reached out with a tissue.

People seated around the courtroom, on the press benches, began talking amongst themselves. The judge called out, 'Could we have some order please.' He thanked the jury members for discharging their civic responsibility in such a conscientious manner and excused them from jury duty for ten years. He then spoke about me as a politically misguided individual who completely disregarded the safety of others: a criminal adventurer and callous terrorist causing reckless endangerment to human life.

I pretended the judge was referring to someone else, a stranger I'd never met, but there was no escaping the staring eyes and assenting nods endorsing the judge's outrage.

'You will go to prison for twenty years,' he said. 'Take him down.'

I was still in automatic best-behaviour mode, as urged by Neil and Ken all through the trial: 'Don't do or say anything that could possibly upset the judge or alienate the jury.' Now the damage was done, I could say or do what I wanted, but there would be no defiant speech from the dock: an IRA ceasefire had been in operation for eight months and care was needed to avoid public utterances the media could exploit.

I looked up to the public gallery, then raised my hands and clapped them together in appreciation of my loved ones' support, a gesture that felt totally inadequate.

My two guards closed in, one on either side, and led me from the dock.

Tuesday, 24 February, 4.45 p.m. – Mary

Neil is waiting for me at the side of the concourse. He apologises for Ken, who's had to leave on urgent business.

Neil's face is even paler than normal. He puts his hand lightly on my arm; I shake it off and sit down on a wooden bench nearby. Neil remains standing.

'Are you okay?' he asks.

'I just can't believe it. How's Michael?'

'He's a bit shaken but trying to be positive.'

'Can I see him?'

'Afraid not, not today, but I'll try to arrange a short visit for tomorrow.'

'What happened to Stockdale? Why wasn't he here?'

'We did everything possible, Mary. When I contacted him, he said he couldn't see a reason to change his report.'

'In other words, my opinion means nothing?' I say it quietly. 'So, I take it there's no question of an appeal on that basis?'

'I'm afraid not,' Neil says.

'But we do have grounds on other matters. We could start with the jury's request to be screened. Some, at least, had decided Michael was guilty.'

'I'm not so sure they did.' Neil hugs his folder to his chest. 'The judge refused their application anyway.'

'The jury, at that time, hadn't even heard all the evidence. I appreciate how hard you've worked. Ken too,' I add. But in my head, I'm thinking that if he had stressed the phrase 'presumption of innocence' and also 'beyond reasonable doubt' a little more, maybe Michael would be sitting here beside me right now.

I lift my briefcase and get to my feet. 'I'll head off now, try to beat the rush hour traffic.'

Neil suddenly leans in close. I worry he'll give me a consolatory hug, a gesture that would be really uncharacteristic and also leave me unsure how to react. Instead, he has a quick look around, reaches inside his file, takes out a small piece of paper already folded in two and places it in my hand. 'I managed to get you this message out from Michael – don't open it here.' I almost expect him to add, 'And make sure you swallow it after reading.' I shove the letter in my jacket pocket.

Heading outside, blinding flashes from cameras momentarily disorient me. Photographers and journalists brandishing notebooks shout my name:

'Over here, Mary!'

'Can you comment on the case?'

'What's your reaction to the verdict?'

I half run towards the car park, hearing a clatter of chasing feet behind me. When I reach the Fiesta, I look round. Thwarted by two policemen, the photographers are drifting back towards the court.

Once in the car, I take out Michael's note.

> Tuesday 4.05 pm
>
> Dear Mary
>
> Please don't get too upset. You have to stay strong for me (well most of the time anyway – I'll allow you a temporary depression).
>
> Give my love to all the family. Tell them I'm fine.
>
> I (still) sing Athenry to you
>
> Your Michael
>
> X

Underneath, he's drawn his usual sign-off whiskered smiley face, but the crease on the paper makes it look like the face is grimacing.

I join London's commuter traffic. In the rearview mirror, the faint flickers of cell lights beyond the walls of Belmarsh gradually disappear as I get further and further away from Michael.

Twenty-one

Consequences

Tuesday, 24 February, 6 p.m. – Michael

Prison Officers Baggot and Muir escorted me, my arms handcuffed behind my back, through the tunnel leading into the prison. Baggot's announcement through the intercom at the security gate, 'Long-sentenced convict coming through', gave me a sick-to-the-stomach reminder of my new status.

Taken to the hospital wing, I sat on the side of one of its two beds. Baggot unlocked my handcuffs. 'Let's have your clothes, Gallagher.'

I took my jacket off and gave it to him. He shoved it inside a black bin liner, the soft flannel material crushed in one hand.

'Hey, take it easy. That's new,' I said.

Ignoring me, Baggot turned to Muir. 'Star Trek outfits will be in fashion by the time this clobber next sees the light of day.'

'You two!' came a gruff call from the direction of the doorway. 'We'll have less of the smart-arse comments.' The voice's owner, a dumpy figure with a short haircut and wearing a nurse's uniform, came striding into the room wheeling a medical trolley. At her reprimand, delivered in a broad Glasgow accent, the two screws retreated, taking seats in armchairs in front of a television set where an announcer had just begun reading the six o'clock news.

'This is just the routine check-up given to all long-sentenced prisoners,' said the nurse sitting down facing me on the side of the other bed. She reached out and took hold of my right wrist to take my pulse. In contrast to the coarseness of her bark to the screws, her hand had a comforting softness.

'What did he give you?'

'Twenty years.'

'Not bad.'

My laugh was short. 'Seriously?'

'That judge is notorious,' she said, letting go of my hand. 'Most of you IRA lot get twenty-five or thirty.'

She picked up a clipboard from the trolley, and her eyes quickly scanned a document attached. 'It says here you're from Glasgow.'

'And you too, by the sound of it.'

'Govan, born and bred.'

'How long have you been down here?'

'Thirty years.'

'And no time off for good behaviour?'

She smiled. 'Are you married?'

'Partner.'

'Was she in court?'

I nodded.

'What will she do now?'

The question echoed what I'd asked myself a thousand times during the latter days of the trial.

'I'm hoping to get a visiting order arranged for tomorrow; maybe find out then.' My tone feigned nonchalance and I tried to ignore the ache deep inside me. 'If I get a visit at all.'

'Lucky you, pal, if you do.' She stood up, wrapped a blood pressure monitor cuff around my upper arm and began inflating it. 'Lots of woman in her position would have already skedaddled.'

'She still might.' I managed to keep my tone light. 'But first I have to see her. We've a lot to talk about.'

'I bet you have.'

After taking my blood pressure, the nurse placed a thermometer in my mouth. Just as I managed to manoeuvre it under my tongue, I heard the news announcer say the name Michael Anthony Gallagher. I turned with incredulity to look at the television: my mugshot covered the whole screen.

Reporting on the trial, the newsreader quoted the judge's closing remarks: 'Gallagher had helped the IRA wreak a five-day campaign of terror, causing widespread destruction at Heathrow, the world's busiest international airport. Each salvo of five mortars was launched with the help of pre-set electronic timers. Although coded phone warnings were given, the judge said, it does not bear thinking about the carnage which would have ensued had those mortars exploded. It was only for great, good fortune not one of them did.'

The nurse looked at me, shaking her head, daring me to counter the newsreader's words, while I sat breathing through my nose and juggling the glass thermometer under my tongue. Had I been able to speak, I would have been tempted to tell her the judge knew very well why there was no carnage: a scientific report commissioned by the prosecution, but not used in the trial, admitted it was plausible the mortars had been constructed in such a way so as not to explode.

The nurse removed the thermometer, shook it and took a quick look. 'You'll live,' she said.

The TV pictures switched to an outside broadcast camera. It focused on the red-brick front of the court building and slowly zoomed in on the figure of a woman. She was hurrying away from the entrance, her long hair conspicuous in the middle of a throng of photographers and reporters.

'That's her!' I pointed at the TV. 'That's her!'

The news film followed Mary jogging along the pavement in her high-heeled shoes, her two hands clutching her briefcase to her chest. Several photographers scampered behind, aiming their cameras. The film sequence closed with two policemen standing at the court's car park entrance stepping aside to allow Mary through, then barring the entry of her pursuers.

In years past, Mary's advice to fellow activists when up before a local magistrate following demonstrations had always been to smile for the photographer.

She wasn't smiling now.

'Poor lassie,' exclaimed the nurse, staring down at me. 'Men!' she said, her lips pursed. 'You've no idea the trouble you cause.' In spite of the stern words, her tone was compassionate, her voice soft. She jotted down some notes on her clipboard and turned her trolley in the direction of the doorway. I wanted her to stay, to talk some more, even if it was just to scold me.

Wednesday, 25 February, 7.30 a.m. – Michael

Without opening my eyes, I knew from the cold feel of the metal bed frame and the hardness of the mattress below that I was still in jail.

The Glasgow nurse, in a plain no-nonsense way, had been kind but realistic. I might never see Mary again. The screw's mocking remarks about my jacket had been prompted out of malice, the nurse's comments out of compassion. She reminded me of another small, rounded female exile from Glasgow, Sister Jude, who I'd met fourteen years earlier at the Crisis at Christmas gathering in a disused warehouse on the Thames Embankment. This former NHS chiropodist allowed me to call her Judy while, with my foot resting on the coarse fabric of the nun's habit covering her knees, she tended to corns and callouses caused by months of homeless foot slog. She said she would say a prayer for me and promised me better days ahead.

And they had been, until now.

Sounds of footsteps coming to a stop outside the cell forced my head off the pillow. Through the dim daylight I saw a slip of paper appear under the door. I got out of bed, picked it up and read, 'Emergency compassionate visit between prisoner XK1660 Michael Gallagher and Mary Attenborough. 1.30 pm Wednesday, 25 February 1998. Duration: Twenty minutes.'

My mind was made up. I'd say my short piece, and Mary could then do all the talking – if she didn't just walk out, as she had every right to do. One way or another our relationship would come to an end. There would be no lingering farewells.

Wednesday, 25 February, 1.30 p.m. – Mary

The female officer unlocks a door, and I go through prepared to have to pick out Michael from a sea of red-bibbed bodies in the crowded visits room. Instead, I find myself in a small anteroom, empty except for Michael. The officer takes a seat next to the door and brings out a folded crossword puzzle magazine from inside her jacket.

Michael, dressed in a faded, baggy tracksuit, stands at a low table next to equally low-slung chairs. We hug, tightly but briefly, and then sit down.

'So, when do they serve the sushi?' I joke.

Michael doesn't laugh or even shape his face into the usual mock grimace at my corny remarks. He smiles for a moment but then stares at the ground as if the words he's searching for might be found on the chessboard black and white linoleum.

'I have an appeal form here,' I say, patting the side pocket of my denim jacket. 'We can talk about your grounds.'

'I'm sorry, Mary,' he says, 'there's no point.'

'Of course, there is. It's important it's done straightaway.'

He lets out a long sigh. 'It's not as important as what I have to tell you.'

'Go on,' I urge, convinced he's going to propose some hare-brained scheme, maybe about escaping or going on hunger strike.

'I know this will come as a terrible let-down for you. And an awful shock.' He takes my hands in his.

'Tell me.'

'There can't be an appeal.'

'Why not?'

'I really was involved at Heathrow. I'm sorry, Mary, the jury got it right.'

I stare at him in shock while trying to absorb what he has just said and wondering which version of the truth to accept – his previous denials or this new admission.

'How? Why? I don't believe you. I'd have known.'

I pull my hands away from his, get to my feet and back away from the table. The officer also stands up. She gives me a rueful, sympathetic look. On consideration, however, I think I need more explanation, so I sit down again and she does too, like we're involved in some sort of ritual dance of indecision.

'Why didn't you tell me all this earlier?' I blurt out.

'I did make hints, through the stories about Malachy, and I told you I thought I was being followed.' The resigned hunch of his shoulders tells me he knows how pathetically inadequate his explanation is.

'When you told me about someone following you, all that crossed my mind was that you were a fantasist, imagining things based on your writing scenarios. I asked you outright and you told me you were not in the ...' I stop, aware I'm talking loudly and the officer has looked over. I lower my voice again and add, 'You could have told me when you were arrested.'

'We didn't have any time alone. Later, had I owned up after getting bail, it would have put you in a terrible dilemma with the sureties – or even with the police.'

It now occurs to me that he could really, this time, be telling the truth. I've a mind to have a real go at him about his deceit to our family and friends, which I am now implicated in, but as I imagine Michael going back to his lone prison cell, I don't have the heart to summon up admonishments, and I can see the guilt he feels about his duplicitous behaviour by the pain on his face. 'Poor Michael,' I mutter, repeatedly, the two words almost entirely summing up my feelings. He was prepared to risk our twelve-year-long relationship while carrying on his secret involvement with the IRA and, having lost the gamble, he now faces the consequences of his actions. He may have made a terrible choice, but he is still the man I have loved for over a decade. Yet, despite still having feelings for him, I know I must now turn away.

I worry about how he will manage without me and me without him – but unlike Michael, I have a world of freedom in which to recover. I look at his baggy prison-issue tracksuit with the faint spattering of food on its front. 'How will you cope?' My voice is so low it's almost as if I'm talking to myself. And then I start to cry – I cry for my lost love, and I cry out of concern for him, and I cry because perhaps he doesn't deserve that concern.

The officer reaches across and hands me a packet of tissues. She has seen it all before. I smile and nod my thanks.

Michael puts his hands around my shoulders and draws me towards him until our heads are almost touching. I don't resist, burying my face in the crook of his neck. We stay locked like this for what seems like an age, until the bell sounds for the end of the visit.

'I know I've no right to expect anything,' Michael says, his face a picture of helpless abandonment, 'but I have a visitor order for Saturday. Will I see you then?'

I stand up, saying nothing but knowing the reply I should and had decided to give – but at the door I turn and call out to him, 'I'll be there.'

Twenty-two

Please Go – Please Don't Go

Wednesday, 25 February, 3 p.m. – Mary

Walking along the tarmac path towards Plumstead station, head bowed, eyes watering, I nearly collide with an approaching pedestrian – a woman, I think. I avoid looking up, not wanting anyone to show concern or, even worse, ask if I'm alright. How can I explain that my partner of twelve years has lied to me, put my life in danger and carried on the deception for sixteen months since that police raid?

At the station, I hear the weird wail of the approaching electric train. Was this for the last time? I'd rashly promised a visit for the weekend – but would I actually go?

On the train, I pick up a morning newspaper lying abandoned on the unoccupied seats opposite. A front-page photo of Michael leaps out at me; a police mugshot showing a dull-eyed, emotionless face.

I read the article underneath, going through the details of the verdict and sentence until I reach the passage at the end: 'Yesterday, Gallagher was found guilty of conspiracy to cause an explosion after a trial lasting almost two months. Commander John Grieve, the head of the anti-terrorist branch, said: "Gallagher was quite an unusual creature. He took great risks. He lived in London ready to do the IRA's bidding and was essential to the IRA's campaign on the mainland. Without people such as him the IRA's campaign would be impossible."'

I doubt if endangerment of our relationship would have been considered by the commander or, indeed, by Michael himself, in any assessment of 'great risks' taken.

Back in my flat, I look around and realise he's never coming home. Twenty years. No appeal. I can't realistically promise to wait twenty years for a guilty man – but can I walk away leaving him in misery and despair? Will my family and friends think I'd known all along? Will they judge my earnest pleas for sureties insincere or, worse, dishonest? I have to tell them the truth at some point, but it can wait for another day – I don't have the strength right now. There's nothing to do but sit. Maybe he'll ring? Then I realise that's an old thought, an innocent Michael thought. Would I want him to ring now?

The room is getting dark. I've sat, immobile, for maybe two hours. When the phone does ring, I rush to answer. It's Becky. She's heard about the verdict and asks about the appeal. I say we're seeking legal advice. I can't bring myself to tell her the truth and certainly not by telephone – I don't want to give the security services the satisfaction of hearing the full details of my misery.

To my relief, she quickly moves on to optimistic news about her business. She has a big contract beginning shortly and feels she needs a break before starting. Why don't we head for the beach? – she mentions a bargain last-minute deal for Tenerife. I thank her for the invite and say I'll get back to her. After I hang up, I sit in silence and think: the beach?

I must have fallen asleep because I'm slumped on the settee. I switch on the TV for some light. Films, I think, I like films. Searching through my handbag I find the Blockbuster video-shop card. God knows when I last used it, but it doesn't have a 'valid to' date. I drag myself off the settee and head for Earl's Court Road. I might even get some crisps and popcorn. My thoughts are insane. Perhaps I've just lost all sense of reality. I decide I'd like strawberry popcorn.

Thursday, 26 February, 10 a.m. – Mary

Walking downstairs with video in hand, I check for post on the hall ledge. There is a small, inconspicuous white envelope for me, addressed in Michael's handwriting, and now I wonder if, subconsciously, I came downstairs to check the post and not on a change of video mission at all. I head back upstairs with almost the old spring in my step, but then the reality hits again: this is no longer my poor innocent Michael but the man who deceived our friends, family and me. Nonetheless, once back in the flat, I open the envelope with the same eagerness as in the past.

> XK1660 CAT A Belmarsh Wednesday 25/2/98
>
> I am writing this after your visit today. Your whole demeanour throughout this very harrowing time in our lives has made me feel quite humble. I just wonder at times why I've been so blessed to have us fall in love. So, you see I put our separation into a more realistic perspective. In the next few days, I will try to get my head around what all this entails. I will not be in any hurry to make sense of it all but I know we will both come through. I think you must be the strongest person I've ever met and without your resilience, I would not have coped so far. Anyway, my love, that is how I feel tonight. I ache to have you near me so much but I console myself that I can have such strong feelings and one day all our dreams will come true.

He then asks after the family and ends with:

> For the foreseeable future, a day at a time, the highlight of my life will be our phone calls, letters and visits. You are my inspiration and

I am madly and passionately in love with you. Until I see you on Saturday, I will count the minutes.

Your Michael

Still singing Athenry

Again, I find myself sitting silent and motionless on the sofa. I don't know what to think or how to react to this letter. Did I really promise just to carry on as though he had never told me of his big lie and been given a twenty-year sentence?

Then the sensible piece of my brain – the bit that never completely leaves me, the analytical bit – intrudes with the thought that it doesn't matter what I said or might have said. Even if I implied I'd made up my mind to carry on as before, decisions are only permanent until they are not, and sometimes lying is the kindest thing to do. I'm even self-possessed enough, I realise, to marvel at my own self-possession.

I don't know what to make of these thoughts streaming through my head – though again, I wonder if they, like my thoughts about strawberry popcorn, are a symptom of insanity.

Then I notice the bottom of Michael's letter where he has drawn a musical stave formed into a smiley by a tie between the notes. I laugh and cry simultaneously, and I think: only one day to wait until I see him again.

Saturday, 28 February, 3 p.m. – Michael

Before the visit, I reread Mary's first letter since the verdict. She had written of people asking after me and wanting to know about a possible appeal, with no hint of the devastation she must have felt about last Wednesday's revelation. She finished with: 'Anyway, my love, writing to you has cheered me up because I imagine I'm sitting talking to you. I know you'll be fine, and we will come through this difficult time together.'

Despite her upbeat attitude, 'let's just carry on as before', I knew I needed to provide more explanation about my deception. Mary could ask the questions, and I'd try to answer as fully as possible.

The visiting room was filled with squealing children and squeaking toys. For once, I didn't get annoyed: it meant we could talk freely with less risk of being overheard. I stood as I saw Mary enter the room. As she approached, her red-rimmed eyes and the droop of her shoulders showed clear distress, but still we hugged as though grasping for the life we knew we'd never have again.

She didn't take off her coat, as she always had done before, and she sat back in her chair, keeping as much distance as possible between us. I could hardly blame her – but now I felt a pulse of panic. I plunged in.

'I know you'll want to hear all about the whys and hows,' I said as soon as she sat down. 'The first thing I want to say is if I'd thought for a minute what I'd been up to could threaten you in any way, I'd have stopped as soon as we began our relationship. You have to believe that.'

Mary leant forward to grasp the plastic teacup on the table in front of her. The manoeuvre was so sudden I wondered if she intended to drink from it or fling it at me in disgust.

'Okay, Michael.' She calmly addressed the teacup cradled in her hands. 'What I don't understand is how you could have been involved before we got together. I mean, for one thing, it was less than two years since you sobered up and stopped living on the streets: how did the IRA possibly think you would be a reliable member?' Now, at last, she looked up.

'I'd known people from way back. You'll remember me telling you about the Anti-partition League in Glasgow that I went along to with my father and how I'd met all those old IRA men and woman.' I was gabbling, I could hear the anxiety in my voice. I paused, slowed, thinking, *For God's sake keep it together.*

I talked about considering joining the IRA after it got going again in the 1970s but didn't because I was just married to Cathie. But I had an old mate, Brendan, active during the '50s border campaign, who I kept in touch with after he'd gone back home to Tyrone – even through my drinking times.

Mary was tentatively sipping from her plastic cup, but I could tell she was listening, paying attention.

'Just a few months after I sobered up in 1984, I got a phone call from Brendan. He was impressed I'd started in recovery. Then, later in the summer, he paid me a surprise visit here in London, said he was here on some of that business and told some story about how a volunteer had dislocated his shoulder and couldn't risk getting treated locally. He asked if I'd drive the lad back to Ireland.'

I carried on, telling her about the local chief in Tyrone who was impressed by my help and how, after discussing the political situation at a time when feelings were still running high after the hunger strikes, he had asked if I was willing to help out in England.

'And what did you say?' Mary sounded calm – or did she sound cold? I couldn't tell; I rattled on.

'Well, I went up to Donegal to think about it. I realised that during the years of my drinking, all I'd done was mouth off about injustices and sing about them. After I spent a week there, I went back to Tyrone, told my contact I wanted to join up and was sworn in.'

'Simple as that.' Mary slowly shook her head and gave an ironic laugh.

I felt … how did I feel? Did I feel relieved? I still felt a sense of panic but something else too: I felt the beginnings of calm. I was telling the truth at last. Whatever happened now – and I still didn't know, I still couldn't read Mary; was she going to walk out on me? – at least now I was telling the truth. There would be no more need for self-censorship: elliptical nudges, using language so vague it had been impossible to decipher or Malachy's scenarios and his near misses, some of which were, despite my previous denials, my own experiences.

'Your role then was as a fixer – like they claimed at the trial?' Mary said, straightening up in the seat but keeping her hands in her pockets. 'Providing back-up and the like?'

'And accommodation and false IDs if needed. There wasn't really much to it, Mary.'

'That's why you thought your activities were risk free?'

'It became second nature. I thought I was invisible,' I said ruefully. And at once I knew this was the wrong thing to say, that I was blowing it, that I had blown it, because now, suddenly – now, at last – Mary looked furious.

'How can you say that, Michael?' she said, her voice – not raised but hissing. 'Quite apart from anything else, from everything else, how could you have been so stupid, so naïve? Just like your fictional Malachy had worried: no matter how careful you are, when dealing with other people, you can be shopped or your cover exposed inadvertently. As you were eventually by Garneys, and all he had to do was spy through his window from the block of flats across from the lock-up.'

Uncomfortable as I was at reliving such past experiences, I felt I owed it to Mary. 'Garneys, as we know from his statement, had noted the registration number of the Sierra car I'd bought for the unit,' I said, speaking quickly, anxious to get the explanation over with. 'But instead of reporting his suspicions, he went on holiday, and the Heathrow attacks took place while he was away. It was only after he got back five days later and saw the police's appeal for information that he contacted them.'

'But what made him suspicious?'

'It was probably the balaclavas we were wearing,' I said, straight-faced and, for a split second, I thought she was going to slap me.

'Ha ha,' she said scornfully. 'What *did* make him note the number of that Sierra?'

'I really don't know. Possibly the Neighbourhood Watch scheme: it was just taking hold in London around that time.'

'The poor man,' said Mary. 'Going to all that trouble for the measly

£500 your trial judge awarded him. What happened to the million pounds and relocation to a sunny place abroad like they offered you in Canon Row – just for the names of those involved? Surely, Garneys was more deserving. And I suppose the story about "John" giving you the lock-up key in thanks for a lift to Manchester was made-up rubbish. *You* were the John Fraser who hired the garage.'

I nodded meekly.

'And knowing that there could be evidence left behind,' said Mary, looking me in the eye, clearly warming to her inquisitorial role, 'you still went back to collect the deposit.'

'Our people were convinced no clues had been left behind in the lock-up: but there was one decision left to make – whether or not to return the key when the lease expired seven weeks later. In the aftermath of the attacks, the police had issued a plea for anyone in the Greater London area involved in the rental of lock-ups or storage space to get in touch if they had noticed anything suspicious. One plausible reason for a landlord to respond would have been if a tenant had upped and offed without returning the key and picking up the deposit. So, in the positive atmosphere after the successful operation, as the men packed up to return home, the consensus was that, unless I became aware of an untoward happening in the intervening period, I should return the key at the end of the lease; by then, the attacks would be well off the front pages, and, if not given a reason to raise any suspicion, pushed to the back of the lock-up owner's mind. Even in the worst-case scenario, I could only be held and questioned about renting a garage under a false name, and that's not even a crime.'

'Oh my God,' exclaimed Mary. 'No matter how careful you were, there was always a possibility you could have left traces of evidence.'

'Come on, Mary. It was you that showed both the soil and fibre evidence to be bogus. And the explosives traces were very probably caused by accidental contamination by police or in the forensic lab. You saw the television news pictures afterwards – dozens of police walking all over the ground around the mortar launching sites without wearing any forensic covering. Our team was meticulous by comparison.'

Mary's 'nobody's perfect' frown stopped me from elaborating further: about the heavy-duty plastic sheeting that covered the garage floor and high up the walls – removed with painstaking care; or the thorough decontamination processes undertaken; or using our own padlock, identical in appearance to theirs, before swapping them back at the end, just in case, in-between times, the estate agent decided to visit the garage using a spare key.

'I mean Mary: how could anyone account for someone like the nosy neighbour?'

'But why go back at all,' she said, her voice low, laden with exasperation, 'when there's even the slightest chance of being caught?'

'It was still incredibly unlucky, you must admit.'

'You could argue that all you want,' she said, sitting upright, looking me in the eye. 'But what about eighteen months later, when you decided to hang around London knowing you had been followed. Why didn't you recognise then that your luck had run out?'

'It was so long after Heathrow. I was sure they couldn't have been following me in relation to that, and there was nothing else I'd done to warrant such attention. I mean, who would have imagined the police would put me under surveillance for months instead of just arresting me on the spot when I returned the key?'

'Anyone else but you, probably,' Mary said without a trace of humour on her face. 'Blinkered, crazy,' she muttered. We sat in gloomy silence for the next long minutes. It was warm, but she still had her raincoat wrapped around her, as if needing extra protection from me and my pathetic explanations. I thought sadly back to those long hours she had spent using her scientific background and reasoning powers to deconstruct the prosecution's case.

I tried to recall some amusing incidents that might lighten the mood.

I mentioned finding a volunteer kneeling, frozen with fear, praying at the bedside of the Paddington flat I had rented for an operation and having to arrange for him to be taken back home to Cork. Then I described a time when I'd been asked to help with a jailbreak plan at Gartree Prison. I'd been crouching in the long grass behind a tree, taking pictures of the perimeter wall so we might identify possible blind spots for the watch-tower guards, when I heard sirens coming from the prison.

'I stuck the camera inside my jacket and lay face down. After about a minute, the noise stopped,' I said, lowering my voice to emphasise the tension. 'Very slowly, I got to my feet, but then I saw a uniformed security guard coming in my direction with a large Alsatian dog.'

Here I paused, waiting for Mary's usual 'what happened then' prompt, in response to my dramatised tales. Greeted only by silence, I struggled to maintain the dramatic flow as I reached the story's finale: 'As the man passed, I put my hands at my fly, as if zipping up my trousers and made a rueful remark about lack of nearby public toilet facilities.

'"Another bloody false alarm," the dog handler said, ignoring my mild complaint, as he headed back towards the prison. "The noise doesn't half get these beasts going."'

When I'd finished speaking, I gave Mary a smile, but she didn't return it.

'I'm not going to start finding your activities funny, Michael. What about all the casualties there could have been at Heathrow?

'The mortars weren't armed to explode; you saw that yourself in the police's statement.'

'I realise everything you did was, in your mind, Michael, for a just cause, but you were reckless and lacking in consideration – for so many people, and for *me*.'

'I just never thought my actions would have consequences for you. I know now I should have left the organisation when we settled down together. I didn't put you first and, for that, I'm very sorry.'

Perhaps I just looked worn down at this point, or maybe Mary was considering accepting my apology – but, for whatever reason, her expression softened. 'Poor Michael,' she said and then leaned forward so unexpectedly I almost jumped in my seat. What was this? She wanted to give me a hug – and in that moment, there was nothing I wanted more. And so I put my arms around her, hugging her tightly, for what seemed like ages, ignoring the people and noises all around us.

The visit nearly over, our conversation turned to the topic of a holiday proposed by her friend Becky to Tenerife. 'Of course, you should go,' I whispered hoarsely. 'You need the break.'

'You wouldn't worry if we couldn't communicate for a week?'

'No, of course not,' I said gamely.

'You're a kind man, Michael,' she said but looked at me pityingly, remotely, like a stranger would when passing a wretched beggar lying on a park bench. 'Get a hold of yourself,' she added. 'Of course, I'm not going to bloody Tenerife. What, to drink piña coladas?'

The visit had ended positively, but I knew I had to take a decision. However much I relied on Mary to keep me going in this awful place, for her sake I had to let her go. She had to move on and forge a new life. I took out my jotter and pen. I would write and ask her to agree that we stop all communication between us right away so we might adapt more easily to our new situation: better that at least one of us could be free.

Three hours passed, but the pain of my proposed plan to split hadn't eased. My attempt at a letter had been a waste of time: I hadn't got beyond 'Dear Mary'. I cursed my foolishness. Of course, I couldn't do without her, couldn't let her go. Listening to the music coming from all around the wing – the 'Saturday night concert' before lights out – I turned my head and burrowed my face into the pillow, my misery only fading as sleep finally came.

Sunday, 1 March, 9 a.m. – Mary

I think about yesterday's visit. Despite his deception, he's still the same Michael who I was always keen to get back home to after work or a night out.

He acknowledged he should have withdrawn from any IRA involvement when entering into a serious relationship with me. Was it reasonable that he thought there could be nothing to implicate him and that the worst that could happen was that he'd get arrested with a tap on the shoulder and have to spend a few days in a police cell held under the PTA? It's just like him to be oblivious to the potential dire consequences of his actions. And the fact of the matter is – and this is sort of the point – his untroubled positivity had been a big part of what attracted me to him.

I could also see how, once the legal process started, with my enthusiastic promotion of his innocence and organising his bail, it would have been increasingly difficult for him to tell me the truth.

But whether or not I decide to forgive him, I have to consider the practicalities of maintaining a relationship with a man facing twenty years in jail. And what about the potential consequences to the public of his actions? There were no casualties, but does that make it easier to forgive his role?

There are so many painful thoughts, thoughts I've been pushing to the back of my mind. I consider myself an ethical person; caring for humanity is at the heart of who I think I am. So many ethical reflections for my whole life – and yet here I am considering a future with someone convicted of violence-related offences, a deceiver, a liar. What does this say about me?

I can't think about this now. Instead, I think about the phantom piña coladas on my phantom beach holiday and I manage a smile. I hope Becky can find someone else to go – I suspect she only suggested the idea to help me out anyway.

Just as I'm about to call her, the phone rings. It's Keith. I feign positivity as I recount Michael's good spirits at the visit and side-step questions about the appeal. Keith is in London next Wednesday, at The

Royal Society, giving a review paper on outdoor sound propagation. I arrange to go along.

Wednesday, 4 March, 7 p.m. – Mary

As I approach the venue, near The Mall, I'm not concerned that anyone at the lecture will be aware of my relationship 'problems'. The only national paper that made a big deal of my involvement was the *Daily Mail*, which had a giant photo of me on page 10 taken with a telephoto lens on the day of the verdict. In the anonymous London domain, your fifteen minutes of fame lasts about fifteen seconds.

The lecture room on the third floor seats about thirty. I'm late and make my way towards the back of the room. Keith has already started to speak. After the applause and questions and answers, I stand alone near the exit and wait while he chats with several people gathered around him, fellow academics probably. On previous occasions he would have introduced me.

After about a minute Keith comes across to me. Uncharacteristically formal, he thanks me for attending and suggests we meet for a coffee at a café he knows just off Trafalgar Square, saying he'll be along shortly.

After a short wait, I find a table for two. When Keith arrives, I stand and wave, smiling effusively, affecting a relaxed attitude: inwardly nothing can hide my sense of shame.

As soon as he sits down, I tell him of Michael's confession. Keith is never very expressive, but his face has taken on a look of frozen disappointment. He'd visited Michael in prison, had pledged all his equity and savings for the bail, even Jean's little Skoda. My nephew, David, had told all his student friends and had them collectively exercised about Michael's innocence.

I repeat over and over again that I didn't know. Keith says nothing: I can't tell if he believes me. He has never been someone to verbalise his feelings, and we part now with an unspoken remoteness. I just have to hope we mend this rift with time.

Saturday, 7 March, noon – Mary

On the journey to Aldridge, I can predict my parents' attitude. My mother, who used to say no country had gained independence without an armed struggle, has lately become far more reticent on the subject. Dad, I know, will stick to his position, communicated even before the outcome of the trial, that the best option is to end the relationship.

I've spent over eleven years living with Michael, years of closeness, discussing our mainly shared politics, human insights, jokes, mock competitiveness through Scrabble games and the *Countdown* TV game show, all interspersed with moments of intimacy and times talking into the night. Even since his incarceration, we have maintained that connection through visits and letters. We shared the moment of triumph when he got bail and the moment of defeat when he was found guilty. There's too much of Michael that's now a part of me and vice versa. I may need to take the decision in the future to leave him, to protect my own well-being, but I just can't do it right now.

I arrive at the house, and Mum greets me with a warm hug. I explain that I have to tell her something.

'No need, love,' she says, 'Keith told us.'

She hands me a copy of the *Walsall Observer* from Friday 27 February:

> **Ex-lecturer's lover was IRA sleeper**
> **20 years for bomb plot boyfriend**
>
> A former university lecturer from Walsall watched as her boyfriend was jailed for 20 years for his involvement in an IRA plot to mortar bomb Heathrow Airport. Dr Mary Attenborough blew a kiss to her lover as IRA sleeper Michael Gallagher was led from the dock at Woolwich Crown Court on Tuesday. Earlier the court had heard how detectives had secretly recorded hundreds of conversations involving Gallagher at Dr Attenborough's London flat, where he

> lived at the time of the failed bomb attempt in 1994. The court heard there was no evidence Dr Attenborough was aware of her boyfriend's terrorist connections. The daughter of a retired Walsall local government officer, Dr Attenborough set up the National Union of School Students at the age of 18 and joined the Young Communist League as a schoolgirl. She went on to study mathematical physics at Imperial College London, and after getting a doctorate, lectured in maths at South Bank University, London. Throughout the trial she backed Gallagher's defence that his interest in the IRA was prompted only by a novel based on the Provisionals which he claimed to be researching. Dr Attenborough left the court in tears after he was convicted of conspiring to cause explosions, still insisting she believed in his innocence.

I'm happy the article is sort of sympathetic towards me.

'Has there been any other reaction?' I ask my mother.

'I phoned our John, but he wasn't in,' she says. 'I spoke to Barbara and told her everything. She thought it was heroic of Michael to keep it from you until afterwards.'

'Well done, Barbara. I might not agree, but it's good somebody's positive.'

'And Pat Biggs too,' says my mother. 'On hearing the news, she called round and left a book for you.' Mum turns round to the shelf in the corner of the room, picks out a worn, slim volume, *The Ulster Reciter*, and hands it to me. 'Pat said that one of the poems – "The Man from God Knows Where" – about Thomas Russell, a member of the United Irishmen who helped organise the rebellion in 1798, was written by her mother, Florence Mary Wilson.'

I open the book donated by Mum's friend and read on the flyleaf: 'To Michael and Mary, with Best Wishes from Pat Biggs'.

I'm pleasantly surprised. I've known Pat for many years and she has never mentioned her Irish poet mother. How strange to discover this connection in an obscure English town. The thought of Pat's gesture and Barbara's reaction cheers me enough to face the prospect of listening to Dad's repeated salutary advice.

Tuesday, 10 March, 8 p.m. – Mary

'I'm not staying long – leaving for Tenerife in the morning,' says Becky as she arrives at my flat and hands over a bottle of wine. 'I thought a quick tipple might just cheer you up.'

I'm glad she seems up-beat despite my turning down her beach holiday offer. As I wrestle with the corkscrew, I decide to wait until she's on at least her second glass before I tell her of Michael's guilt.

Returning to the sitting room, I find my friend, her coat and shoes off, seated sideways on the couch, her feet tucked under her. I leave the wine glasses on the coffee table, pour us each a drink and retreat to a chair at the table.

'Poor Michael,' she says. 'How is he coping after that awful verdict?'

'Not too badly, considering,' I say, and when I've searched my mind unsuccessfully for something banal to add, I just blurt out, 'But there is something I have to tell you.'

'Go on, Mary.'

'Michael says he really did help the IRA with the Heathrow attacks.'

Becky stares at me for a moment of echoing silence and then at last, 'What the fuck!' She untucks her feet and sits up straight. 'You're kidding. So why are you still visiting him after he put you through all that?'

'He's apologised – anyone can make a mistake,' I reply, with a feigned nonchalance. I swallow a mouthful of my drink.

'A mistake!' Becky clatters her glass on the coffee table. 'For fuck's sake. It was a betrayal – he was lying to you for years. It's a bit more than a bloody mistake, Mary.' She looks like she can hardly believe her ears and, well, no wonder. But I forge on.

'To be a betrayal it would need to have entered his head that I could be harmed. Michael believed he could keep his IRA activities isolated from our day-to-day relationship. Okay, a *big* mistake but not betrayal.'

'God almighty, Mary, I should have you writing our company's PR scripts.'

'I've thought about this a lot, Becky,' I say and move across to sit at the other end of the couch. *Keep going*, I think; it helps that I do actually believe what I'm about to say. 'Michael can be accused of foolishness and denial, which is not the same as betrayal. He should have reconsidered his activities when he entered into a serious relationship with me. And it wasn't just his wife and children he felt guilty about after so many years just getting pissed. He'd always regretted not helping out when it all kicked off in the North. In fact, he hadn't long stopped drinking when he joined the IRA.'

There, I've said my bit.

'So, he put down his bottle and picked up a gun.' Becky gives an ironic laugh then becomes more serious. 'Couldn't he have made his political case without going around bombing people?'

'Michael didn't hurt anyone. The Heathrow attacks were timed to highlight the renewal of the Prevention of Terrorism Act in Parliament and the mortars weren't intended to explode. Michael has always believed there is a political justification for an "armed struggle" – a mistaken belief, in my opinion, but one he genuinely holds. There's an element of ethics, here, Becky.'

'Ethics?'

'Yes, ethics, self-sacrifice and dedication even. You don't have to share them, but ethics just the same.'

'At one time,' Becky says, and I hear the note of forced cool and calm in her voice, 'there was a justified excuse to take up arms: but that all ended with the 1921 Treaty, voted for by a majority in the new Irish Parliament.'

I feel taken aback and also sort of annoyed. Becky's ready grasp of Irish history isn't what I need just at the moment. I was relying on philosophical talk of ethics to shut things down. Now I'm forced to depend on my own, sometimes unreliable, historical knowledge. So, I talk about the 1921 Anglo-Irish agreement being controversial, the outbreak of civil war and nationalists in the North being left as second-class citizens, suffering years of discrimination and attacks against their communities: out of sight, out of mind from those in the South. 'So, Becky, many people, not just Michael and not just the IRA, continued to feel violence was necessary. From a republican standpoint, the armed struggle is a *moral* struggle, needed to save a stranded minority and to reunite the country.'

I feel like the two of us are jousting with bits of stick and see that Becky is far from convinced.

'Quoting his political justifications, Mary, doesn't take away from the fact that he is *your partner*,' and now Becky sits forward, 'and this is my point: its utterly unforgivable for him to carry on with his lies throughout your relationship and right to the very end of the trial, without so much as a hint. Surely you can see that?'

I pause and think back to conversations, so many discussions, over dinner or late at night in bed. Michael did give some vague indications he was in the know with the IRA, but I never took him seriously. How could I? But now I say, 'He did hint, Becky, but he was busy with his writing. I just thought fact and fiction were getting blurred.'

'Well, you never mentioned anything like that to me.'

That's true, I think as I look at Becky's face, annoyed and yet still kind. She deserves a decent explanation after putting her house on the line for Michael – no, not really for Michael, for me – she trusted *me*.

'I was probably embarrassed. No one wants to admit their partner might have lost it slightly. You'll remember Benny and Budgie, the two guys from Glasgow we met at that function, mouthing off as if they were actually in the IRA. Had I seriously thought that Michael was involved, I'd have wondered at the absurdity of it all. I mean, why would an organisation reputed to be so disciplined even consider an alcoholic not long in recovery as being a reliable candidate for membership?'

'But why did he claim to be innocent after he was arrested?' asks Becky.

'He was surrounded by eavesdropping prison staff and remote listening devices and his letters were censored.'

'How about when he got bail?'

She's right: he could have told me then – some time when we were outside, as we were always aware of possible listening devices – but would I even have believed him? Even if I hadn't, I'd have felt duty bound to let the bail sureties know. I look across at Becky – I owe her so much.

'You would have withdrawn your support, which would have been tantamount to him admitting his guilt and leaving him without a defence. Barbara, my brother John's partner, actually thought Michael was heroic in not telling me, protecting me from difficulties I could have faced had I found out the truth earlier. The point is, Becky, he was so deeply inside the rabbit hole by then, he couldn't get out. I hate that this happened, I really do hate it, but I can see how he ended up in this situation, lying and lying.'

Becky looks at me. 'Okay, I do too, actually, I get that bit.' She holds the bottle up to me, but I shake my head. She empties the remaining wine into her glass. 'I hope you at least gave him a good tongue-lashing when you found out?'

'Sorry, I couldn't. The revelation was so shocking. I just thought "Poor Michael" and cried because I thought I had to leave him and how lonely he would be without my support. Even now, I miss him so much and, more than anything else, I look forward to seeing him, even if it is in the dingy prison visiting room.'

'You could have been killed as a result of his actions and all you can think is "poor Michael"?' She flares up again. 'Get a grip here, Mary, for God's sake.'

'But consider the circumstances. MI5 had been following Michael for months. They knew he didn't have any guns. They had broken into our flat to place the bugging devices, so they knew there were no armaments there and also that I was completely innocent. The armed police raid was for publicity only. They could have just tapped him on the shoulder and arrested him, but that wouldn't have looked impressive on the news, so I blame the British State for nearly killing me.'

'So, you're letting Michael off the hook?'

'Not at all; I blame the State, but I also blame Michael: since when did the IRA trust the British to behave responsibly?'

Becky sighs and straightens up on the couch. She reaches out to me, touching my hand. 'I know you say it was a mistake, but can you forgive him? Anyway, he's in jail, so you need to move on. Can you honestly see yourself five years from now travelling possibly hundreds of miles to whichever prison he ends up in?'

'Well, I think I do forgive him but, on the other hand, because it was a mistake of such magnitude, I don't feel obliged to stand by him. He's the architect of his own demise. But I'm not ready to leave him yet.'

I'm conscious as I speak that this is the important bit, this is the crucial bit, this is the bit I've been leading up to all this time. 'It would be like voluntarily cutting off my arm to save the rest of my body. I love him, Becky. *I love him*. He's funny and interesting. We've spent so much time together, and I stand by my belief that he's the kindest man I've ever met, even if occasionally blinkered as to the consequences of his actions. And you've always liked him too.'

Becky sits back and the expression on her face has softened. 'Of course I do, or did. Right at this minute though, I could wring his neck for putting you through all this.' She stops for a moment, taking a breath. I know what she's going to say before she says it. 'But just consider this: it might be time to move on. It might be, Mary. And, maybe, the sooner you do, the sooner you'll get over him.'

'You're probably right,' I say, suddenly very matter-of-fact. 'I've given him the impression I will remain committed to him going forward, so I'm lying about that certainty, but it's probably the kindest approach in the immediate circumstances.'

I don't say what's really in my head: I could never, ever imagine being able to reach that moment of deciding to leave him. I've realised this just in the last few moments and my head is spinning. Suddenly I can't wait for Becky to leave.

We head downstairs to the waiting taxi. At the front door, as we break off from our tight hug, a serious expression crosses Becky's face. 'If you're going to come through this you'll have to concentrate less on poor Michael and give more thought to poor you.'

As I climb back to the flat, my head down, I see on the vinyl the eighteen-month-old scuff marks and welts made by the boots of the armed police – still there, ingrained.

Wednesday, 18 March, 7.30 a.m. – Michael

My cell door opened.

'Pack your gear, Michael,' said Officer Priddy, 'you're on the move.'

'Where to?'

'You know better than to ask.' He smiled apologetically. 'You'll find out when you get there.'

There weren't many positives to life in Belmarsh, but Priddy's good-humoured manner was one of them. I could complain about anything and everything, including the behaviour of his colleagues. Sometimes he'd say, 'Rise above it, Michael. They don't know any better, but you should.' I'd miss him.

I had dreaded the inevitable move to a dispersal prison. I prayed it would not be Frankland in Durham or Full Sutton in Yorkshire. How long would Mary put up with a 400–500-mile round trip up north every week or even every month?

As we journeyed away from Belmarsh, by peering through the frosted glass in the prison van's locked cubicle, I could make out some road signs and directions. We went through the Blackwall Tunnel and headed west through Central London. At every roundabout I prayed we'd travel straight on, that there would be no right turn in a northerly direction. To my great relief, when we reached the roundabout at Shepherd's Bush and took the access road to the M40, I knew we were bound for Long Lartin.

Wednesday, 18 March, 8 a.m. – Mary

I wake up to the sound of ringing on my phone.

'Good morning. Is that Mary?'

'Yes.'

'I have a message for you.'

'Go on.'

'Whisper it darling: your Michael is being ghosted this morning to Long Lartin.'

'Really? You know this for certain?'

'Gospel. Got the word from a pal inside; he gave me your number.'

'It's very kind of you to let me know … er … can I ask who's calling?'

'Fraser's the name,' he said.

'Thanks again: have you a first name?'

'Frankie,' he said. 'Mad Frankie, if you must.'

'Thanks, Frankie.'

'No trouble.'

Twenty-three

Long Lartin, Long Wait

Wednesday, 18 March, 5 p.m. – Michael

I'd been locked up all afternoon without my property bag, not just clothes but phone cards, notepaper and pen, all separated from me during the four-hour-long journey from Belmarsh. Will Mary even know I've been moved? One of my acquaintances had promised to get word out to his pal Frankie Fraser and ask him to phone her and tell her I was being transferred to Long Lartin, but I'd no way of knowing if this had happened. And even if the phone call did take place, would she trust the word of an infamous gangster?

At evening mealtime, I approached one of the screws involved in the transfer.

'Do you know what's happened to my property bag?' I asked.

'You'll get it in good time, Gallagher; the contents have to be processed by our security staff,' he replied, hands in pockets, not bothering to look me in the eye.

'The contents were processed through security on the way out of Belmarsh, what the fuck do you think could have happened to them in the meantime?' I said, my voice raised only slightly but probably enough to have been heard by a number of prisoners standing at the nearby hotplate. Determined to behave myself, as I'd promised Mary, I walked off and headed back to my cell.

I was in there barely a minute when the door swung open and a prisoner came through, his small stature almost hidden by the cardboard box he carried.

'Hi mate, I heard you nearly having a ruck with the screw there,' he said. 'Here's something to keep you going: there's a bit of fruit, coffee, some cheese, sweets and a bottle of juice.'

He placed the box on the bed and turned towards me. 'Ronnie O'Sullivan from London,' he said and we shook hands.

'Thanks Ronnie. Mick Gallagher from Glasgow. Pleased to meet you.' Before I could say more, another prisoner came into the cell. A head taller than Ronnie, he introduced himself as Ian McDonald from Glasgow.

'Here's a phone card for you Mick,' he said and handed it to me.

The bang-up bell sounded then, loud and shrill. The two men turned to go before I could properly express my gratitude, particularly for the precious phone card. Just outside the door, they both stopped and turned around.

'Let me know, Mick,' said Ian, 'if you get any grief from any of this lot: cons or screws.'

I smiled. 'So, you can come and help them out,' I said, pointing to the Rangers FC crest on his replica strip.

We all laughed.

Monday, 23 March, 4 p.m. – Michael

While relaxing with a book, my concentration kept being interrupted by the heavier-than-usual footfall in our spur's corridor. At the sound of a voice saying, 'Thanks Reggie', my curiosity got the better of me. I went to the door and put my eye to the spy hole. Reggie Kray, deeply tanned and wearing a Hawaiian shirt, stood outside the cell door opposite mine, shaking hands with Bruce Caufield, a young prisoner on our wing.

Fuck! I'd forgotten. Charlie had told me his brother had been allowed a week-long short-stay family visit here in Long Lartin. But did he have to be my nearest neighbour?

Reggie closed his door and, as Bruce walked away, wearing a broad smile and waving aloft a sketch paper caricature of himself, someone from inside a nearby cell shouted, 'How many blow jobs did that cost you, Bruce?'

I winced for the lad, his triumphant moment so crassly undermined.

With only ten minutes before lock-up, I went to the toilet block. When I got back, Reggie was standing outside his cell door seeing off another prisoner he had sketched. He gave me a neighbourly nod, which I ignored.

Tuesday, 31 March, 5 p.m. – Michael

Charlie Kray and I were seated in armchairs alongside one another, the only two prisoners remaining in the TV lounge. Charlie, an ex-boxer, had been speaking fondly of my old friend Derry Treanor and reminiscing about how he had watched the fight against Howard Winstone for the British featherweight title in 1962, which he thought Derry had been unlucky to lose.

Charlie then turned and leaned slightly towards me, propping his elbows on the chair's armrest. He had a querying look in his eyes as they locked onto mine.

'Do you mind if I ask you something personal?'

I straightened up in my seat. 'Fire away, Charlie,' I said, suspecting my one-man boycott of his brother had been noted.

'I just wondered. You're a sociable fella, Mick, and already in tight with quite a few of us lads here.'

'Yea, Charlie. You're an easy-going crew.'

'But our Reg says when he was here on his visit last week you weren't for having it with him for some reason.'

'Sorry, Charlie, no offence meant but, when he was up on his last appeal, Reg's brief slagged off the IRA, said they were mass murderers and committed crimes far worse than his client.'

Charlie sighed. 'Sorry, Mick, but when you've been doing bird for as long as him, you'll say a lot of things to get out.'

'Yea, Charlie, I understand.'

And I did. The Kray twins had already spent almost thirty years in prison for the murders of two members of rival gangs and, despite the draconian sentences regularly meted out to IRA members, none had languished as long.

'Anyhow, Mick,' he said, getting up to go, 'we ain't going to fall out over it.'

'Yea, Charlie, no problem.'

A problem with the Krays was the last thing I needed.

Saturday, 4 April, 9.30 a.m. – Michael

Mary's first two visits to Long Lartin had been just okay. We had sat on opposite sides of the low table, our hands clasped together, oblivious to the twenty or so other prisoners and their guests in the room. Missing, however, was Mary's engaging enthusiasm, always present before my admission of guilt. I asked about her journey. 'Long, as usual', she said and went on: 'I had Moya St Leger on the phone saying the Connolly Association people, including herself, are very downbeat about your repatriation prospects; apparently there are deliberate hold-ups within the Home Office.'

'Not according to news from Steve.'

'Steve who?' asked Mary.

'He's the young Londoner I met when I first went into the SSU,' I said, keeping my voice low. 'He's now in Whitemoor but keeps in regular touch with his mates in Portlaoise: rumour has it they may get moved soon to an open prison.'

'Planning for the future based on a rumour is the last thing we need.'

'It would be amazing,' I said, undeterred. 'For republican prisoners only and, according to Steve – he has a way with words – set in some sunny upland in the west of Ireland: cells with bathrooms, conjugal visits and Chinese takeaways; the lot.'

'Is this Steve a pipe smoker, by any chance?' she asked, withdrawing her hands from mine and sitting upright in the seat.

I ignored her sarcasm. Steve had no reason to lie, but it did seem too good to be true.

'Sinn Féin has been included in all-party talks next week in Belfast: you never know what concessions they might give us,' I said. Mary didn't answer. Recognising I was fighting a losing battle in my attempts to raise her spirits, I moved on.

'How's your new job?'

'Everyone seems nice enough, but I've only been there a few days.'

'What about your Easter break? Have you any plans?'

'It's not for another week,' she answered. 'I never know what I'm doing from one day to the next.'

It came time to go then. We stood amongst the prisoners and guests, all milling around saying their last goodbyes before going their separate ways. I felt the hand of a prisoner walking past briefly squeeze my shoulder.

I called after him. 'All right, Charlie.'

'Who was that?' whispered Mary.

'Charlie Kray,' I replied.

Mary smiled and shook her head. 'Do all your friends have to be notorious gangsters?' she whispered in my ear.

'Well, not all are gangsters but none are paragons either,' I tell her. 'Blame the environment, Mary. If this was a monastery, all my mates would be monks.'

She laughed loudly. I caught a glimpse then of Mary's old self, the sparkle back in her eyes. I wished I could keep it there for a little longer.

Good Friday, 10 April, 9 a.m. – Mary

Who can that be at this time on a bank holiday morning? I wonder, as I reach for the phone.

Michael's sister Margaret's excited voice calls out from the other end of the line. 'Did you hear the news, Mary? Michael's getting out.'

I sit up. Am I dreaming?

'The peace agreement, the talks in Belfast,' says Margaret, 'It's really happening! And all the political prisoners are to be released!'

'What? When? Is that official?'

'Apparently so. I have to phone over home and let my mother know. She'll just be getting up,' says Margaret, and the line goes dead.

I'm having difficulty processing her news about the talks. Nobody really thought they would end successfully: the Unionists weren't going to sign up to anything before the IRA disarmed. My hand is shaking so much I can hardly pick up the TV remote control from the bed cover. A picture appears on the screen showing Tony Blair, John Hume and David Trimble lined up at Stormont, all smiling, and when I see Gerry Adams there with them, I realise Margaret is right.

I'm getting Michael back.

Friday, 17 April, 1 p.m. – Mary

I'm feeling upbeat. Not only will I see Michael for the first time since the Good Friday Agreement was signed, but also Keith has been in touch suggesting we take part in The Really Big Chorus's performance of Mozart's *Requiem* in the Albert Hall at the end of May – so I think Michael's big lie has been forgotten by him, if not forgiven.

Not long after I book in at reception in Long Lartin prison and sit down to wait, a woman takes the seat facing me, and we exchange friendly nods. Soon, Dawn and I are chatting like old friends, and we arrange to meet up after the visit.

Michael is pleased and relieved about the Irish peace agreement and delighted at my improved mood. I tell him about making a new friend. He knows her husband, Mark. 'A lifer,' he says, 'a pleasant big guy.'

The visit over, Dawn drives us to the 'Thatched Tavern' in Honeybourne.

As we chat, she tells me she was a prison librarian when she met and fell for inmate Mark – believing him when he said he was wrongly convicted of bank robbery. After they were found in a compromising position and she was sacked, they married while Mark was still in prison. However, after his release, her husband relapsed into a cocaine habit and, during a 'bad trip', collapsed and later woke to discover the stabbed dead body of his dealer next to him. Dawn stuck by him, despite the life sentence. As she tells me her story, I reflect on the boundless capacity for irrationality in the face of love. I also realise that no matter how bad my position has been, other people have faced much, much worse.

Thursday, 17 December, 11 a.m. – Michael

A letter from my brother Johnny stood out amongst those I'd received today due to its thicker-than-usual size. Opening it, I saw he had included copies of letters he'd sent to Irish politicians asking them to contact British authorities for assurances that the remaining Irish prisoners would be treated humanely and transferred to Ireland as soon as possible. Johnny wrote of his impression that getting a few prisoners moved from England was very low on the list of the implementation priorities of the Good Friday Agreement.

I wasn't able to tell Johnny – not wanting the family to worry more than normal – of the additional problems I was now facing in the prison. Most IRA prisoners had been repatriated, and the few remaining, like me, had been left in isolation, scattered around the country, in ones and twos. Prisoners with far-right leanings, British National Party members and supporters who had kept quiet in previous years mainly because of IRA prisoners' opposition to their politics, became increasingly vociferous in airing their propaganda around the recreation area. Lately, I'd hear sideways remarks when going around the spur like, 'Why are you being repatriated to Ireland, Jock?' – not one prisoner had called me Jock before this – and comments like 'Why are you lot getting out when we ain't?', which I managed to ignore. No matter how much supportive prisoners like big Ian and little Ronnie looked out for me, it would only take one nutcase when my back was turned to do serious, if not fatal, damage.

Thursday, 17 December, 1 p.m. – Michael

A senior officer stood outside my cell, with several screws hovering behind him. He handed me a letter: 'You better have a read at that,' he said. 'You've five minutes to pack your gear.'

The men looked on impatiently as I ripped open the envelope and began to read. From the Home Office, it informed me my application for repatriation had been granted with immediate effect. I double-checked every word, even making sure it had the right name. Then I began stuffing everything into my prison-issue plastic sack. When I'd finished and left the cell, instead of going towards the screws, I turned and walked to the far end of the corridor and then turned around. As I walked back quickly, I stopped briefly at each locked door to call out my goodbye. From inside, most of the prisoners called out their good wishes and banged on doors. Their voices and the echoing din followed me and the screws all the way to the wing's outer exit gate. As I stepped through, a sharp pang of sadness hit me – most of these men were facing many more years behind bars.

I spent my final night in England at Full Sutton Prison in South Yorkshire. There, I joined five other IRA prisoners who had been brought together from jails around the country. At 7 a.m. we were transported by bus to Humberside Airport in Lincolnshire. Bypassing the terminal building, we were taken directly to a small twin-engine aircraft parked on the runway. Men wearing the dark-blue uniforms of the Irish prison service stood lined up alongside the steps leading to the plane's open door. One by one, the English officers removed our handcuffs and waited while their Irish counterparts secured us with new ones.

'All yours,' said the spokesman for the English and, without another word, turned and led his men back to the bus. As soon as it was out of sight, the Irish warders unlocked our handcuffs and we boarded the plane for home.

Twenty-four

Over and Out

Friday, 18 December, 3 p.m. – Michael

As the bus pulled up to Portlaoise Prison – a relic from before the Victorian era – where soldiers with rifles patrolled the rooftop above, I exchanged a weary grin with Steve, who was seated across from me; the young Londoner had come over on the same plane.

The cold, grey outer walls were soon forgotten, however, in the warmth of the welcome we received on reaching the wing. We climbed the iron stairs to the third floor, the Threes, where around twenty IRA prisoners greeted us with much handshaking and backslapping.

Afterwards, when we'd broken into smaller groups, Joe O'Connell and Hughie Doherty, who I'd never met before, came over to introduce themselves. During my anxious wait for the transfer to Ireland, Joe, from County Clare, had written regularly to me at Long Lartin. His letters, urging patience and offering coping advice in his quiet, philosophical way, had greatly helped to lift my morale.

Hughie shared the same background as me, and I'd often seen members of the Doherty family amongst the many Donegal exiles sailing on the overnight Derry boat during the annual exodus of many of the Glasgow Irish.

Hughie and Joe had spent twenty-three years incarcerated in English prisons before being repatriated to Portlaoise last year. Joe had actually served two years in Ireland as a political prisoner before being locked up in England.

I already owed them a debt. Throughout their sentences they had gained great respect from other prisoners for their readiness to confront and face down threats, and for being prepared always to take part in prison protests against conditions. These two, along with many other Irishmen and the few brave Irishwomen who had served time in England down through the years, had given IRA-connected prisoners like me coming afterwards a certain level of safety in a toxic environment where violence and bullying were commonplace.

I was allocated a place halfway along the top landing, the Fours, next door to Steve. A typical cell, concrete floor and springy metal bed, nothing unusual about it, I thought. Just after I had emptied my property bag, I looked around for a toilet bowl, but there wasn't one. Right away, I came out of the cell and walked along the landing, stopping at Steve's half-opened door.

'I've no toilet.'

'We have to slop out,' said Steve, pointing to a chamber pot under his sink. 'I'm afraid it's old school here.'

'So much for the sunny upland in the west you promised in that last letter.'

Steve laughed. 'Give it time, Mick.'

The transfer to Portlaoise was like having to adapt to a new time zone: the night lock-up at Long Lartin was half past five; here it was nine o'clock. At the end of that first day, on the OC-shouted order 'Paráid', we stood outside our cells and formed lines on either side of the two top landings. We then obeyed the 'Paráid! Aire!' command, standing rigidly to attention until, a short time later, the 'Paráid scaipigí' fall-out was called, ending a simple ceremony that reminded me why I was here.

Saturday, 19 December, 1 p.m. – Mary

Michael's brother Eddie has been here an hour, and I'm still not ready. His removals van is parked at a meter and his time is running out. He is not happy. I'm struggling to organise the remainder of my belongings into boxes and pack a suitcase with enough clothes to see me through a couple of weeks. I don't have time to call in to say goodbye to Roy. I leave a message under his door.

Outside, I look back at the street entrance and think of my twenty years in Earl's Court – so many memories – friendships, neighbours, political meetings, parties, my life with Michael, to say nothing of police raids, arguments, disruption. Now, I'm heading for a new life in a new country. It will be tough at first in Dublin, where I intend to find work whilst Michael is in Portlaoise prison, but at least we're getting nearer to Donegal!

Saturday, 19 December, 8 p.m. – Mary

I've been recommended a B&B in Portlaoise, where another IRA prison inmate's partner sometimes stays. On arrival, I park the hired car in the driveway. The landlady offers tea and homemade scones – I'm the only guest for the night – and we sit by the turf fire and chat about the weather, England, Ireland and her life. She knows the reason I'm in Portlaoise – no need to hide the facts from her – but I can't tell if she disapproves; she keeps her opinion close to her chest and asks no questions about Michael.

Monday, 21 December, 10 a.m. – Mary

Paddy, large and jovial, makes small talk as he leads me along the pathway between portacabins forming part of Portlaoise prison. I'd never met such a friendly prison officer: a different world from Long Lartin and Belmarsh. Michael is waiting and we have an entire room to ourselves, while Paddy waits in the next room. We can hug for as long as we like, with no interference throughout the two-hour visit. He tells me he'll be temporarily released for Christmas, which we can spend in Donegal.

Monday, 1 February 1999, 8 a.m. – Mary

I travel by Dart railway and bus from my one-bedroom flat in Glenageary, Dublin, to Sandyford Industrial Estate. My new job is for a telecommunications company, Eicon Technology, and I'm to work on the user interface software, which has the potential to be a little more interesting than writing software for financial transactions. I arrive, to be greeted by my manager, who looks a decade younger than me, and meet the rest of the team – all in their twenties, except for one other contractor. I'm feeling old and English.

Friday, 9 April, 8.30 a.m. – Michael

As my cell door was unlocked, I heard a shout.

'Something here for you, Mick.'

The warder, Paddy Prendergast, gestured to something outside my cell as he told me, 'Hughie got away earlier.'

'For good?'

Paddy chuckled. 'Less of you now to watch,' he said.

Coming out of my cell, I found, propped up against the landing wall, a framed landscape signed Aodh. This gift, the last of Hughie Doherty's many accomplished works created during his twenty-three years of incarceration, touched me greatly.

Monday, 26 April, 9 a.m. – Michael

Sorting through my mail, just delivered was an envelope marked 'Listowel Writers' Week'. At my writing class, the teacher, Angela, thought my story 'Chill-Out' was good enough to submit to the 'Writing in Prison' short-story competition, but I hadn't given it much further thought, diverted by maintaining my fitness regime and joining in with the others playing snooker and football in the yard.

I was just about to open the letter, when Officer Paddy arrived at the cell door. 'Hey Mick, the governor says to let you know you won first prize in that writing competition. He's going to let you out for the week of the festival and congratulate you in the local paper.'

Friday, 17 December, 11 a.m. – Mary

At morning coffee break, I sit with Neil, Louise, Noreen and Ronan, who are discussing their transport arrangements for this evening's work Christmas party, and I mention I'll be driving there with Michael. My four colleagues know Michael, having socialised with him at two previous after-work get togethers he attended when ostensibly holidaying from refurbishment of our Donegal cottage but actually out of prison on temporary leave.

My mobile rings and I move away from the table to a quiet corner of the room to answer it.

'I can't make your party,' Michael says. 'There's been a change of plans here: they aren't giving me leave this weekend after all.'

'Nothing serious I hope?'

'Possible transfer to Roscommon. Nothing's confirmed.'

'Oh, that's a shame. I'll have to give your apologies.'

'Just say there's a hitch with the renovations that I've had to deal with urgently.'

'Oh well. I'll see you tomorrow morning for a visit.'

'If you don't have too much of a hangover to make the journey,' Michael laughed.

'Not much chance of that now: as my sober driver is indisposed tonight, I'm my own nominated driver.'

Friday, 17 December, 6 p.m. – Mary

Back in my flat, while putting the finishing touches to my makeup, I switch on the TV to see the RTÉ *Six One* news. When I hear the words 'Provisional IRA prisoners', I hastily turn to the screen and see Michael, dressed in joggers and a hoodie, beard dishevelled, carrying a large sack, handcuffed to the tallest, most smartly dressed prison guard I've ever seen. The news item continues: 'Earlier today, the last remaining Provisional IRA prisoners eligible for early release under the Good Friday Agreement were transferred from the high-security Portlaoise Prison to the lower-risk institution at Castlerea, County Roscommon.'

I just have to hope no one from work has watched the *Six One* news. If my lack of honesty gets back to the management, it might be a blot on the good reference I'll need when my contract finishes next month. At least by the time the nine o'clock news is on, everyone will be busy at the party.

As I drive along the M50, heading for the Citywest party venue, I see, ahead of me, work colleagues in a packed car driven by Ronan. Noreen's carefree wave from the back seat partially reassures me, but I still worry that, if anyone knows, word would travel like wildfire around the company, unless I get to the party venue before them and, hopefully, persuade them not to say anything. I tail them for a while, waiting for an opportunity to overtake, until I eventually do.

Arriving just behind me at the function Ronan approaches.

'What the hell were you up to, Mary?' he says, looking at me sternly.

'I couldn't tell you anything earlier ...' I start to say, when he interrupts: 'That overtaking manoeuvre was definitely out of order – you pulled back in too quickly. I nearly had a heart attack.'

'I'm sorry,' I say, greatly relieved. It looks like no one knows, and I relax, focusing now on enjoying my evening.

Tuesday, 21 December, 1 p.m. – Michael

Relieved that Castlerea Prison had brought forward my Christmas temporary release, I paced along a corridor in Letterkenny hospital. As I entered my father's room, his eyes opened and he greeted me with a faint smile.

In an advanced stage of emphysema and pausing often to take deep breaths, my dad told me he was proud of me: I had quit drinking and stayed sober. He also said he had prayed for me every day, especially during my time in London when he knew I was sleeping rough. Of my later hardship, he told me: 'You had it in you, Michael: no shame there.' I was very moved. Despite his difficulty breathing, he had made the effort to let me know he understood why I'd followed the road that had eventually led to my imprisonment.

As he lay then, his eyes closed, muttering prayers, I took his right hand, its back marked like a pin cushion from needle punctures of intravenous drips, and for the next few minutes, I gently massaged his bruises: caresses that let him know I loved him without having to tell him so.

I fell ill the next day with flu and, due to quarantine protocols, was unable to visit him again before he died on Christmas Day, the last one of the twentieth century.

Wednesday, 5 January 2000, 10 a.m. – Mary

We're just leaving for our hill walk, the last before Michael returns to Castlerea at the end of his leave, when the phone rings. When I answer a formal male voice says, 'Can I speak to Michael Gallagher, please?'

I cover the mouthpiece and hand the phone to Michael. 'Someone for you – sounds serious.'

After a couple of seconds Michael whispers to me, 'It's Castlerea,' then resumes listening. Soon, his expression changes from serious to positively gleeful. 'Thanks, goodbye,' he says and hangs up.

'They don't want me back,' he says, 'I'm on permanent leave until the official release date in July.' He puts his arms around me and speaks softly into my ear, 'We need never be parted again, Mary. That's it.'

I'm aware of my eyes filling up with tears of joy. At last, we can leave the awful nightmare behind and move on with our lives.

'There is one downside,' I say, lifting my face to his.

Michael looks puzzled, 'What's that?'

'You only got to spend four days in the sunny upland in the west of Ireland, with its en-suite bedrooms and Chinese takeaways.'

Michael laughs as he hugs me still closer. 'Never mind,' he says, 'the conjugal arrangements here are much better.'

Saturday, 8 July, 3 p.m. – Mary

After eighteen kilometres of the sponsored Glenveagh National Park deer fence walk, the rest of the group have long marched off into the distance and only Martin, steward and regular hill runner, is left accompanying Michael and me. He's demonstrating his superior level of fitness by repeatedly scouting ahead, before doubling back to report our position on his walkie-talkie to the Donegal Mountain Rescue team – on the last occasion referring to us as 'the stragglers'. Despite this discouragement and the increasingly steep terrain, with over 400 punts of sponsorship, mostly from my Dublin work colleagues, at stake, we doggedly keep going.

After climbing an almost sheer section, we find a flat boulder to sit on for a drinks break. With my blistered bare foot resting on the boulder's edge, I'm looking longingly below to the mountain stream running alongside the Doochary Road, when Michael's mobile phone rings. After a short conversation, in which he appears to be uneasy, he says, 'Excuse me a minute, Danny' and covers the mouthpiece.

'It's Danny Boyle, a second cousin of mine,' Michael says. 'Local Sinn Féin want to organise a Fáilte Abhaile reception for me: they're having a meeting at five in the Óstán Loch Altan to discuss it. I've told Danny I'm up here in the mountains and it's a bit inconvenient. Apart from that, I don't want any fuss. It's embarrassing.'

'You should make the effort, Michael,' I say. 'You were doing what you really believed in: it's only right your sacrifices are recognised by your own organisation.'

'Okay, I'll go to their meeting, but I'm not guaranteeing to agree to any function.'

As Michael gets back on the phone, Martin makes a timely reappearance. I tell him we want to abandon our walk. Right away he speaks into the walkie-talkie, his tone of voice revealing his delight as he asks a fellow steward to meet us on the Doochary Road and drive us back to our car parked in Dún Lúiche.

I'm just hoping the eighteen kilometres completed will be seen as sufficiently arduous for my sponsors not to demand a cut to their contributions to the Donegal Mountain Rescue Team.

Friday, 28 July, 8.20 p.m. – Michael

Driving along the high road between Falcarragh and Gortahork overlooking Ballyness Bay, en route to the Fáilte Abhaile event in the Óstán Loch Altan, Gortahork, we were flagged down by local resident Ginger Neddy Jack. As soon as we set off again, Ginger spoke from the back seat. 'Mamie must be very proud of you.'

'Yea,' I grunted and, glancing sideways, caught Mary's mock grimace.

We'd been advised by the organisers to arrive twenty minutes late, so the car park was full, but I managed to find a space on the spare ground facing the hotel. The forecourt was deserted apart from my sister Margaret and, standing alongside her, my mother – quashing family speculation that she might not come. Any show of approval within the family for IRA actions had always been met with my mother's same grim look and her comment, 'I can't stand violence.' With my brother Johnny, then a child, she had been on the street in Claudy when it was bombed back in 1972.

As we crossed the road to meet them, my mother said something to Margaret and then gave a short wave to Ginger.

'Evening, Mamie,' he called back, while shouldering open the door of the hotel's public bar.

We hugged, first Margaret and then my mother. While Mary and my mother complimented each other's dresses and Mary remarked positively on my mother's new hairdo, I edged Margaret away towards the hotel's main entrance.

'What did she say to you there?'

'What's that galoot doing here?'

'Who? Me or Ginger?'

Margaret laughed. 'Mother says he misses nothing: wakes, weddings, the lot, Ginger's there.'

'A bit like herself then,' I said.

'That's not fair, Michael.'

'Only joking.' I looked around me. 'Where is everybody?'

'They're in there, waiting for you and the speakers.'

Mary and I went inside. In a corner of the foyer stood Barry McElduff, an Omagh Sinn Féin councillor, and alongside him was local Ógra Shinn Féin organiser Pearse Doherty. Standing at 6 feet 5 inches, Pearse was as long as Barry was short.

At the entrance to the ballroom, we were met with loud cheering. We stopped to hug my son Damian and Margaret's sons, Kieron and Miney Brady. Going further inside the room, we were applauded past the table where my loyal friend, cousin Bud O'Donnell from Kennington, London, stood with his daughters and grandchildren, alongside another much-loved cousin, Danny Gallagher, with his wife Bridie from Glasgow. At the next table sat my mother's sisters Peggy Gallagher and Frances O'Donnell and her son Gerry, who all clapped their hands.

Moving tentatively on, I looked in a disoriented panic at thirty or so tables placed around the dance floor and waved haphazardly, but in a heartfelt way, towards a blur of faces: Gallagher cousins, and their families from the hillside townlands around Cnoc na Naomh, and many of my mother's neighbours from there too. I saw my mother then, sitting at a table near to the stage. I wanted to run there and hide underneath.

We reached our seats next to Margaret and exchanged cheerful greetings across the table with Johnny, his wife Bríd and their daughter

Siobhán. Next to them my mother sat fussily pinning an ornamental brooch on her granddaughter Róisín's Irish dancing costume, while Mairéad Gallagher and budding dancing champion Suzanne Coyle waited for their turns. As I watched, quite unexpectedly, a sudden surge of love for my mother welled up in my chest.

'She's made a real effort,' I said. 'New hairdo, the lot.'

'It suits her too, that short and stylish look,' said Mary.

'She went to Máire Kelly's in Falcarragh.' Margaret gave Mary and me a knowing look. 'Apparently, Gerry's wife goes there.'

'Gerry?' asked Mary.

'Gerry Adams.'

'What! Mother rubbing shoulders with republicans?' I laughed. 'What's happened to her non-violence principles?'

'Mother maintains his lot are different,' said Margaret, smiling. 'They don't call them "Gerry and the Peacemakers" for nothing.'

'Very funny, Maggie.' Margaret was one of my heroes. During my drinking days, despite the hassle of a full-time job and raising three children on her own, never once had she closed her door to me, no matter how drunk I was.

Sounds of a guitar being tuned came from the stage. We waved up to the three lads of the band Inis Fáil from the Rosses and at guest singer Alanna, who had come with her mother, my cousin Bridie Birt and wee Sean, along with a large contingent of our extended family from Monaghan and Dublin.

I spoke from the stage, thanking Pearse and Barry for coming, and then praised Mary, saying how great she had been. Feeling quite emotional, I covered up quickly by moving on to thank everyone who had supported me, especially those present.

Pearse acclaimed me as a true republican, while Barry eloquently explained how Mamie Gallagher had rallied the family to support me. While he spoke, my mother had her head lowered, smiling with embarrassment but secretly delighted, I was sure.

Nearing the end of the night, while squashed against the bar waiting to be served, I heard Alanna and the band start the last medley of songs. Just as the music became upbeat and rebellious, I got into a barely audible conversation with a young woman who I recognised as one of several Sinn Féin activists hovering around the bar. She introduced herself as Una and said she was fresh from getting her degree relating to the criminal justice system. She hoped now to do a PhD on how ex-prisoners and their families coped with post-incarceration trauma and asked if I might help.

Before I could answer, my drinks were served and, by the time I'd paid, Una had moved to the dance floor with her friends. They joined in a circle with others already there, amongst them Mary and Margaret, and Ginger Neddy Jack, arms aloft, all clapping in time to the tune of 'The Merry Ploughboy'.

I then saw my mother, eighty on her next birthday, skip nimbly across to meet Ginger in the middle of the floor, where she linked his arm and spun around, oblivious, it seemed, to the words of the raucous chorus from the ring of dancers: 'So, I'm off to join the IRA and I'm off tomorrow morn'.

May 2002 – Michael

I agreed to act as agent for Pearse Doherty standing as Sinn Féin candidate in the 2002 general election. Although unhappy with the party's slow drift away from its core 'Brits Out' message since the Good Friday Agreement, I felt somehow indebted: they had got me out of jail. Besides, I'd been impressed with Pearse. Just twenty-three, highly articulate and well read, he had no Dáil political lineage or family patronage and, from the age of sixteen, had been one of only a dozen or so Sinn Féin activists in the area.

One evening before the election, during a Sinn Féin campaign event in the Bridge Inn in Dungloe, I met Una, the young woman researcher I'd last seen at my Fáilte Abhaile event in 2000.

'Have you time for a quick catch up?' she asked right away.

'No problem,' I said.

She excused herself from the group of fellow campaign workers and we got seats at a quiet side of the lounge.

'I'm now working on a study of post-incarceration trauma,' Una said as soon as we sat down. 'How's it been for you and Mary?'

Taken aback at her directness I dithered: I didn't want to have to tell her about arguments or big rows, not that there were too many. Nor did I want to get mawkish either, with something like, 'Oh aye Una, we're so happy in our cottage near the sea, looking down on the golden sands of Ballyness Bay', which was all true. As I searched for a sensible, balanced reply, Una spoke:

'Do you have any traumatic flashbacks?'

'No, not about prison.'

'Not even once?' asked Una.

'Never,' I answered. Her question made me think about my regular dreams of being penniless and living on the streets, not knowing where the next drink was coming from, or longings for my lost family: yet I'd never once dreamed about prison. Then I realised why.

'Prison wasn't easy,' I said, 'but Mary wrote most days, always rallying support for me, and she never missed a visit, so my abiding memory is of her incredible loyalty that sustained me throughout.'

'Well done, Mary!' Una paused, as if to consult a mental list of her next questions. 'Does all the stress and the loss of time in prison make you feel regretful of your IRA involvement?'

'No. If there's something you really believe in, you have to be prepared to take risks.'

Realising I wasn't being completely honest, I got off my high horse quickly: 'But I do have regrets – if I could do one thing differently, I would put Mary first. I'd no right, once we started our relationship, to carry on with my activities: she thought I was innocent until after the trial when I told her the truth.'

'You mean, all that time, she didn't know?' said Una, startled.

'Have you managed to interview many ex-prisoners?' I asked, uncomfortably trying to change the subject.

'Quite a few.'

'Will you be including us all in your study?'

'In due course, possibly.'

Una got to her feet. 'I have to get back to the campaign team,' she said, and looked down at me. 'I think now, though, I'd really like to interview Mary, if she's agreeable. Hers seems to be the most intriguing story of all.'

2003 and beyond – Mary

Two years have passed since Mary Coughlan, Minister for the Gaeltacht, came from Dublin to help launch our fledgling enterprise, e-Siopadóir Teoranta. On the day she said, 'Now they have instant access to the world, on this level playing field of the Internet, companies such as this can inject a fresh dynamism into e-commerce in the Gaeltacht.' Our software developer Bríd then outlined the project *as Gaeilge*. I followed, presenting in English with a smattering of Irish, a slide show of some of e-Siopadóir's main features.

Entrepreneurs fail and so did our first venture: not spectacularly, just slowly and somewhat painfully. The Gaeltacht wasn't ready for e-commerce or maybe e-commerce wasn't ready for the Gaeltacht. We changed the project twice and I eventually developed some very simple online web-building software, with the main feature being search engine optimisation. With Michael in the role of selling, motoring constantly throughout Ireland seeking business, I stayed at home, sometimes working a twenty-hour day. One-time technophobic owners of small firms became less sceptical when they began to get business from the web, and we started to thrive.

So that's us now: citizens of the Donegal Gaeltacht, using a *cúpla focal* daily and telling ourselves we'll soon have enough time to become fluent. Michael does addiction recovery meetings, practises his freestyle football routine and is still an ardent republican. I keep on running, and we walk in the mountains.

I sometimes wonder, if I could do one thing differently, what would have happened if I hadn't turned up at Michael's flat for that game of Scrabble? I'd have saved myself a lot of heartache. But if I hadn't, then I wouldn't now be living with a view of the mountains and sea, nor have by my side someone who quotes Burns and Shakespeare and still sings 'The Fields of Athenry' to me.